Borrowed Identity

128th United States Colored Troops

2nd Volume in a Series

Multiple-name Usage by South Carolina's Black Civil War Veterans

Volume 1: *Voices from the Past: 104th U.S. Colored Troops, 1997*

BORROWED IDENTITY

128th United States Colored Troops

Multiple-name Usage by Black Civil War Veterans Who Served with Union Regiments Organized in South Carolina

Compiled and Edited by
John R. Gourdin

HERITAGE BOOKS
2009

HERITAGE BOOKS
AN IMPRINT OF HERITAGE BOOKS, INC.

Books, CDs, and more—Worldwide
For our listing of thousands of titles see our website at
www.HeritageBooks.com

Published 2009 by
HERITAGE BOOKS, INC.
Publishing Division
100 Railroad Ave. #104
Westminster, Maryland 21157

Copyright © 2009 John R. Gourdin

Other books by the author:
Voices from the Past: 104th Infantry Regiment, USCT, Colored Civil War Soldiers from South Carolina

Title page illustration: "The Price of Freedom" by John A. Nelson
Courtesy of Black Camisards, Inc., ©1998

Cover illustration: "If These Eyes Could Speak" by John A. Nelson
Courtesy of Black Camisards, Inc., ©1998

All rights reserved. No part of this book may be reproduced or transmitted in any form or by any means, electronic or mechanical, including photocopying, recording or by any information storage and retrieval system without written permission from the author, except for the inclusion of brief quotations in a review.

International Standard Book Numbers
Paperbound: 978-0-7884-5007-5
Clothbound: 978-0-7884-8204-5

Table of Contents

Preface vii

Introduction ix

Research Methodology xi

Abbreviations and Definitions xiii

Main Entries 1

Appendix A: Cross Reference – County to District 239

Appendix B: Cross Reference – District to County 241

Appendix C: Cross Reference – Community to County 243

Appendix D: SC Volunteer Colored Infantry Regiment 245

Appendix E: USCT Regiments Organized in SC 247

Appendix F: Structure of an Infantry Regiment 249

Appendix G: Officers of the 128th USCI Regiment 251

List of Sources 253

Name Index 255

About the Editor 273

List of Vignettes

Medal of Honor – Black Soldiers in the Civil War 8

Medal of Honor Recipient – Sgt. William Carney 16

Medal of Honor Recipient – Sgt. Andrew Smith 20

Civil War Pension Benefits 24

The Big Storm of 1893 28

The Butler Medal 38

Gradual and Limited Emancipation during the Civil War 46

Freedom Day in South Carolina 52

Definitions (Conscription vs Impressment) 84

Definitions (Affidavit vs Deposition) 120

Pawning Pension Certificates 128

The Great Earthquake of 1886 138

Black Man's "Bill of Rights" 168

40-Acres and a Mule 184

Explanation ("New Law" vs "Old Law") 190

Preface

Borrowed Identity is a compilation of selected biographical and genealogical narratives and historical perspectives of Black Civil War veterans who served with the 128th United States Colored Troops organized and mustered in South Carolina. These narratives and perspectives are excerpts from Civil War Pension Records stored and preserved by the National Archives and Records Administration in Washington, DC.

This work is not intended to be a history of a Civil War military regiment, nor is it an exposé or treatise on contributions and conquests of colored soldiers during the Civil War. Those topics are covered in many other books written by individuals infinitely more knowledgeable on the subject than I. The sole intent and purpose of this book is to provide genealogists, family researchers and historians with a selection of genealogical and biographical information extracted, transcribed, compiled and edited from military pension records on some of the enlisted members of the 128th U.S. Colored Infantry regiment organized in South Carolina during the Civil War.

Most of those soldiers served under the surname borrowed from their former owners but many adopted new names or used multiple names after being discharged from service. These borrowed and multiple names are captured in this book from depositions, affidavits, declarations, medical records, and correspondence used to verify the colored veteran's service in the War.

It is my hope and desire that the content of this book will be a valuable aid to researchers in identifying soldiers after the War and connecting them with their plantations of origin and with their antebellum owners.

Readers should be aware of the relative reliability of information provided in this book. Be mindful that any inconsistency between data found in various documents in pension records is the rule rather than the exception. In most cases, during the processing of pension applications, it was necessary for pension examiners to conduct follow-up interviews in order to resolve conflicts between testimonies of different witnesses –

Preface

and in many cases between statements made by the same individual at different times.

As a means of standardizing the acceptability of information, whenever available, I used data accepted by the Bureau of Pension as a basis of determining the eligibility of pension applicants. In other cases, where discrete data were not available, "best judgment" assessments of relevant data were made in order to draw reasonable conclusions.

I am most fortunate to have had so many knowledgeable individuals who unselfishly shared their expertise with me during this research and wish to acknowledge and express my gratitude to the staff of the National Archives for their assistance and patience over the past several years; to the very able editors and other professional assistances at Heritage Books for their critical evaluation of the layout and format of the manuscript; to leaders and members of the **United States Colored Troops Institute**, the **United States Colored Troops Living History Association** and the **African American Civil War Memorial and Museum** for the wonderful and inspiring work they do to tell the story of our ancestors; and, to my family, friends and associates for their encouragement and support as I pursued my goal of gathering and publishing the *Borrowed Identity* about some of *South Carolina's Black Civil War Veterans*.

John Raymond Gourdin
September 15, 2008

Introduction

Undisputedly the most imposing obstacle faced by historical and genealogical researchers is the challenge of crossing the 1870 Census "barrier" and identifying individuals of African descent who resided in America prior to the Civil War.

This barrier is a result, in part, of the scarcity of data on black Americans in the U.S. Census Records, and other public documents, prior to 1870. Prior to 1870, most blacks in America were enumerated as chattel or property. Only "free" people of color were listed in the general census records while slaves were listed in schedules only by age, gender, and color, or merely as a head count. The 1870 Census was the first census that provided full descriptions of black Americans. Subsequent to the 1870 census, all legal inhabitants in America were and are similarly enumerated in census records by name, age, gender, race, occupation and family units, and several other descriptive categories.

Surmounting the proverbial "1870 obstacle" is a particularly daunting task when conducting research in southern states where the vast majority of the black population was held in slavery. Compounding this task was a tendency of black Civil War veterans to use multiple names after returning home from the war.

At the beginning of the Civil War nearly 90% of blacks in America were held in bondage, and it is highly likely that many of the remaining 10%, residing in the North and South, were descended from slaves. So this research objective is not isolated to African descendants in southern states because after the turn of the century the grand majority of black Americans who migrated out of South Carolina settled in northern states. In fact, during the period of 1930 to 1940, more than 50 percent of blacks that migrated out of South Carolina settled in two northern states – New York, with 37.2 percent and Washington, DC, with 13.4 percent.[1]

This migratory pattern is evidenced by the change in the ratio of

---

[1] George A. Devlin. *South Carolina and Black Migration, 1865-1940: In Search of the Promised Land* (New York: Garland Publishing, Inc., 1989). p. 379-382.

Introduction

Afro-inhabitants in southern states versus northern states during the first half of the twentieth century. The black population of South Carolina shrunk from 58.4 percent[2] in 1900 to 42.9 percent[3] in 1940 – an amazing decrease of 15.5 percentage points.

During that same period the black population in New York grew from 1.4 percent[4] to 4.2 percent[5] of the state's population – an astonishing increase of more than 200 percent.

Even though many other factors contributed to this tremendous growth in the black population of New York during that forty-year period, it is still important that genealogical researchers from northern states look to the South as a valuable source of information on the ancestry of black Americans residing in New York and other northern states.

As well, northern researchers must remain keenly aware of the possibility that their ancestral surname may have evolved during the years shortly after the Civil War. That evolution of surnames can result in false or misleading ancestral information during genealogical research of census records and other public records.

Therefore, an awareness of the multiple-name usage by black Civil War veterans can potentially save researchers countless hours of nonproductive work as they explore the connection between antebellum slave laborers and post-War veteran soldiers.

---

[2]U.S., Department of Commerce, Bureau of the Census, *Twelfth Census of the United States, 1900: Population*, Volume 1, Part 1:cxiv. NOTE: The black percentage of the population in South Carolina in 1900 (58.4%) is second only to the state of Mississippi (58.5%).

[3]U.S., Department of Commerce, Bureau of the Census, *Sixteenth Census of the United States, 1940: Population*, Volume IV, Part 4:345. Note: Race classification was grouped as 'White' and 'Nonwhite'. The percentage used in this article is based on the Nonwhite representation of the total population, which include 'Other Races.'

[4]Ibid., *Twelfth Census of the United States, 1900*.

[5]Ibid., *Sixteenth Census of the United States, 1940*, Volume II, Part 5:17.

Research Methodology

Borrowed Identity consists of seventy-six genealogical and biographical entries of black Civil War veterans who mustered and served in the 128th United States Colored Troops, and is indexed with more than 500 surnames and nearly 1500 individual names. Data for these entries were excerpted, compiled and edited from pension files stored and preserved at the National Archives in Washington, DC.

Genealogical Entries

Genealogical entries provide descriptive information about selected veteran soldiers including, but not limited to: service rank; service unit; date and place of birth; name of previous owner (as applicable); given name and maiden name of his spouse; date and place of marriage; name of official who performed the marriage; name and date of birth of each child; and the date and place of soldier's death.

Data were compiled primarily from pension application summaries; Soldier's and/or Widow's Pension Declaration forms; Bureau of Pension's data collection sheets; depositions and affidavits submitted by claimants (veterans, widows, parents, court appointed guardians) and witnesses in support of claimants.

Biographical Entries

Biographical entries, usually in the voice of selected veteran soldiers, document the reason why they used multiple names after the War and are based on excerpts extracted and edited from depositions, affidavits, letters and other official correspondence, based on sworn statements by veteran soldiers, widows, parents and court appointed guardian of minor children (in cases where both parents of a minor are deceased or incapacitated).

Based on a review of the pension indices (T288 and T289), a total of 706 discrete pension applications were filed by veterans, widows and other legal claimants of the 128th U.S. Colored Infantry regiment. Since the focus of this research was to identify individuals who used multiple

Research Methodology

names after the war, a stratified selection process was used to select only those records that convey the most useful information - as determined by this researcher.

Five criteria were used to select only relevant records:

- **Enlisted Soldiers**: Officers were omitted, and only enlisted soldiers were included in the selection process – leaving 679 candidate records.
- **Pension Recipients**: Of the 679 applications filed by enlisted men of the 128th, 220, because they were denied pensions for a variety of reasons but in many cases because the applicant's name could not be located at the War Department in Washington, DC.
- **Multiple-name Usage:** Only records where multiple names were used by veteran soldiers were included in the final analysis. A thorough search of the Pension Card Indexes yielded 136 records where veteran soldiers used multiple names after the War and those 136 records were pulled and reviewed.
- **Veteran Descendants**: Selected pension files must identify descendant children of the veteran soldier. Out of the 136 records cleared for review, only 76 were acceptable for this research.
- **Biographical Data**: Selected pension files must contain sufficient documentation to assimilate biographical entries. All 76 records selected were acceptable for this research.

Criterion (1), (2) and (3) were determined from a review of the T288 and T289 Pension Card Index. In order to determine criterion (4) and (5), a thorough review of the 136 files (along with other relevant files and other files of interest) was undertaken. Pension files selected for this research averaged more than 200 pages each, so no less than 25,000 pages of genealogical and biographical documents from pension records were reviewed and edited to produce *Borrowed Identity*.

Abbreviations and Definitions

{ } .... Entry is not a validated transcription
( ) ....Comment or entry made by the Pension Examiner
[ ] ....Comment or entry made by the Editor
1stSgt/1stSergt. .... First Sergeant (Non-Commissioned Officer)
Abt. .... About
Aft. .... After
bef. .... Before
b. .... Born
bur. .... Buried
c. .... Circa (or about)
Capt. .... Captain (Commissioned Officer)
Co. .... Company
Col. .... Colonel (Commissioned Officer)
Cpl/Corp/Corpl. .... Corporal (Non-Commissioned Officer)
d. .... Died
Dist .... District
Gen/Genl. .... General (Commissioned Officer)
JP .... Justice of the Peace
LNU .... Last Name Unknown
Lt/Lieut. .... Lieutenant (Commissioned Officer)
LtCol/LieutCol. .... Lieutenant Colonel (Commissioned Officer)
m. .... Married
Maj. .... Major (Commissioned Officer)

Abbreviations and Definitions

MC	Minor's Certificate (Pension Authorization)
Min.	Minister
MNU	Maiden Name Unknown
New Law	Pension Act of June 27, 1890
Old Law	Pension Act of July 14, 1862
OrdSgt /OrdSergt	Ordnance Sergeant (Non-Commissioned Officer)
Pvt.	Private (Enlisted Man)
Regt.	Regiment
Rev.	Reverend
SC	Soldier's Certificate (Pension Authorization)
Sgt/Sergt.	Sergeant (Non-Commissioned Officer)
sic	[sic] means an exact transcription
USCT	United Stated Colored Troops
U.S.C. Inf.	United States Colored Infantry
VR	Very Respectfully
WC	Widow's Certificate (Pension Authorization

Snow AIKEN
alias
Snow Flagg

Private, Company F: Born on 31 Mar 1846, at Cooper River, Charleston, SC; a Slave of William Harleston, then Dr. Arthur Flagg; Enlisted on 27 Mar 1865, at Charleston, Charleston, SC; Honorably Discharged on 10 Oct 1866, at Morris Island, Charleston, SC. Married to Ellen Boykin, during 1874, in Effingham County, GA, by Magistrate Thomas Hinckley. Children: Joseph (b. c1878); William (b. c1885) and Carrie (b. c1887). **Snow Aiken** died on 03 Apr 1925, Charleston, Charleston, SC.[6]

Snow Aiken (Veteran Soldier)
Date: 18 Mar 1913
Residence: Charleston County, SC
Occupation: Unknown

Snow Flagg, now known as Snow Aiken, who served in Company F, 128th U.S. Colored Volunteers, declares that he is an applicant for increase of pension under the Act of May 11, 1912; that he was born March 31, 1844, which information he got from his former owner; that he cannot find any recorded evidence to substantiate his age as all records of the plantation are lost and those concerned are dead; that he would ask that his age be based on the age given on his discharge; that he cannot read or write; that his discharge is also lost having been so by

---

[6] Civil War Pension Record for Snow Aiken alias Snow Flagg, SC No. C-2.499.026, Private, Company F, 128th USCI, Records of the VA, RG 15, NARA, WDC; 1900 U.S. Federal Census, South Carolina, Berkeley County, St. James – Goose Creek, ED: 19, Page: 39B, Line: 88 (Roll: T623-1519. Note: The 1900 Census Record indicates that Snow & Ellen Aiken had no children, which is a contradiction in Private Aiken's testimony in his pension application.

general moving which caused him to lose said certificate. He would ask that his age be accepted from the record of his discharge.[7]

Emile L. Hare (Executrix for the Estate of the Veteran Soldier)
Date: 08 Apr 1925
Residence: #70 Radclift St., Charleston, SC

Dear Sirs: This is to inform you of Snow Aiken's death, one of your pensioners whose Pension Certificate is number 1.110.564. He passed away four days after he received his check for April - 1925. He was sick for four years and unable to leave his room for two years – having lived in a place in my yard for about 6 years. I used to do his writing, etc, for him. His check was soon gone having to get a woman to nurse him, doctor, rent, medicine, nourishment, etc.

We thought he saved some of his money but found only $27.01 to his credit in the Mutual Bank and he carried no life insurance. Now the undertaker had to be paid and there is nothing to pay him with and that I beg that you help me out as I am responsible for it and the old man empowered me to act as his Executrix before his death.

There was nothing to settle, save a few personal belonging he willed to the faithful nurse who received almost nothing for her services, for $50.00 per month meant very little to a man 84 years old, ill for so long, at times with no one who is a blood connection save some distant cousins who did not notice him at all. I was compelled to bury him in Potter's Field (Public Cemetery).

Let me hear from you as early as possible, and I trust favorably. Very Respectfully, Miss Emilie L. Hare.[8]

---

[7] General Affidavit for Snow Flagg, now known as Snow Aiken (Charleston County, SC), dated 18 Mar 1913.

[8] Letter from E.L. Hare, 70 Radcliff St., Charleston, SC, to Office of Disbursing Clerk, U.S. Bureau of Pensions, Washington, DC, dated 08 Apr 1925.

Peter ARMSTRONG
alias
Peter King

Corporal, Company G: Born c1840, on St. Simons Island, Glynn, GA; a Slave of Capt. Mallory P. King; Enlisted on 10 Mar 1865, at Savannah, Chatham, GA; Honorably Discharged on 10 Oct 1866, at Morris Island, Charleston, SC. Married to Julia Robinson (b. c1858, St. Simons Island, Glynn, GA; d. 07 Mar 1930, Brunswick, Glynn, GA), on 07 Feb 1874, on St. Simons Island, GA, by Rev. Andrew Oneal. Children: Harry (b. c1878); and Rena (b. c1881). **Peter Armstrong** *died c1886, on St. Simons Island, Glynn, GA.*[9]

Julia Armstrong (Widow of the Veteran Soldier)
Date: 06 Jun 1899
Residence: Brunswick, Glynn, GA (Corner of London and Cleveland Sts)
Occupation: Cook

I am about 41 years of age. I am an applicant for pension as the widow of Peter Armstrong who served in the army under the name of Peter King. My husband said that he had been a soldier and Jupiter White or Gardner, who served with my husband, told me what company my husband served in.

We were married on St. Simons Island at the colored church over there. It was a small house owned by someone but in which preaching was sometimes done. Andrew Oneal, a colored preacher, performed the

---

[9] Civil War Pension Record for Julia Armstrong, widow of Peter Armstrong alias Peter King, WC No. 438.743, Cpl, Company G, 128th USCI, Records of the VA, RG 15, NARA, WDC; 1900 U.S. Federal Census, Georgia, Glynn County, Brunswick, ED: 40, Page: 219B, Line: 87 (Roll: T623-200).

ceremony for us. There were lots of people present at our marriage but it has been a long time and I can't say now who they were, except my father, my mother, and my brother. {Tona and} {Simon} Robinson, Dennis {Terriel} and, I think, Jupiter White were also present.

My husband died on our own place of 3 acres on St. Simons Island - about 3 miles from St. Simons Mill post-office. The asthma was the cause of his death. He also had a pain in the side and a cough. I have not remarried since the death of my husband. I have not lived with and not cohabitated with any man since his death. I have no record of my husband's death and can't say how long he has been dead, but it is 12 or 14 years – I think. I was never married before I married the soldier and did not live with any man as his wife before marriage to the soldier. My husband had no other woman before he had me - that I have heard of. I have no idea how old my husband was when I married him.

I have given birth to one child before I married the soldier but I was not married to the father of the child. I had four children by the soldier. Two of them are dead. Rena and Harry are the names of the living children. Harry is the oldest, about 20 to 22 years old. Rena is 18 years old. I was raised on St. Simons and was a slave of Mr. Jim Postell (now deceased). I lived on St. Simons all my life until I moved to Brunswick – since the death of my husband. My husband was born right here on St. Simons. He was a slave of Capt. Mallory P. King (now deceased).

Jupiter White, Toby {Farm}, Betty White, Robert White, Robert {McAbout}, Robert White, Jr., and Tyra McIntyre have known me all of my life and can testify that I was not married before I married Peter.

I don't know how old my husband was when he died. He was a good deal older than me. His father's name was Harry or Henry Armstrong (now dead). His mother is dead. He has one sister living. Her name is {Sue} Armstrong. She is a single woman. He has one brother living. His name is William Armstrong. He is here in Brunswick now.[10]

---

[10] Deposition of Julia Armstrong, case of Julia Armstrong (Brunswick, Glynn, GA), dated 06 Jul 1899.

Randol BECKETT
alias
Randol Ward

Private, Company D: Born on 12 Oct 1843, at Brook Green, Georgetown, SC; a Slave of Dr. Josh Ward; Enlisted on 27 Mar 1865, at Beaufort, Beaufort, SC; Honorably Discharged on 10 Oct 1866, at Sullivans Island, Charleston, SC. Married to Lois Winry (b. c1845), on 13 Nov 1882 or 9, at Oak Plantation, Georgetown, SC, by A. B. Flagg. Children: Edith (b. 1892). **Randol Beckett** *died on 20 Jan 1912, at Brook Green, Georgetown, SC.*[11]

Randol Beckett (Veteran Soldier)
    Date: 08 Mar 1911
    Residence: Brook Green, Georgetown, SC
    Occupation: Farmer

I am the Randol Ward that served in Company D, 128th U.S. Colored Volunteer Infantry. I was born in this county on Brook Green plantation, and I was the slave of Dr. Flagg – now dead. He was killed in the storm of 1893. He lived here all the time I knew him. None of the old family lives here now except Dr. J. Ward Flagg. He has some brothers and sisters but they are out west.

My father was named William Beaty and my mother was named Charlotte Beaty. We all belonged to the same owner. Both of my parents are now dead. When I enlisted in the army I titled after my master. They

---

[11] Civil War Pension Record for Lois Beckett (widow of Randol Ward now known as Randol Beckett), WC No. 742.386, Pvt, Company K, 128th USCI, Records of the VA, RG 15, NARA, WDC; 1900 U.S. Federal Census, South Carolina, Georgetown County, Waccamaw, ED: 53, Page: 208B, Line: 51 (Roll: T623-1528).

Randol Beckett alias Randol Ward

gave me the name of Ward because I was a slave and lived with Josh Ward on his plantation. I was married during slave time and had two children before freedom. My father was titled as Beaty in slave time, but he took the name of Beckett after freedom, and when I came out of the war, I titled after my father.

When I enlisted they stripped me and searched me to see if I was an all right man. Israel Carr, Archie Ward and Frank Pyatt enlisted at the same time I did. We were all off of the same plantation and all belonged to the same man and all of these men live right here now.

During my service I stood guard and drilled with the other soldiers. On guard we stood two hours and rested four. We had Guard Mount in the morning and Dress Parade in the evening. When I first enlisted, after doctors examined me, I drew a gun and uniform. I drew a knapsack for clothes; a haversack for rations; and a canteen for water.

We were made up at Georgetown, S.C and went first to Beaufort, S.C. We were in Beaufort over a year. We then went to Charleston and remained there until muster out. We went to Charleston in the summer and was mustered out the following fall.[12]

Dr. J. Ward Flagg (Attending Physician)
    Date: 08 Mar 1911
    Residence: Brook Green, Georgetown, SC
    Occupation: Physician, Surgeon and Planter

I am 50 years of age. I am the physician, surgeon and planter at this place. I have known this claimant all my life. He was a slave of my grandfather, J.J. Ward. I have known him as Randol Beckett ever since the war. He has been on this plantation ever since the war.

Before freedom, I suppose that he had the same name as his owner – Ward. I have always understood and believed that he was a soldier in the Federal Army during the Civil War. Several of his comrades have been on this plantation ever since the war, and I get my information from them. I cannot tell how old he is, but I would judge him to be about 70.

---

[12] Deposition of Randol Ward, case of Randol Beckett (Brook Green, Georgetown, SC), dated 08 Mar 1911.

I have here a list of my grandfather's slaves. Under the heading: "Little Niggers – 1843," I find Randol's name. I do not know just what that heading means, but it shows that Randol was in existence at that time. He may have been any age from one to anything that would be classed as a "little nigger." Anything I might say about that would be my own supposition and conjecture.[13]

Israel Carr (Comrade of the Veteran Soldier)
  Date: 08 Mar 1911
  Residence: Brook Green, Georgetown, SC
  Occupation: Farmer

I am 74 years of age. I served as a private in Company D, 128th U.S. Colored Volunteer Infantry during the Civil War. I am a pensioner at $15.00 per month on account of said service. I have known this Claimant since he was a boy. I am not related to him, nor have I any interest in his claim for pension. He is near my age. He was married and had children before the war came up. We belonged to one owner in slave time. He titled Ward in the Army. We have both lived on this place ever since the war. We have been in sight of each other all our lives.

He titled Beckett after the war – after his father. I know his father well. Randol Beckett and Randal Ward is one and the same person. This Randol Beckett is the same man that was soldier in my company during the war. I am the same Israel Carr that testified before you about this same man several years ago, and he has the same right to pension as I have. [14]

---

[13] Ibid., Dr. J. Ward Flagg.
[14] Ibid., Israel Carr.

Medal of Honor
Black Soldiers in the Civil War

During the Civil War, a total of seventeen black soldiers earned the Medal of Honor for "Gallantry under Fire" – the highest honor bestowed on a service member, of any race.

Fifteen of those medals were earned in battles in the state of Virginia – fourteen at the Battle of New Market Heights (sometimes called the Battle of Chaffin Farm) near Richmond, on September 30, 1864, and one was earned during the ten-month Siege on Petersburg (in an event usually referred to as the Battle of the Crater), on July 30, 1864.

Amazingly, the other two medals were earned in battles in the Palmetto State of South Carolina.

William Harvey Carney, a Sergeant with the famed 54th Massachusetts Infantry regiment and native of New Bedford, Massachusetts, earned the medal during the Assault on Battery Wagner, in Charleston Harbor, on July 18, 1863 (See Page 16).

and

Andrew Jackson Smith, a Sergeant with the 55th Massachusetts Infantry regiment and a native of Clinton, Illinois, earned his medal during the Battle at Honey, near Grahamville, on November 30, 1864 (See Page 20).

WE HONOR THOSE GREAT AND NOBLE MEN

Duncan BETTERSON
alias
Stephen Lawton

Private, Company E: Born on 10 May 1849, near Bluffton, Beaufort, SC; a Slave of Joe Lawton; Enlisted on 07 Mar 1865, at Beaufort, Beaufort, SC; Honorably Discharged on 10 Oct 1866, at Morris Island, Charleston, SC. Married to Tamar Wilson, on 10 Dec 1868, at {Camp Green Church}, by Rev. Gilbert Taylor. Children: Maggie (b. 1868); Martin (b. 1870); Anna (b. 1873); Stephen (b. 1887); Samuel (b. 1889); Chloe (b. 1890) and Henry Rabbit (b. 1897). **Duncan Betterson** died on 13 July 1928, Garnett, Hampton, SC.[15]

Duncan Betterson (Veteran Soldier)
Date: 09 May 1901
Residence: Brighton, Hampton, SC
Occupation: Farmer

I am 58 years of age. I am the Duncan Betterson who served under the name of Stephen Lawton as a private in Company E, 128th U.S. Colored Infantry during the War of the Rebellion and was pensioned under the General Law at $8.00 a month for rheumatism.

I was born near Savannah on the S.C., side of the river. I was born the slave of Joe Lawton and remained his slave until freedom. My father was named January Betterson. He belonged to Lawton also. I do not know where my father got his name. I and my father were both Lawtons

---

[15] Civil War Pension Record for Duncan Betterson alias Stephen Lawton), WC No. 928.531, Pvt, Company E, 128th USCI, Records of the VA, RG 15, NARA, WDC; 1900 U.S. Federal Census, South Carolina, Hampton County, Lawton Township, ED: 57, Page: 93B, Line: 77 (Roll: T623-1531).

Duncan Betterson alias Stephen Lawton

when we were slaves and I gave my name as Lawton when I enlisted. When I came home I found that my father had changed his name and I changed mine too. I am sure I have never been known by any other names than these two. I have always had the name Stephen. Dunc or Duncan is a nick name. I gave my name as Stephen Lawton when I enlisted. I enlisted at Beaufort, S.C. I think I was about 18 when I enlisted. I do not remember who recruited me.

After I enlisted the doctor examined me. He took me in a room and stripped me and made me run up and down the floor and put his ear against my breast and then sent me to camp. Company E, 128th U.S. Colored Infantry was my only U.S. service except I now carry the mail. I was not in the Confederate Army in any capacity. I was never on detached duty. I remained with my Company all the time. I have lived in this county all the time since the war.

Joe Frazier and John Baily were my tent mates. I was in no battles. I was never in the hospital but, I had pneumonia a couple of days and it ran into rheumatism and that was all the sickness I had in the army. I have been drawing a pension for 4 or 5 years. I think I got $700 the first draw. Jerre Solomon and Joe Butler were two of my original witnesses. I testified for Baily in his pension claim. I paid them $1.00 each. Billy Wine was a witness for me. He was in my Company. I testified in his claim also, but I paid him nothing. I have applied for an increase but have never heard from it. I was last examined about two years ago at Beaufort, S.C.

I have been married but once. I married the wife I am living with now soon after I came out of the army. I knew her from a girl and know that her marriage to me was her first marriage. We were married by a minister in this county. I have four living children under 16 – aged as follows: Stephen, aged 14, Samuel, aged 12, Henry, aged 8 and {Murvin}, aged 4.[16]

---

[16] Deposition of Duncan Betterson, case of Duncan Betterson (Brighton, Hampton, SC), dated 09 May 1901.

Hilton R. BOSTICK
alias
Hilton Shipman

Private, Company D: Born c1849, on St. Stephen Parish, Charleston (later Berkeley County), SC; a Slave of F.N. Shipman; Enlisted on 07 Mar 1865, at Beaufort, Beaufort, SC; Honorably Discharged on 10 Oct 1866, at Morris Island, Charleston, SC. Married to Elizabeth "Betsie" McDonnell (d. c1902), at St. Stephen, Berkeley, SC, by Rev. Walker. Children: Lula (d. bef 31 Jan 1922); Aron Elijah (d. bef 31 Jan 1922); Charity (d. bef 31 Jan 1922); Mrs. Martha Armstrong (b. c1890). **Hilton Reddy Bostick** *died on 10 Dec 1926, at Bonneau, Berkeley, SC.*[17]

Hilton Bostick (Veteran Soldier)
Date: 09 Aug 1923
Residence: Osborne, Charleston, SC
Occupation: Farmer

I think I was born in the year 1850. My post office station is Adams Run. I live here with my son-in-law, John Granderson, and my sister, Harriet Bennett. Harriet is a pensioner. My full and complete name is Hilton Reddy Bostick and I am the same Hilton R. Bostick who is applying for pension on account of my service in Company D, 128th U.S. Colored Infantry in the Civil War. I served in that organization under the name of Hilton Shipman as I was owned by a man named F.N. Shipman. My father was named Bostick. I enlisted at Beaufort, S.C., and was discharged

---

[17] Civil War Pension Record for Hilton Bostick alias Hilton Shipman, SC No. C-2.412.831, Pvt, Company D, 128th USCI, Records of the VA, RG 15, NARA, WDC; 1880 U.S. Federal Census, South Carolina, Charleston County (later, Berkeley County), St. Stephens Parish, ED: 90, Page: 499A, Line: 1 (Roll: T9-1224).

Hilton R. Bostick alias Hilton Shipman

at Morris Island, Charleston County, S.C. I do not remember the date of my discharge or of my enlistment. I served as a private.

My colonel was named [Charles H.] Howard and my lieutenant colonel was [William M.] Beebe. My major was [William H.] Danielson and my captain was F[rederick] K. Field. I do not remember the name of the lieutenant but the first sergeant was James White. After my enlistment the regiment stayed at Beaufort all the time until we came to Charleston where we were mustered out.

I think I was about 5 feet 6 inches tall when I enlisted and had black hair, eyes and complexion. I had a discharge certificate but I misplaced it somewhere and I do not know what became of it. After my discharge from the army I went to St. Stephens where I was raised and lived there for a while and then went to Florida and lived there 17 years and then came back here where I have lived ever since.

I have been married only one time. My wife was named Elizabeth but she has been dead over 20 years. She died at St. Stephens and is buried there. I tried for a pension about 20 years ago and I filed the claim through a Mr. Webb in Washington, D.C., but I never heard anything more about it. I think it was after my sister, Harriet Bennett, got her pension. I did not file another claim because I never heard anything from that one but I finally decided to try again.

I had no other military or naval service except my service in the 128th U.S. Colored Infantry. No member of my family served in the World War and I am not receiving nor have I applied for compensation on account of the service of any person in the Civil War.

I have no photograph of myself, and I do not know whether any member of my company is living now or not. I have not seen any of them for many years. I positively did serve in Company D, 128th U.S. Colored Infantry. William Fletcher & Company, of WDC, are the attorneys in my claim. I have not paid them anything for services in my claim.[18]

---

[18] Deposition of Hilton R. Bostick, case of Hilton Bostick alias Shipman (Osborne, Charleston, SC), dated 09 Aug 1923.

Mrs. Harriet Bennett (Sister of the Veteran Soldier)
Date: 09 Aug 1923
Residence: Osborne, Charleston, SC
Occupation: None

I do not know my exact age but I am older than the claimant, in this case, Hilton R. Bostick, who is my brother. I am a widow and pensioner. I am pensioned at the rate of $30 per month as the widow of David Bennett who served in Company C and B 128th U.S. Colored Infantry.

I was living in Charleston at the time the claimant enlisted in the army and I saw him while he was in service. I saw him when he was on Morris Island just before he was discharged. He was in uniform at that time and I know that he served in the army. He served in the same regiment as my husband but in a different company. The claimant was in Company D. The claimant, in this case, positively is my brother and I know he served in the army as he claims.

I do not know why the claimant waited so long before he applied for pension. If the claimant is allowed pension it will benefit me financially as he is helpless and I have to wait on him all the time. The claimant has to have help in bathing and dressing as he is entirely unable to help himself. He has been that way for four years. He has been living with me for four years and he has been that way ever since he came here.[19]

John Granderson (Son-in-Law of the Veteran Soldier)
Date: 09 Aug 1923
Residence: Osborne, Charleston, SC
Occupation: Farmer

My age is 58. The claimant, in this case, Hilton R. Bostick, is my father-in-law and I first met him four years ago when he came here to live. I have seen him every day since he came here. I have always understood that the claimant was a soldier in the Civil War.

---

[19] Ibid., Harriet Bennett.

Hilton R. Bostick alias Hilton Shipman

Since the claimant has lived here he has been entirely unable to help himself. I have bathe and dress the claimant as he is not able to do these things for himself. He has to be helped to the toilet as he is not able to attend to the calls of nature unassisted. He has been that way ever since he came here.[20]

E.F. Fewell (Pension Special Examiner)
    Date: **08 Mar 1911**
    Office: **Charleston, Charleston, SC**
    Occupation: **Special Examiner**

The Commissioner of Pensions: Herewith are returned all papers in the case of Hilton R. Bostick alias Hilton Shipman, together with my report.

This claim was referred for special examination for some inquiry into the matter of identity of claimant with the man who rendered the service of which the claim is based, and for some explanation of his long delay in asserting title to pension. The claim came to this district for the initial examination.

Notice of special examination was served on the claimant and his rights and privileges were fully and carefully explained to him, all o which he waived. He was not present at the examination of the witnesses.

I was favorably impressed with the claimant's manner of testifying and he appeared to be trying to tell the exact truth. He is almost entirely helpless and had to be helped from his bed into the room where I was as he can not walk unassisted. His mind is clear and he seemed to have a very good memory of his service. He bears a good reputation for truth as far as I could learn. The witnesses are all rated good for truth.

There seems to be no doubt that the claimant is the man who rendered the service on which the claim is based. He lives with his sister, Harriet Bennett, in whose claim he testified at the time her claim was filed. Harriet's husband served in the same regiment but in a different company. Claimant gave the names of his officers and some of the men in the Company without hesitation and he remembered the initials of his Captain although he could not remember his first name. He claims that

---

[20] Ibid., John Granderson.

he filed a claim for pension through one Webb soon after his sister was pensioned and states that he never heard anything of it. Soon after that he went to Florida to live and it is possible that that is the reason that he never heard from his claim.

I called on Jonas Mitchell of 4 Holmes St., Charleston whose name was given as one of claimant's comrades. Mitchell is very old and his memory is poor and he was unable to recall claimant. I did not think it necessary to take his deposition.

As claimant requires the regular aid and attendance of another person, I took some testimony on that point. It is plainly evident that he is unable to take care of himself. W. D. Blumenberg is a white man and although he has never seen the claimant he told me that he had often heard from members of claimant's family and others that claimant was entirely helpless. I could have secured a great deal of testimony on that point but to do so would have required another day as I had very little time before the last train to Charleston. I believe the evidence submitted is sufficient.[21]

---

[21] Letter from E.F. Fewell, Special Examiner, Charleston, SC to Commissioner of Pensions, Washington, DC, dated 20 Aug 1923.

Medal of Honor Recipient
Sgt. William Carney

William Harvey Carney was the first African American soldier to earn the Medal of Honor.

Carney was born a slave in Norfolk, Virginia, but escaped to Massachusetts and enlisted in the Union Army and served with the 54th Massachusetts Volunteer Infantry as a Sergeant and took part in the July 18, 1863, assault on Fort Wagner in Charleston, South Carolina. He received his medal for saving the American flag and planting it on the parapet and although wounded, holding it while the troops charged.

When the Federal troops were overwhelmed by Confederate fire, Carney struggled back across the battlefield, and although wounded twice more, returned the flag to the Union lines. Before turning over the colors to another survivor of the 54th, Carney modestly said, "Boys, I only did my duty; the old flag never touched the ground!"

During the heat of battle during the Civil War, the flag was an important visual contact for troops. Many medals were awarded for protecting and displaying the flag under fire, or for capturing enemy flags. Carney was awarded the Medal of Honor on May 23, 1900, nearly 40 years after his heroic act.

He died in Boston, Massachusetts, and is buried in the family plot at Oak Grove Cemetery New Bedford, Massachusetts. Engraved on his stone monument is a gold image of the Medal of Honor.

Source: http://en.wikipedia.org/wiki/William_Harvey_Carney

Francis BROWN
alias
Francis Lawton

Private, Company B: Born c1840, Beaufort, Beaufort, SC; a Slave of the Lawton's; Enlisted on 27 Feb 1865 or 07 Mar 1865, at Beaufort, Beaufort, SC; Honorably Discharged on 10 Oct 1866, at Morris Island, Charleston, SC. Married to Louisa Ellis (b. c1850, near Columbia, Richland, SC; d. 05 Jan 1912, Charleston, Charleston, SC), on 31 Aug 1870, at St. James Goose Creek, Charleston (later, Berkeley County), SC, by Rev. Charles Small. Children: Boston (b. c1874). **Francis Brown** *died on 31 Dec 1895, at Charleston, Charleston, SC.*[22]

Louisa Brown (Widow of the Veteran Soldier)
Date: 18 Jun 1901
Residence: #11 First St., Charleston, Charleston, SC
Occupation: Washer Woman

I don't know my age but I was eleven years of age when the War of the Rebellion commenced. I am a pensioner as the widow of Francis Brown.

Before the war he went by the name of Francis Lawton and I always heard him say his owner's name was Lawton. He was known both as Lawton and Brown. He died either five or six years ago – the first of last January. He died on Meeting Street near the {Palmer} House. He could not lift his hand. I can't say whether it was paralysis or not. He was sick

---

[22] Civil War Pension Record for Louisa Brown (widow of Francis Brown alias Lawton), WC No. 438.478, Pvt, Company B, 128th USCI, Records of the VA, RG 15, NARA, WDC; 1900 U.S. Federal Census, South Carolina, Charleston County, Charleston – Ward 10, ED: 105, Page: 89A, Line: 40 (Roll: T623-1520).

Francis Brown alias Francis Lawton

nearly a year. Dr. {McClenan} had been his Doctor but was not present when he died. We sent for him but the soldier had died before he arrived.

I married the soldier at {Sinas} Station, St. James Goose Creek Parish, S.C., on Mr. Parker's Place. We had been married 25 or 26 years when he died. Rev. Charles Small (colored) performed the ceremony. I married him under the name of Louisa Ellis and he married me under the name of Frank Brown. Shortly after the marriage Rev. Small gave us a certificate but it was lost in the fire the year after we were married.

I have no bible entry of our marriage or any record of any kind. We were married in Mission Hall Church, a Calvary Baptist Church on Sunday morning. The church was full of people. {Hippy} Jones and her husband Thomas Jones, who lives back of the {power} house, were present at my marriage. Diana Steward, who lives at Goose Creek, was present. Also present was my granddaughter, Caroline Warren, who resides in Goose Creek.

I only knew soldier for about a year before we married. He was working for the Charleston Mining Company, but had only been there a little while. He said he had come from Charleston. I inquired among his friends and was told he had never been previously married. I never heard the soldier say whether he had been previously married or whether he had lived with any woman before he married me. I had never been previously married.

I was born 25 miles this side of Columbia, 12 miles from Kingswell. I belonged to Boston Clarkson. My father was David Ellis (dead). My mother was {Lavay} Ellis and she died during the War of the Rebellion. I had never lived with anyone as his wife before I married the soldier.

The first year after freedom I was living on my owners place and a colored man named Thomas Jones courted me and we agreed to marry but his mother objected to the {match} and we did not marry. We never lived together but he slept with me and I became pregnant with his child but it was not born alive. He is the only man I ever had intercourse with before I married the soldier and I have not remarried or lived any man or had intercourse with any man since the soldier died.

I lived for five years on Butler Street and then moved to First Street about five years ago and have lived here ever since. I own the place I live in. I agreed to pay $300 for it but I owe $200 on it yet. This is all I own and I am wholly dependent on my labor and my pension for my support. Soldier and I had only one child. His name is Boston Brown. He is about 27 years old. He is married and has five children and he and his family have lived with me ever since the soldier died.

Soldier and I never separated but were living together at the time he died. We moved to Charleston when Boston was two years old and have lived here ever since.[23]

Thomas Lastry (Comrade and Friend of the Veteran Soldier)
    Date: 19 Jun 1901
    Residence: #110 Coming St., Charleston, Charleston, SC
    Occupation: Farmer

I am 56 years of age. I served in Company I, 128th U.S. Colored Infantry Regiment.

I met Francis Brown in the war and I saw him around here for a few months after the war and then he went away and I did not see him again until about 1893 when I met him here one day. He said that he was living up on Meeting Street and was trying for a pension and got me to make an affidavit for him. I heard that he died soon after that but I do not know the date of his death.

He was a small dark skin man about 4 feet 5 inches. I'm sure that the Francis Brown who was living on Meeting Street in 1894 was the same man who served in Company B of my regiment under the name of Lawton.[24]

---

[23] Deposition of Louisa Brown, case of Louisa Brown (Charleston, Charleston, SC), dated 18 Jun 1901.
[24] Ibid., Thomas Lastry, dated 19 Jun 1901.

Medal of Honor Recipient
Sgt. Andrew Smith

Andrew Jackson Smith was a Union Army soldier during the American Civil War and a recipient of America's highest military decoration the Medal of Honor for his actions at the Battle of Honey Hill.

By November 30, 1864, Smith was serving as a Corporal in the 55th Massachusetts Volunteer Infantry. On that day, his unit participated in the Battle of Honey Hill in South Carolina, and it was for his actions during the battle that he was awarded the Medal of Honor.

Smith was promoted to Color Sergeant before leaving the Army. After the war, he lived in Kentucky, where he bought and sold land. He died at age 88 and was buried in Mount Pleasant Cemetery, Grand Rivers, Kentucky.

Smith was nominated for the Medal of Honor in 1916, but the Army denied the nomination, citing a lack of official records documenting his case. Smith's commander at Honey Hill had not included an account of Smith's actions in the official battle report. It was not until January 16, 2001, 137 years after the Battle of Honey Hill, that Smith was recognized; President Bill Clinton presented the Medal of Honor to several of Smith's descendants during a ceremony at the White House on that day.

Source: http://en.wikipedia.org/wiki/Andrew_Jackson_Smith_(Medal_of_Honor_recipient)

John BROWN
alias
John Owens

Private, Company H: Born c1845, at Mathews Bluff, Savannah River, Colleton, SC; a Slave of William Owens (previously – Mr. Mike Brown); Enlisted on 07 Mar 1865, at Beaufort, SC; Honorably Discharged on 10 Oct 1866, at Morris Island, Charleston, SC. 1st Marriage to Margaret [MNU] (d. c1889), about 1866. Children: Mrs. Millie Edwards; Mrs. Ella Thompson; Mrs. Josie Smith; Morris; Keith; John Samuel; and Jonas. 2nd Marriage to Amelia Warren, on 18 Jun 1889, by Dr. C.E. Kinsey (d. 03 Jun 1913), at Williams, Colleton, SC. **John Brown** *died on 30 Jul 1910, at Williams, Colleton, SC.*[25]

John Brown (Veteran Soldier)
Date: 12 Jan 1909
Residence: near Williams, Colleton, SC
Occupation: Farmer

I don't know my age and never did know, but I was just grown when I went in the army. I was about 21 years old – I think. I was never married up to that time. I was first owned by Mr. Mike Brown and then by Mr. Wm. Owens – both dead. Mr. Brown lived on the Savannah River and Mr. Owens up in Barnwell County.

I am the man who served in Company H, 128th U.S. Colored Troops under the name of John Owens. I was born in Barnwell County, S.C. I went to Beaufort, S.C., during the war and soon after I got there, in

---

[25] Civil War Pension Record for Amelia Brown (widow of John Owens now known as John Brown), WC No. 787.059, Private, Company H, 128th USCI, Records of the VA, RG 15, NARA, WDC; 1900 U.S. Federal Census, South Carolina, Colleton County, Warren Township, ED: 51, Page: 377B, Line: 76 (Roll: T623-1525).

John Brown alias John Owens

March – I think, I was put in the army. My brother (dead), Charles Owens, went with me and served as a Corporal in the same company. We were in Beaufort most of the time – never in a fight. We were also at Grahamville and other places in Beaufort County and then were taken by boat to Morris Island and were mustered out there – but I think we were discharged from a boat in a {eack} near there.

While I was in the army I heard that my mother had been brought near here, so when I got out I came up here and have been here ever since. I lived near Walterboro the first year and then came here and have been here ever since. My mother and father and all my family – except one sister up in the states are dead.

My name before and while I was in the army was John Owens, but as soon as I came here I took the name of Brown because that was my father's name and was my name before I went to Mr. Brown. I have been known by the name of John Brown ever since I have been here. No one who was in my company lives near here, but Hector Tracy and Cuffie Simmons were in my regiment and knew me in service and have known me ever since; and Alex Ladson did also, but he is now dead.

I have been married twice. My first wife was Margaret who I married the year I came here and lived with her until she died about 19 years ago. Two years later I married Amelia – 16 or 17 years ago. We were married by Dr. Kinsey of this place. We have no certificate and I do not know of any record of it in a bible or anywhere else.

I have no children under the age of 16. Jonas is the youngest and he is about 21. Amelia has never had a child by me.[26]

Amelia Brown (Widow of the Veteran Soldier)
    Date: 16 Dec 1913
    Residence: near Williams, Colleton, SC
    Occupation: None

Amelia Brown made oath that she was the wife of John Brown alias John Owens, and that she was married to him on the 18th day of June 1891 by

---

[26] Deposition of John Brown, in the case of John Brown (Williams, Colleton, SC), dated 12 Jan 1909.

Dr. C.E. Kinsey, a Justice of the Peace, at Williams, S.C., and that Dr. C.E. Kinsey died on June 3rd 1913, and that the same can be found on his private record at his former home, and that John Brown died on July 30th 1910 with kidney trouble, and that Margaret, his former wife, died a few weeks and one year before my marriage to him, and that I lived with him until his death, and that none of the parties were divorced as South Carolina don't allow divorces, and that I was married to John Warren on about July 1872, and that he died thirty two years ago, and that her husband, John Brown, was a soldier and served in the Civil War about 1865, and that I have his certificate of record of his service in Company H, 128th U.S. Colored Infantry.[27]

---

[27] Sworn Statement of Amelia Brown (Colleton County, SC), dated 16 Dec 1913.

John Brown alias John Owens

Civil War Pension Benefits

After the Civil War concluded, the process of being compensated with war pensions swept the land as an accommodating federal government intervened to assist families whose lives were destroyed because the veterans and families of veterans who were incapable of providing for themselves. By 1893, more than 40 percent of the federal budget supported widows, orphans and elderly and invalid soldiers.

Between 1865 and 1890, Congress vastly expanded the pension system by extending deadlines, increasing benefits and liberalizing evidentiary requirements Thus for blacks and for whites alike, the Civil War pension system became its own social welfare system. Between 1861 and 1890, the federal government approved more than 700,000 pension applications stemming from the Civil War.

Source: Abstracted from Megan J. McClintock. "Civil War Pensions and the Reconstruction of Union Families," *The Journal of American History*, 83 (September 1996).

Richard CANADY
alias
Richard Kennedy

Private, Company I: Born c1838, at Goose Creek, Charleston, SC; a Slave of the Stoney family; Enlisted on 07 March 1865, at Charleston, Charleston, SC; Honorably Discharged on 10 Oct 1866, at Morris Island, Charleston, SC. Married to Elsie Nelson, during Nov 1866, at Oakley, Charleston (now Berkeley), SC, by Rev. Samuel Dickerson. Children: Mrs. Rosa or Rose Smith* (b. c1856); and Gracie (b. c1871). **Richard Canady** died on 02 Jul 1881, at Charleston, Charleston, SC.[28]

Thomas Lasty (Comrade and Friend of the Veteran Soldier)
Date: 31 Aug 1901
Residence: #67 Bafain St., Charleston, Charleston, SC
Occupation: Laborer

I am about 60 years of age. I was a soldier in the War Between the States. I served in Company I, 128th U.S. Colored Troops and was enlisted March 7th 1865, at Charleston, S.C., and was mustered out at Morris Island, October 1866.

About two days after enlistment I was sent to Beaufort with the regiment. The regiment was made up in Charleston and transferred to Beaufort. The regiment remained intact at Beaufort until about March 1866 when the regiment was sent to Sullivans Island, then the different companies forming the regiment were scattered about. Some went to the

---

[28] Civil War Pension Elsey Cannedy, widow of Richard Cannedy alias Richard Kennedy, WC No. 424.241, Private, Company I, 128th USCI, Records of the VA, RG 15, NARA, WDC; 1880 U.S. Census Records, South Carolina, Charleston County, Charleston, ED: 69, Page: 348B, Line: 25 (Roll: T9-1222); * Rosa is the daughter of Elsie and her first husband, Jack Spann, and is therefore Richard Canady's step-daughter.

Richard Canady alias Richard Kennedy

Islands and some went to different places inland. Our company was stationed at Sullivans Island.

They then took men from the different companies and sent them on detached service. I can't remember the names of the men who were detached. At Morris Island, the companies were all called together in 1866, about September, and then in October they were all mustered out. I recall to mind the names of a good number of my comrades in Company I: Adam Bennett, March Bennett, Stephen Terrell, Henry {Lloyd}, Clarence Palmer, Edward Alston, Richard Kennedy, Edward Garrett, Boston Jackson, Samuel Holmes, Brutus Butler, Griffin Green and there are many men who all names I cannot recall.

I did know a Richard Kennedy in the service. I don't know how he spelled his name. I never saw him write his name neither did I ever hear him spell it. I don't think he could read or write. The Richard Kennedy I knew was from the Stoney Place near Goose Creek somewhere. I don't know just where the place is. I heard him say this while in the service and I have heard him say it often. I have also heard his wife say it.

His wife was Elsey Kennedy who lives on Drake Street. He was a man with dark skin. His eyes and hair were dark. He was an older man than me. I was about 22 in 1865 and he was about 26 or 27 – I guess.

I first met Richard at Beaufort. That was sometime in the spring of 1865. I don't know if I enlisted before he did. We were tent mates for a while – for about three or four months.

I belonged to the patrol under Capt. Manning - patrolling the streets of Beaufort. Every time I went back to the company I would see Kennedy, continuous once a week and sometimes once in three weeks. Our company was ordered to Gillisonville and staid there – I should say about 3 or 4 months. This was about the last of 1865. Then the company came back to Beaufort and later was sent to Hilton Head. I did not go with the company because I was on patrol. It was about this time I lost sight of him. I don't know what became of him for quite a while.

The last time I saw him was along in 1866 on Sullivans Island – this was when the companies and detached men came together just before being mustered out on Morris Island.[29]

Isaac D. Stoney (Acquaintance of the Widow)
Date: 02 Dec 1901
Residence: Mt. Holly, Berkeley, SC
Occupation: Farmer

I am 59 years old. I am well acquainted with Elsey Kennedy. She was born a slave of my father. She was first married by ceremony in my father's house to Jack Spann. I cannot recall who married them, but I can remember that there was a ceremony. I cannot tell the date of this marriage but it was before the commencement of the War Between the States and while Elsey was a slave. Jack Spann was living on James Island the last I heard from him. Elsey was called Elsey Nelson before her marriage to Jack Spann. They had one daughter born to them called Rose who was born before the war began.

Elsey and Jack Spann lived together as husband and wife for several years or until just about the time of the evacuation of Charleston about the 17th or 18th of February 1865. Jack Spann never lived with Elsey after peace was declared or after the evacuation of Charleston. Elsey lived on my father's plantation during the whole of the war and Jack Spann, who was not a soldier, lived with her all that time until he was told that he was free when he left and went to live on James Island.

I was in the Confederate service and was discharged in May 1865 and when I reached home Jack Spann was gone and Elsey was still on our place. Jack left her and took up with a fellow slave named Patience Cash and I know that he lived with Patience for several years on James Island. I don't know if he was married by ceremony to Patience or not. I think not. I know that he never returned to Elsey and never lived with her after the close of the war.

---

[29] Deposition of Thomas Lasty, case of Elsey Cannaday (Charleston, Charleston, SC), dated 31 Aug 1901.

Richard Canady alias Richard Kennedy

Elsey was next married to Richard Kennedy or Kannedy. I cannot tell how he spelled his name. Elsey and Richard were married in the latter part of 1866 or the early part of 1867. They lived on our plantation for a number of years and then went to Charleston, as I understand, and he died there about 20 years ago. I cannot be definite as to exact time.[30]

[The remains of Richard Canady was returned to the plantation, in Goose Creek, for interment]

The Big Storm of 1893

On August 27, 1893 a major hurricane, which came to be known as the Sea Islands Hurricane, struck the United States near Savannah, Georgia. It was one of two deadly hurricanes during the 1893 Atlantic hurricane season. The storm killed an estimated 1,000-2,000 people, mostly from storm surge, and an estimated 20,000-30,000 were left homeless and with no mean of subsistence. Property damage was estimated at $10 million, equal to $119 or 330,000 in 1985 dollars.

Source: http://en.wikipedia.org/wiki/1893_Sea_Islands_Hurricane;
http://www.dnr.sc.gov/climate/sco/Tropics/hurricanes_affecting_sc.php
(South Carolina State Climatology Office. South Carolina Hurricane Climatology.

---

[30] Ibid., I. D. Stoney, dated 02 Dec 1901.

* * * * * * * * * * * * *

Gibson W. COLEMAN
alias
Gibson Westpoint

Corporal, Company K: Born on 05 Mar 1848, at Wadmalaw, Charleston, SC; a Slave of Constantine Bailey; Enlisted on 06 Mar 1865, at Beaufort, Beaufort, SC; Disability Discharged on 06 Oct 1865, at Hilton Head, Beaufort, SC. 1st Marriage to Lavinia Wright (d. c1888, Charleston, Charleston, SC). Children: Ephraim (b. c1871); Moses (b. c1877); Samuel (b. c1880); and William (b. c1882). 2nd Marriage to Isabella Rebecca Dobson, on 13 Feb 1890, at Charleston, SC, by Rev. J. Bunch Williams. ***Gibson Westpoint Coleman*** *died 02 Nov 1907, at Charleston, Charleston, SC.*[31]

Gibson Westpoint Coleman (Veteran Soldier)
Date: 30 Oct 1901
Residence: #45 Queen St., Charleston, Charleston, SC
Occupation: Laborer

I am 53 years of age. I was 17 years of age when I enlisted in the army but they put me down as 19. The old folks told me I was born on March 5th. I was born on Wadmalaw Island about 35 miles from Charleston on the sea coast. I was born a slave of my master named Constantine Bailey. My father was named Huckey Coleman. I was known as Gibson Coleman when I enlisted in the army. My mother had been twice married. Her first husband was named Hardtime Westpoint and I have kept the name of Gibson Westpoint. When I enlisted it was with my half brother

---

[31] Civil War Pension Record for Gibson Westpoint Coleman alias Gibson Westpoint, SC No. C-2.503.077, Pvt, Company K, 128th USCI, Records of the VA, RG 15, NARA, WDC; 1900 U.S. Federal Census, Charleston County, Charleston City, ED: 74, Page: 3A, Line: 1 (Roll: T623-1520).

Gibson W. Coleman alias Gibson Westpoint

Peter Westpoint and I took the name of Gibson Westpoint and I have kept the name of Westpoint ever since and I made my full name Gibson Westpoint Coleman, but I am mostly known as Gibson W. Coleman or G.W. Coleman.

I enlisted at Beaufort, S.C. in Company H, 128th U.S. Colored Troops about the 6th day of March 1865 and was discharged because of sickness or disability on October 6, 1865 at Hilton Head, S.C. I was never in any other company or regiment. I was never in any other Army or Navy of the United States before March 1865 or subsequent to October 1865. I was never enlisted in the Confederate Army. I never had anything to do with the Confederate Army except that I waited on the sick soldiers at the hospital in Summersville, S.C., when I was a boy carrying around the food to the sick in the cots.

I served in Beaufort up to September 1865 when my Company was ordered to Grahamville, S.C., and during the march I fell out senseless from the heat and marching and when I came to my senses I was in an ambulance and was taken to Grahamville. I staid in Grahamville about a month and was sent to the hospital at Hilton Head and from there I was discharged and I went right to Edisto Island where my mother and father were living. I was taken with the small pox and was healed at my mother's house by a 'free' army doctor. I lived on Edisto Island until 1887 when I moved to Charleston, S.C., and have lived here ever since.

I am presently married. I have been married twice. I was married on Edisto Island first – in February 1867. I married Lavinia Wright. She is dead. She died on the 1st day of Sept 1888. I again married Feby 12, 1890 at #4 Chapman St., Charleston, S.C. I married Isabelle Dobson. We were married by Rev. Bunch {A.} Williams, of the A.M.E. Church. She was never married before. I was never married but once before. I have no children by my present wife.[32]

---

[32] Deposition of Gibson Westpoint Coleman, case of Gibson Westpoint Coleman (Charleston, Charleston, SC), dated 30 Oct 1901.

Allen DAVID
alias
Allen Yaney

Private, Company A: Born during 1847, at Yaney's Plantation, Barnwell County, SC; a Slave of John Yaney; Enlisted on 01 Mar 1865, at Charleston, Charleston, SC; Honorably Discharged on 10 Oct 1866, at Morris Island, Charleston, SC. Married to Phoebe Mole (b. c1846; d. 13 May 1932, at Varnville, Hampton, SC), on 03 Nov 1869, at Beaufort, Beaufort, SC, by Stephen Kearse. Children: Francis (b. 12 May 1886); Wesley (b. 25 Nov 1888); and, Stewart (b. 10 Jan 1890). Allen David died on 13 Sep 1909, at Varnville, Hampton, SC.[33]

Allen David (Veteran Soldier)
Date: 10 May 1902
Residence: Varnville, Hampton, SC
Occupation: Mill Hand

I am 55 years of age. I was born in Barnwell County, S.C. on Yaney's plantation and was born the slave of John Yaney – now dead. Only his nephews are now alive – Wyman and John. They live in Barnwell County and know me well.

My father was named David Cope and he belonged to George Cope. My mother was Adaline Harvey and she belonged to Owen Harvey – all of Barnwell County. My father titled after his master. My parents were never known by any name except that of their owners. I enlisted under

---

[33] Civil War Pension Record of Feby David (widow of Allen Yaney now known as Allen David), Widow's Certificate No. 723.942, Company A, 128th USCI, Records of the VA, RG 15, NARA, WDC; 1900 U.S. Federal Census, South Carolina, Hampton County, Pepples Township, ED: 59, Page: 145B, Line: 96 (Roll: T623-1531).

Allen David alias Allen Yaney

the name of Allen Yaney and was called that name all through the army. I was known as Allen Yaney before I enlisted and never had any other name until I came out after the war.

I enlisted before Lincoln was killed and served about a year and ten months. I enlisted when the regiment was first made up. We were organized at Beaufort, S.C., and remained there for about a year. We then went to Charleston and remained there about 10 months and were sent to Morris Island, S.C., and then mustered out. These were all of my stations during my service.

When I came out of the army I thought I would go by my father's first name which was David. He went by Cope in slavery because Cope owned him. He was David Cope until he died. I just took my father's first name, David. I am known now as Allen David.

After my discharge I lived one year near Beaufort; 12 years at Brunson; then 15 years at Almeda; then here. Daniel George and Thomas Hamilton lived near me at Almeda. Henry Harvey and Mike Goodin knew me well at Brunson. E.R. Gin and Josiah Pope both know me well.

Henry Williams of Sheldon and Hector Tracy of Williams Post Office are the only witnesses who signed for me in my claim. They both appeared in person. They both get pensions. I did not witness in either of the claims. I gave Hector Tracy about $1.50 and Williams about the same.

Some of my comrades were Jesse Folk, Richard Rankin, Frank Jones, Bill Dosier, Adam Brant, Hector Tracy and Henry Williams. Folk is in Charleston. Rankin, Dosier and Brant are dead. Williams is at Shelton, S.C. Hector Tracy is at Williams, S.C.[34]

---

[34] Deposition of Allen David, case of Allen David (Varnville, Hampton, SC), dated 10 May 1902.

* * * * * * * * * * * * * *

George Washington DEAS
alias
Washington Diss

Private, Company G: Born c1840, at Georgetown, Georgetown, SC; a Slave of Francis Weston; Enlisted on 08 Mar 1865, at Charleston, Charleston, SC; Honorably Discharged on 10 Oct 1866, at Morris Island, Charleston, SC. 1st Marriage to Mary Jane Izzard (d. 06 Nov 1893, Charleston, SC), on 15 Mar 1887, by Rev. G.C. Boone. Children: Annie V. (b. 1888); Emily (b. 1890); Frank (b. 1892); George (b. 1893) and {Gretus} E. (b. 1896). 2nd Marriage to Rosa E. Martin, on 22 Mar 1909, at Charleston, SC, by Jesse D. Lyker, Rector Calvary P.E. Church. **George Washington Deas** *died on 22 May 1912, at Charleston, Charleston, SC.*[35]

Clarence Palmer & Elias Phoenix (Comrades of Veteran Soldier)
Date: Abt May 1912
Residence: Charleston, Charleston, SC

Clarence Palmer states that he has known Washington Deas before marriageable age; that he has known him before they enlisted in the army, some six or seven years before they enlisted; that Deas was not married at that time, and he did not get married while a soldier; that they enlisted in the 128th Regiment; that Deas enlisted in Georgetown, and that he enlisted in Beaufort, S.C.; that he always kept their friendship the same as before they enlisted and up to his death; that Deas got married to his first wife somewhere in 1888, or about that time; that her name was be-

---

[35] Civil War Pension Record for Washington Deas alias Washington Diss, SC No. C-2.466.262, Pvt, Company G, 128th USCI, Records of the VA, RG 15, NARA, WDC; 1910 U.S. Federal Census, South Carolina, Charleston County, Charleston – Ward 4, ED: 28, Page: 65A, Line: 43 (Roll: T624-1452).

fore her marriage, Mary Jane Izzard; that there were no other marriages between his first wife, Mary Jane, and his second wife, Rosa E.; that if there had been he would have known it, as they always had kept company continuously; that he knew his first wife as well as his second wife, now living; that his full name was George Washington Deas; that he only went by the name Washington Deas; that he seldom gave his full name.

and

Elias Phoenix states that he has known George Washington Deas from boyhood; that they were slaves to the same owner, Francis Weston; that they have always been together; that both enlisted in Georgetown, South Carolina, in the 128th Regiment; that Deas was enrolled in Company G and that he was enrolled in Company F; that Deas never married until he married to his first wife in Charleston, S.C., Mary Jane Izzard (deceased); that there was no other marriage between Mary J. and Rosa E., the present wife, and; that claimant's deceased husband always called himself Washington Deas, and he lived with his wife, Rosa E. up to his death and never was parted from her.

and

Clarence Palmer and Elias Phoenix and further states that George Washington Deas, now deceased, and Rosa E. lived as man and wife up to his death and have never been separated during the marriage, and; that they give these statements from their own personal knowledge, and of their acquaintance with Deas from boyhood up to his death and if it were otherwise they would know it.[36]

---

[36] General Affidavit of Elias Phoenix and Clarence Palmer, case of Rosa E. Dias, widow of George Washington Deas (Charleston County, SC), dated about Jun 1912.

Harry DICKSON
alias
Harry Lewiston

Private, Company K: Born c1830, in Virginia, (brought to South Carolina a Slave of John Livingstone, but Freed before enlistment); Enlisted on 07 Mar 1865, at Beaufort, Beaufort, SC; Honorably Discharged on 10 Oct 1866, at Morris Island, Charleston, SC. Married to Essie [MNU] (d. 29 Sep 1925, at Orangeburg, Orangeburg, SC), during May 1869. Children: Mrs. Rose Cooper (b. 1893). **Harry J. Dickson** *died on 27 Mar 1919, at Orangeburg, Orangeburg, SC.*[37]

Harry Dickson alias Lewiston (Veteran Soldier)
Date: 13 Oct 1893
Residence: Orangeburg, Orangeburg, SC
Occupation: Farmer

I am 62 years old and reside 10 miles East of Orangeburgh, S.C., which is my post office. I am the same Harry Dickson who is an applicant for pension on account of service during the late war as a member of Company K, 128th U.S. Colored Infantry.

I was born in Virginia and was sold as a slave to South Carolina when I was 12 years old. I belonged to the Lewistons or Livingstons in Orangeburgh County, S.C. When I enlisted I gave my name as Harry Livingston and I think that was the name on my discharge papers. The same year that peace was declared the Federal Army came through here

---

[37] Civil War Pension Record for Essie Dickson (widow of Harry Dickson alias Harry Lewiston), WC No. 882.012, Pvt, Company D, 128th USCI, Records of the VA, RG 15, NARA, WDC; 1910 U.S. Federal Census, South Carolina, Orangeburg County, Limestone Township, ED: 55, Page: 57B, Line: 59 (Roll: T624-1470).

in January and I went with them to Wilmington, N.C. At Wilmington, they put a whole lot of us on a transport boat and took us to Beaufort, and then I was enlisted in Company K, 128th U.S. Colored Infantry.

We staid at Beaufort for several months doing garrison duty and drilling. Then my company and Company E were sent to Parris Island and staid there till Christmas. We did not do much but 'coal' boats. From there I went to Sullivans Island and Castle Pinckney, S.C. Then a certain number out each company were detached to do prison guard duty. We did duty at the Big House where Major {Bogers} had his headquarters. Then I did duty in Charleston at the Citadel assigned under Captain Field. I was mustered out at Morris Island about this time of the year.[38]

Harry Dickson (Veteran Soldier)
Date: 15 Dec 1899
Residence: Raymond, Orangeburg, SC

Harry Dickson declares that his owner previous to the Civil War was John Livingstone; that his Christian name is and always has been Harry; that according to custom he assumed for a surname Livingstone, the surname of his master; that during the war and immediately afterwards this name Livingstone was corrupted by his associates into Lewiston; that shortly after the war he assumed the name Dickson by which name he has been since then and is known now; and that Harry Livingstone, Harry Lewiston and Harry Dickson are one and the same.[39]

Sheck Thomas and Irving Rowe (Comrades of the Veteran)
Date: 09 Jun 1900
Residence: Orangeburg County, SC

Sheck Thomas and Irving Rowe, comrades of Harry Dickson, declares that Harry Dickson is the same Harry Lewiston who served in the 128th Regiment U.S. Colored Volunteer Infantry; also, that Harry Dickson was

---

[38] Deposition of Harry Dickson alias Lewiston, case of Harry Dickson alias Lewiston (Orangeburg, Orangeburg, SC), dated 13 Oct 1893.

[39] General Affidavit of Harry Dickson, in the matter of Harry Dickson, Application for Pension (Raymond, Orangeburg, SC), dated 15 Dec 1899.

born in Virginia, but was brought to South Carolina when he was very small; that he has lived here ever since; that he was about thirty-five years old when he enlisted; that he was then a freed slave; that he was about five ft. and 6" or 8" high; and that he is a negro, with black hair (now turning gray) and black or dark eyes.[40]

Abstracted Summary of Response from Department of Pensions
Date: 15 Nov 1900
Office: Bureau of Pension, Washington, DC

Sir, Herewith are referred to you the papers, in the claims of Harry Dickson alias Harry Lewiston alias Harry Livingston, Company K, 128th U.S. Colored Volunteer Infantry; of Irwin Nero and of Jacob McAllister.

Irvin Nero applied under that name and was pensioned. It is now shown in his testimony to establish the identity of Harry Dickson, that his name is <u>Irwin Rowe</u> alias Irwin Nero.

Jacob McAllister applied for and was pensioned under that name. In testifying to the identity of Harry Dickson, that his name is <u>Scheck Thomas</u> alias Jacob McAllister.

Both Irwin Rowe alias Irwin Nero and Scheck Thomas alias Jacob McAllister have, as above stated, testified as to the identity of Harry Dickson alias Harry Lewiston alias Harry Livingston.

In view of the various aliases, as stated, the papers were referred to this division [Law Division] under Order 244 for an investigation as to identities.

It is desired that the accompanying papers be referred to a Special Examiner whose district embraces Orangeburg County, S.C, and for such other reference as may be necessary, to establish the identity of the soldiers herein named. This letter should appear as an exhibit in the final report of the Special Examiner. VR / Chief of Law Division.[41]

---

[40] Ibid., Sheck Thomas and Irving Thomas, dated 09 Jun 1900.
[41] Letter from Chief of Law Division, Bureau of the Pension, Department of the Interior, Washington, DC to Chief of S.E. Division, dated 15 Nov 1900.

The Butler Medal

The Butler Medal, officially known as the *Army of the James Medal*, was named for General Benjamin F. Butler, commander of the Army of the James, who commissioned a medal to honor African-American troops in his command for gallantry during the Battle of New Market Heights on September 29, 1864.

The medal is silver, inscribed on the obverse with "Ferro Ilis Libertas Perveniet" and on the reverse with "Distinguished Courage Campaign Before Richmond 1864."

The Butler Medal holds the distinction of being the first and one of the only medals ever struck for black servicemen.

Source: William A. Gladstone. *United States Colored Troops, 1863-1867*. Gettysburg: Thomas Publications, 1990, p.70

Quintus FAVORS
alias
Quintus Hunt

Private, Company C: Born c1840, at Hunt's Ferry, Charleston, SC; a Slave of Dr. William Hunt; Enlisted on 07 Mar 1865, at Beaufort, Beaufort, SC; Honorably Discharged on 10 Oct 1866, at Morris Island, Charleston, SC. Married to Lucinda Middleton (b. c1851, near St. Stephens, Charleston, SC), "Common Law," c1870 and "Ceremonial," c1886, at Mt. Pleasant, Charleston, SC, by Rev. North. Children: Susan (b. 15 May 1884); and Daniel (b. 07 Oct 1886). Quintus Favors died on 12 Jun 1895, at Mt. Pleasant, Charleston, SC.[42]

Lucinda Favors (Widow of the Veteran Soldier)
Date: 02 Jul 1904
Residence: Mt. Pleasant, Charleston, SC

I don't know my age but I think I am about 50. I receive pension as the widow of Quintus Favors who served in the war as Quintus Hunt. I was born near St. Stephen, S.C., and was taken to Colleton County just before and during the war, then was taken back to St. Stephen and left there just at the time of peace and came down here with my father (dead) and have been here ever since.

All of my family is dead except one sister. I was owned by Mr. R. Press Smith (dead). I was only 15 years old when I came here and I went by the name of Middleton. I never went by any name except Middleton

---

[42] Civil War Pension Record for Cinda Favors (widow of Quintus Favors alias Quintus Hunt), WC No. 578.713, Pvt, Company C, 128th USCI, Records of the VA, RG 15, NARA, WDC; 1880 U.S. Federal Census, South Carolina, Charleston County, Christ Church, ED: 78, Page: 3B, Line: 23 (Roll: T9-1223).

Quintus Favors alias Quintus Hunt

until I lived with Quintus as man and wife. I was never married and never lived with a man until I met him about a year after the war and decided to live with him within a year. I lived with him from that time until he died. Quintus and I did not get married until the year of the "big shake" (Page 136). We were married by Reverend North. He got after us to marry and we got married but we had been living as man and wife for nearly 20 years before we were married by him. Quintus died in June – I don't know the year, but it has been about nine years.

I have not remarried nor lived with a man since Quintus died and all the land I own is a 1/2 acre lot with a two-room shed on it which cost me $25.00 for the land and $15.00 for the house and shed. That is all the property I own.

When I met Quintus he was single and he did not have a woman until he had me. He was then known as Quintus Favors, but he told me he served in the war under his owner's name of Hunt. He went by both names after he came here to live with me.

My youngest children are Daniel and Suky. Daniel was born a year after the "big shake." He was born in October. I am positive of that. Suky was born the middle of May and she was born the year of the storm that we had just before the "big storm" (Page 38) and I am positive she is two years and just a little more older than Daniel. They are still living with me.

Quintus was born and lived near here before the war and was owned by William Hunt at Hunt's Ferry.[43]

---

[43] Deposition of Cinda Favors, case of Cinda Hunt Favors (Mt. Pleasant, Charleston, SC), dated 02 Jul 1904.

Dennis FLOYD
alias
William Saunders

Private, Company I: Born c1847, in Barnwell County, SC; a Slave of Mr. Chamberlain; Enlisted on 07 Mar 1865, at Charleston, Charleston, SC; Disability Discharged on 04 Oct 1865, at Hilton Head, Beaufort, SC. Married to Diana Washington, on 05 Mar 1874, at Charleston, SC, by Rev. John Everette. Children: Mrs. Ellen Lewis (b. 03 May 1880); Mrs. Florence J. Smith; and Rebecca (b. 15 May 1882). **Dennis Floyd** *died aft 1909, prob at Charleston, Charleston, SC.*[44]

Dennis Floyd (Veteran Soldier)
Date: 10 Oct 1902
Residence: #12 Butler St., Charleston, Charleston, SC
Occupation: Unemployed

My age is 55. I am the man who served in Company I, 128th U.S. Colored Infantry as William Saunders. I was born in Barnwell, S.C, but was raised in this city. I was last owned by Mr. Chamberlain (dead) of this city. Before the war I was called Dennis Floyd. My father (dead) was Jacob Floyd.

I enlisted at this city in March 1865 and was sent to Beaufort, S.C., where I was mustered into service. I was only 17 or 18 when I enlisted. My father did not want me to go in the army so I took the name of William Saunders when I enlisted so he could not find me, and I served as

---

[44] Civil War Pension Record for Dennis Floyd alias William Saunders, SC No. C-2.535.862, Pvt, Company I, 128th USCI, Records of the VA, RG 15, NARA, WDC; 1910 U.S. Federal Census, South Carolina, Charleston County, Charleston – Ward 10, ED: 53, Page: 300A, Line: 23 (Roll: T624-1452).

Dennis Floyd alias William Saunders

William Saunders, but when I came home I took my name of Dennis Floyd and have gone by that name ever since.

I first did duty at Beaufort and then went to Gillionville and from there I was sent to Hilton Head with several others. I was examined and mustered out and sent home. I don't know what the doctor said was the matter with me but I could not get my breath at times. I had suffered that way nearly all of my life and when I took a cold {I couldn't do any} marching. I would feel like I was going to {smother}. I was that way before I went in the army and have been that way ever since.

I had no other sickness in the service and I was not injured in any way, but since the war I have had the 3rd and 4th fingers of my right hand cut off. I was working at {someone} saw mill about 3 years ago when my hand was caught by the saw and the fingers cut off. Sam {St. Oliver}, who was my [first]/ordnance sergeant during the war, was working with me at the time.[45]

---

[45] Deposition of Dennis Floyd, case of Dennis Floyd (Charleston, Charleston, SC), dated 10 Oct 1902.

* * * * * * * * * * * * *

Jacob FRAZIER
alias
Jacob Kitt

Private, Company K: Born during 1840, near Orangeburg, Orangeburg, SC; a Slave of Daniel Kitt; Enlisted on 08 Mar 1865, at Beaufort, Beaufort, SC; Honorably Discharged on 10 Oct 1866, at Morris Island, Charleston, SC. 1st Marriage to Caroline [MNU] (d. c1867). 2nd Marriage to Elizabeth [MNU] (d. 12 Jul 1880, Jacksonville, Duval, FL). Children: Robert (b. 07 or 20 Mar 1874); Susie R. (b. 12 or 14 Mar 1876); and Mrs. Selina B. Wheaton* (b. 21 Jul 1878). 3rd Marriage to Sylvia Davis or Presley, (d. 18 Jan 1905, Jacksonville, FL), 03 Sep 1883, Jacksonville, Duval, FL, by Judge W.A. McClain. **Jacob Frazier** *died on 22 Oct 1912, at Jacksonville, Duval, FL.*[46]

Jacob Frazier (Veteran Soldier)
Date: 01 May 1899
Residence: #1154 Oakley St., Jacksonville, Duval, FL

Jacob Frazier declares that there is no one in the City of Jacksonville or in the State of Florida who can testify from personal knowledge that he is the identical person who served in Company K, 128th U.S. Colored Volunteer Infantry under the name of Jacob Kitt.

He further says that he was born near Orangeburg in the State of South Carolina; that he was about nineteen years of age when he enlisted; that he was by occupation a servant; and that he was five feet six

---

[46] Civil War Pension Record for Jacob Frazier alias Jacob Kitt, SC No. C-2.559.745, Pvt, Company K, 128th USCI, Records of the VA, RG 15, NARA, WDC; 1910 U.S. Federal Census, Florida, Duval County, Jacksonville, ED: 72, Page: 118B, Line: 73 (Roll: T623-167). *Note: Selina is married to Edward E. Wheaton.

Jacob Frazier alias Jacob Kitt

inches tall, black complexion, black hair and eyes, and; that his discharge paper, together with his clothes and other effects, were stolen from him by some person or persons unknown, in the City of Charleston, South Carolina, more than twenty years ago.[47]

Henry Morse (Acquaintance of the Veteran Soldier)
Date: 06 Sep 1894
Residence: Jacksonville, Duval, SC

Henry Morse (48) declares that he is personally acquainted with Jacob Frazier for 13 years and states that he is all the time complaining of being sick ever since knowing him and knows that Frazier is not able to do any kind of work; that to the best of his knowledge and belief that the sickness of Frazier is not caused by any vicious habits; that sometimes Frazier look like a diseased man and then he picks up a little and looks a little better; that he gain knowledge of Morse's condition by seeing him weekly – and sometimes every day; that when Morse is able to be up he sees him every day; that when he does not see him he ask about him and hear he is sick; that they both live in the City of Jacksonville, Florida.[48]

Major & John Thomas (Acquaintances of the Veteran Soldier)
Date: 24 May 1897
Residence: Jacksonville, Duval, FL

Major G. Thomas (48) and John T. Thomas (42), each declare that they have known Jacob Frazier for thirteen years; that they have seen him frequently during that time, and have worked with him off and on a good deal during all these years; that they know of their own knowledge and from their intimate acquaintances with him that the disabilities of which he complains and with which he is afflicted – pneumonia on the left side, general debilities & lung disease, are not the results of vicious habits.

---

[47] General Affidavit for Jacob Frazier, in re the Pension Claim of Jacob Frazier, alias Jacob Kitt, Company K, 128th Reg't U.S.C. Volunteer Infantry, #976773 (Duval County, FL), dated 01 May 1899.
[48] Ibid., Henry Morse, dated 06 Sep 1894.

They further states that Jacob Frazier has always been a sober hard working man, very steady, and decent in all his habits; and that he has been in feeble health for some years; and that they are thoroughly satisfied that his troubles are not the result of vicious habits.[49]

Mrs. Florence J. Smith (Daughter of the Veteran Soldier)
Date: 17 Apr 1922
Residence: #14 Davenport St., Boston, MA

Dear Sir: The information required concerning my father's first wife I am unable to furnish. I was told by my aunt, my father's sister, that Caroline Frazier left Spencertown soon after the war, and died somewhere in New York State, about the year of 1867. No one has heard of her since.

My father has lived with me all his life until he died, and I have taken care of him ever since I was grown up large enough, and even all through my married life. He depended upon me for everything; a good many things he was not able to do for himself. Now, Mr. Gardener, in reference to the money that is legally due to him, I am not asking for a penny for myself in person, I am only asking for that which is right and that which covers the funeral expenses, doctoring and nursing, as they have asked me several time if I have their money yet.

If it is your desire you make the different amounts out in separate checks to whom these bill are due which you have in your possession so that I may give each one what is due them providing you don't care to sign the whole amount to me. I will be perfectly satisfied either way. I can't see why his first wife, even if she was living, could have anything to do or say in regards of money for my father's funeral expenses. Hoping this will be satisfactory. I remain Respectfully. (signature) Florence J. Smith[50]

---

[49] Ibid., Major R. Thomas and John T. Thomas, dated 24 May 1897.
[50] Letter from Florence J. Smith (daughter of Jacob Frazier), Boston, MA to Mr. Washington Gardner, Commissioner, Department of the Interior, Bureau of Pensions, WDC, dated 17 Apr 1922.

Gradual and Limited Emancipation during the American Civil War

Almost from the beginning of the Civil War, progress was being made to end the dreaded Institution of Slavery in the United States. Following are examples of the gradual process.

1st Confiscation Act
06 Aug 1861

An act permitting seizure of any property, including slaves, being used by the Confederate Service to support insurrection during the American Civil War. It did not free the slaves but did strip their owners of claim to them. The Confiscation Act was an attempt to set a uniform policy throughout the army.

2nd Confiscation Act
16 Jul 1862

This Act declared that all slaves taking refuge behind Union lines, as captives of war, were to be set free. Essentially, the Act prepared the way for the Emancipation Proclamation and solved the immediate dilemma facing the army concerning the status of slaves within its Jurisdiction.

Emancipation Proclamation
01 Jan 1863

This proclamation was a presidential order issued to emancipate all slaves in the United States. Emancipation, was limited, freeing only slaves in southern states (or part of a state) still in rebellion with the Union.

Source: http://en.wikipedia.org/wiki/Confiscation_Act_of_1861; http://www.civilwarhome.com/confiscationact1862.htm; http://en.wikipedia.org/wiki/ Emancipation Proclamation.

Frank GADISON
alias
Thomas Trowell

Private, Company G: Born Feb 1846, in Barnwell District, SC; a Slave of James Trowell; Enlisted on 08 Mar 1865, at Beaufort, Beaufort, SC; Disability Discharged on 07 Dec 1866, at Hilton Head, Beaufort, SC. Married to Martha Wilkinson, during Aug 1869, at La Grange, Fayette, TX, by Minister Murray Cole. Children: Mrs. Mahalia Kimble (b. 28 Apr 1872). **Frank Gadison** *died on 15 Jun 1927, at Rutersville, Fayette, TX.*[51]

Frank Gadison (Veteran Soldier)
Date: 13 Mar 1912
Residence: LaGrange, Fayette, TX

My name is now Frank Gadison, but my name was formerly Thomas Trowell and I enlisted in the Army under the name of Thomas Trowell. My owner's name at the time of the Civil War was James Trowell and he lived in Barnwell District, S.C. I changed my name to Frank Gadison because I did not wish to return to my father in South Carolina, and so I came to Texas under the name of Frank Gadison.

I was born in Barnwell District, South Carolina, but I do not know the date of my birth. I was 19 years of age when I enlisted in the Union Army. I enlisted March 8, 1865, at Beaufort, S.C. I was discharged about October 8, 1866, at Charleston, S.C. I had no Confederate service. I had no prior or subsequent service. I was in the hospital at Charleston, S.C. I

---

[51] Civil War Pension Record for Thomas Trowell now known as Frank Gadison, SC No. C2.476.756, Private, Company G, 128th USCI, Records of the VA, RG 15, NARA, WDC; 1910 U.S. Federal Census, Texas, Fayette County, Justice Precinct 1, ED: 52, Page: 39A, Line: 44 (Roll: T624-1552).

Frank Gadison alias Thomas Trowell

was in no battles. I cannot remember the names of my Captain or Lieutenant. My 1st Sergeant was Joseph Pino. Of my comrades, I remember Seabron Jones, Henry Stokes and Corporal Frank Frazier.

I was married in August 1869, to Martha Wilkinson, at La Grange, Texas. I secured the marriage license at La Grange, Texas. This wife and I live together at the present time. I have had no prior marriage.[52]

Louisiana Gadison (Widow of the Veteran Soldier)
Date: 15 Feb 1928
Residence: LaGrange, Fayette, TX

Gentlemen: I am the widow of the late Frank Gadison, G-128 U.S.C. Infantry, I.C. 1149567, WIDOW DIVISION

Now, I have not received any money since his death outside of the above mentioned $72.00 and I am too old to work for myself. I certainly need the money now as much as when he was living. I am his legal wife and do not see why the bureau did not continue to send the stipulated amount for widows. Please let me know what to do so as to secure the pension. With thanks in advance, Yours Truly, Louisiana Gadison.[53]

==========

Madam: In response to your letter of recent date, I have to advise you that as your marriage to the above mentioned soldier did not occur prior to Jun 27, 1905, you have no pensionable status under the existing pension laws, and you were so advised in a letter addressed to you July 2, 1927. If you desire to receive the accrued pension due the soldier at the time of his death, for which you filed an application, July 27, 1927, you should furnish the evidence indicated in the accompanying circular letter, which is a duplicate of the one sent you Sept 20, 1927, at your former address, Rutersville, TX. Respectfully, Winfield Scott, Commissioner.[54]

---

[52] Deposition of Thomas Trowell now known as Frank Gadison, case of Thomas Trowell now known as Frank Gadison (La Grange, Fayette, TX), dated 13 Mar 1912.

[53] Letter correspondence from Louisiana Gadison (widow), R 2, Box 64, La Grange, Texas, to the Pension Bureau, Washington, DC, dated 19 Jan 1928.

[54] Letter correspondence from Winfield Scott, Commissioner – Bureau of Pension, Washington, DC, to Mrs. Louisiana Gadison, R. #2, Box 64, La Grange, TX, dated 15 Feb 1928.

Richard GEDDIS
alias
Dick Richards

Private, Company H: Born c1840, at Summerville, Dorchester, SC; a Slave of Daniel Postel; Enlisted on 13 Mar 1865, at Beaufort, Beaufort, SC; Disability Discharged on 31 Jul 1865, at Beaufort, SC. Married to Rebecca Smalls (b. c1849), on 24 Dec 1865 or 1866, at James Perry Plantation, Beech Hill, Dorchester, SC, by Rev. Cato Waring. Children: Jessie; Henry; George; Catherine; Henrietta; Rufus; Samuel and Louis (b. Sep 1895). Richard Geddis died 12 Jul 1906, Summerville, Dorchester, SC.[55]

Richard Geddis (Veteran Soldier)
Date: 02 Apr 1902
Residence: Summerville, Dorchester, SC
Occupation: Farmer

I was owned by Daniel Postel during slave days. I was born and reared on his plantation. His plantation was about 15 miles from Summerville on Beech Hill. I now own a part of the place and have resided on the same plantation all my life.

My correct name is Richard Geddis. My father was named Moses Geddis. My mother was named Margaret Latsen before marrying my father. I enlisted into Company H, 128th U.S. Colored Troops early in March 1865 and served until August 1, 1865. I served under the name of

---

[55] Civil War Pension Record for Rebecca Geddis (widow of Richard Geddis alias Dick Richards), WC No. 688.006, Pvt, Company K, 128th USCI, Records of the VA, RG 15, NARA, WDC; 1900 U.S. Federal Census, South Carolina, Dorchester County, Collins Township, ED: 67, Page: 42A, Line: 8 (Roll: T623-1526).

Richard Geddis alias Dick Richards

Dick Richards. My first name being Richard but some people call me Dick and when I went to give the enlistment officer my name as Dick, I stopped short and said Richard, and so they put down as Dick Richards and so I went by that name during my army service.

I remember meeting a man here since the war who belonged to my company, but I cannot remember his name. I remember Richard Fallin, Prince Hamilton, Joseph Albright, Cyrus Lewis, Samuel McNeill, William Porcher, David Robinson, Daniel Samuels, July Tenant and Gibson Westpoint. I think they would recognize me but they may not as it has been a long time ago.

I was discharged on account of bladder trouble – cystitis was the name of the ailment on my discharge. I had the measles during my service but had no cough, throat or lung trouble. Dr. [Henry K.] Durrant (Regimental Surgeon) examined me when I was discharged. I was discharged about the time I was getting over the measles.

The reason I never applied for a pension sooner was because I was able to work until a few years ago. I was paralyzed in my right leg and left arm in June 1901 and applied for a pension right away. I have defective eyesight and kidney trouble and general debility.[56]

Richard Geddis (Veteran Soldier)
Date: 03 Apr 1902
Residence: Charleston, Charleston, SC

I was married to Rebecca Smalls in 1865 or 1866 by a preacher named Cato Waring. We were married on the James Perry plantation 12 miles from Summerville. Edmund Aiken, Frank Gelzer, March Middleton, Frederick Goodwine and Joseph Jenkins were among those that saw us married – all residing at Club House Cross Roads, Dorchester County, S.C. Neither of us had been previously married.

I have one child only under 16 years of age. His name is Lewis Geddis. He was about 10 years old last September. There is a record of his birth in the family bible and I believe there is a church record also. The

---

[56] Deposition by Richard Geddis, in the case of Richard Geddis alias Dick Richard (Charleston, Charleston, SC), dated 02 Apr 1902.

only record of my marriage is in my bible. The preacher put it down the same day I was married.[57]

Primous Geddis (Friend of the Veteran Soldier)
Date: 08 Jul 1909
Residence: Summerville, Dorchester, SC

Primous Geddis declares that: I knew Richard Geddis all of my life and up to the time of his death. He died July 12th 1906 at Beech Hill, Dorchester, County, S.C. I was at his burial. I also know Rebecca Geddis, the claimant in this case, and know her all my life. She was Rebecca Smalls before she married Richard Geddis.

Richard Geddis and Rebecca Smalls were married December 24th 1865 by Rev. Cato Waring, a Methodist preacher on Jim Perry plantation, and I was at the marriage ceremony. Neither Richard Geddis nor Rebecca Geddis were previously married; if they were I would have known it being near neighbors all my life, and the said Rebecca Geddis has not married since the death of Richard Geddis.

Rebecca Geddis has no means of support except her daily labor and there is no one legally bound for her support. She has no property what so ever, no bonds, stocks, or investments at all, and does not pay any taxes because she has nothing to taxes on. All of the above statement is from personal knowledge of all of the facts above stated and being near neighbors all my life.[58]

---

[57] Ibid., Richard Geddis (Supplement), dated 03 Apr 1902.
[58] Sworn Declaration by Primous Geddis, in the matter of pension application no. 858.002 of Rebecca Geddis, widow of Richard Geddis alias Dick Richards (Beech Hill, near Summerville, Dorchester, SC), dated 08 Jul 1909.

Freedom Day in South Carolina

Freedom Day in South Carolina is analogous to the more famous Juneteenth Celebration Day in Texas.

Juneteenth, also known as Freedom Day or Emancipation Day -- June 19th -- is in general a celebration of the ending of slavery in the United States. More specifically it started in Galveston, Texas on June 19, 1865 after the end of the civil war when Union forces landed at Galveston and proclaimed that the war was over, the Confederacy had lost and all slaves were free.

While this happened two and a half years after President Lincoln's Emancipation Proclamation the Proclamation had little effect in Texan as there were no federal forces in Texas to enforce the order.

Similarly, on February 22, 1865, as General Sherman's Army passed through the Low Country of South Carolina, Charleston capitulated and torched the city and slaveholders in the vicinity abandoned their lands and moved their families and selected slaves (house slaves and skilled slaves) to the interior leaving field hands to fend for themselves.

This action opened the area between the Cooper & Ashley Rivers on the south and the Santee River on the north. Slaves in the general area of present day Berkeley were afforded the opportunity to run away from the plantations. This they celebrated as the time of liberation or Freedom Day.

Source: http://en.wikipedia.org/wiki/Juneteenth

Lewis S. GLOVER
alias
Lewis S. Cooner

Private, Company H: Born on 07 March 1849, at Branchville, Orangeburg, SC; a Slave of James Cooner; Enlisted on 07 March 1865, at Charleston, Charleston, SC; Disability Discharged on 01 Oct 1865, at Beaufort, Beaufort, SC. 1st Marriage to Amy [MNU] (d. c1910 or c1911), during Jan 1864, at Albany, Dougherty, GA., by Rev. Henry Harris. Children: Julius (b. Jun 1865); Mrs. Josephine Franklin (b. Mar 1866); Mrs. Leila Gordon (b. May 1867); and Mrs. Darcus Smith (b. Sep 1868). 2nd Marriage to Emma Mandy, near Moultrie, Colquitt, GA. **Lewis S.** *Glover died on 11 Nov 1923, at Warwick, Wilcox, GA.*[59]

Lewis S. Glover (Veteran Soldier)
Date: 19 Jun 1918
Residence: Rochelle, Wilcox, GA
Occupation: Farmer

I do not know my correct age but I was sixteen when I joined the army. I served during the Civil War in Company H, 128th U.S. Colored Infantry. I went in the last year of the War. I enlisted just before the winter was over and was discharged the following fall but I do not recall month of discharge nor can I give month of enlistment.

I was born and raised near Branchville, S.C. I was raised five miles from the Village of Edisto River. I lived there from birth to enlistment in

---

[59] Civil War Pension Record for Lewis S. Glover alias Lewis S. Cooner, SC No. C-2.454.256, Pvt, Company H, 128th USCI, Records of the VA, RG 15, NARA, WDC; 1920 U.S. Federal Census, Georgia, Wilcox County, Pleasant Grove Precinct, ED: 153, Page: 149B, Line: 63 (Roll: T625-286)

Lewis S. Glover alias Lewis A. Cooner

the army. My father was Squire Cooner and my mother was Darkis Cooner. I had one brother when I enlisted. His name was William Cooner. I had two sisters; Mary and Darkis. The oldest child was Mary, William followed her and then I came and Darkis was the youngest. All were dead when I left S.C., but Mary, and I have never been able to hear from her. She was the wife of Richard Freeman and was living near the old home place when I left there. If there is a record of my age I do not know it. I am satisfied for my claim to be settled as me being sixteen at date of enlistment. My mother always told me I was born in March and on either the second day or second Sunday – I am not sure which.

The way I came to enlist is that I heard the Northern soldiers were near Branchville where I was living and I ran away and went to them. I had an uncle named Isham and another fellow named Oliver Metts started with me but we scattered and I got with the Northern troops and they took me with them to Charleston and there I enlisted and then was carried to Beaufort. We staid there more than a month and then we were carried to Hilton Head and after that I was there till muster out except for a short trip to Grahamville or Honey Hill. We were only there for a night. It was not very far from Hilton Head. Was only about a day's march away. I was discharged from Hilton Head before the remainder of the Company were. The reason I was discharged was because I broke down and could not perform the duties of a soldier as I should.

One thing I had was sore eyes and I had on another occasion a pain in my side that carried me to the hospital. I don't remember being to the hospital but once and then I fainted on drill and later I had the pain in the side. I don't remember being in the hospital any other time but I went to the doctor and he excused me from duty several times. I remember once I had a fever but I did not go to the hospital. The doctor let me stay in my tent. When I told you about having a pain in my side it was a mighty bad pain and I had in my right side for several days. I was mighty sick with it but I didn't know what the trouble was called. I was never in prison in service.

In camp, the first thing in the morning we had roll call. We had to fall in line before the roll was call. After dinner we drilled for about two hours. About once a week we had what was called dress parade. Then all the soldiers turned out and the General would review them.

Before I enlisted I worked on the farm of my owner whose name was James Cooner. His wife was Sarah Cooner. They had three children. The oldest was Henrietta, William followed her and then Jim. They were all alive when I left S.C., except William and he was killed in the Confederate Army. They did not bring him home to bury him. During the war my father died and after the war it was customary for colored people to change their names and mother had married a man named Tom Johnson but he changed his name to Tom Glover and I also concluded to take the name Glover from him and I have gone under that name ever since.

I waited many years before making application for a pension because I lived in a section where there were no pensioners and I never knew a man could get a pension till recent years. Wesley Wood, which is a pensioner himself and lives in Rochelle, told me about two or three years ago that as I had been in the army that I could get pension. I had talked with him before that and he knew I had been in the army and when he learned about my service he told me he had been a soldier and that he was drawing a pension and that I could one. I had heard rumors before that there were such things as pensions but that was the first information that I had any faith in. He advised me to have a letter written to Lockwood* in Washington. In fact he wrote the letter himself and that is the way I got started in this matter. Had it not been for Wesley I would probably never have made application. I paid Lockwood three dollars for a discharge paper because I didn't know what became of mine. And that is how I come to be a pensioner.

I knew Wesley years back but he then got no pension and then he disappeared from me and I did not come in contact with him anymore till three years back and then he told me about getting a pension and that I could get one and that is the way I came to put it in.

I have been married twice. My first wife was named Amy. She died seven or eight years ago. She died twenty miles from Moultrie, Ga. She died near where Jim Holmes lived on the Culpepper Place. Cottoner was the Post Office. It was three miles from me. All the neighbors will know of her death. Isaac Manor and family, and Ben Franklin and his family

Lewis S. Glover alias Lewis A. Cooner

will know it. My last marriage was to Emma Westbrook. We are still living as husband and wife. We married at Fitzgerald. My wife was a widow when she married me. She was the widow of Ki Westbrook. He died near Cordele, Ga. He was dead a long time when I married claimant. We have small children.

I was only married the two times. I staid in South Carolina where I was raised some seven or eight years after my discharge. John Cary, who kept the post office knew me well at Branchville. Jim Grimes who ran the hotel, Burn Mile, and Maria Byrd, all of Branchville knew me well but they may be dead for all I know. From Branchville I moved to Warwick, Ga. I then moved to Calhoun County, then to Barrien County, then to Colquitt County, and then to Mitchell County. I lived eight miles from Pelham. I have been four years in this County.[60]

---

[60] Deposition of Lewis S. Grover, case of Lewis S. Cooner alias Lewis S. Grover (Rochelle, Wilcox, GA), dated 19 Jun 1918; Note: * Lockwood is P.J. Lockwood & Company, Attorneys in Pension and Patent Claims, Washington, D.C.

Alfred GOODWIN
alias
Benjamin Adams

Private, Company D: Born c1844, at Gadsden, Richland, SC; a Slave of James Adams; Enlisted on 22 Mar 1865, at Beaufort, Beaufort, SC; Honorably Discharged on 10 Oct 1866, at Morris Island, Charleston, SC. Lived with Mandy Brown. Children: Simon; Eugene; and Mrs. Cherry Silas*. Married to Molly Washington (b. c1867), c1881. Children: Willie. **Alfred Goodwin** *died on 07 Apr 1904, Charleston, Charleston, SC.*[61]

Alfred Goodwin (Veteran Soldier)
Date: 28 Oct 1895
Residence: #53 Mayzick St., Charleston, Charleston, SC
Occupation: Unemployed

I am 51 years of age. My name is Alfred Goodwin and I served in Company D, 128th U.S. Colored Troops as Benjamin Adams. The name of Alfred Goodwin is the one I used as a slave and when I joined the army I took my owners name of Adams and I was pensioned under the name I served under though I now go by my former name of Alfred Goodwin.

Miss Annie Adams, a sister of my owner, is the only one of the family of my former owners that I know of who is still alive and she resides where I was raised.

I was drawing a pension of eight dollars per month which was cutoff on the 8th of July 1894. I was pensioned for a pain in my right ankle, right knee and right elbow, and I still suffer from those pains and I was

---

[61] Civil War Pension Record for Alfred Goodwin alias Benjamin Adams, SC No. 581.173, Pvt, Company D, 128th USCI, Records of the VA, RG 15, NARA, WDC. Note:
* Cherry was the wife of Houghton Silas.

Alfred Goodwin alias Benjamin Adams

taken with shortness of breath with which I was taken after months ago. I claim pension for rheumatism as above.

I was mustered into Company D, 128th U.S. Colored Troops, in March 1865 at Beaufort, S.C., and was promoted a corporal and served seven or eight months when I failed to go out one Sunday morning to inspection and for such failure I was reduced to the ranks. I was mustered out October 11, 1866 at Morris Island, S.C. This was my only service either in the army or navy.

I was raised near Gadsden Post Office, Richland County, S.C. and was owned by James Adams (deceased). I ran away from my owner and joined the army soon after I arrived in Beaufort.

About seven or eight years before I was mustered in the service and while I was a slave I had a severe attack of scarlet fever when my life was {despaired} of and I was laid up for three months. This was the only attack I had of any kind prior to my enlistment and I was entirely restored when I joined the army. The physician, Dr. {Doil}, who treated me, is dead.

I was stripped when I was examined for enlistment by three doctors and I do not know their names. I first felt rheumatism, as I have described to you, in Beaufort, S.C. in April 1865 and it was contacted by exposure we had to lie on an old cloth blanket covered with a blanket under a canvass tent and when it rained the water ran in under us and we lived in this condition for three months. I was not in the hospital on account of it. I did not receive any treatment for it and it was not severe until I was on Morris Island waiting for our discharge. We were there three or four weeks lying on the ground.

I had small pox here in Charleston in March, April and May 1866. Our company had quarters in the City Jail where I contracted small pox and was sent to the small pox hospital three miles west of town and when I was better of it I was transferred back to the Roper Hospital in the city and I joined my company at their quarters in the jail where I had left them and from there we went to Morris Island to be mustered out.

I had no other sickness in the service that I have not told you of. I never had syphilis in the service or at any other time. I was born with a mark on my penis and I never told Dr. {Nelson} that I had a sore on my penis the year I was mustered out. I was not excused from duty at any time during the service except when I had smallpox and was in the hospital.

I cannot really tell you what is the matter with my eyes. I cannot see well. They are not sore but feels tight, that is all, and they have been failing me for the last six years. My hearing is good. My throat is alright. I suffer with pains in the back of my head and temples.

I went back where I was raised after I was mustered out and remained there a year then I came back to Ten Mile Hill where I remained until five years ago then I moved here. My brother, Jim Goodwin, resides at Hopkins, Richland County, S.C., and Berry Goodwin, another brother, resides near Gadsden, and my sisters, Irena {Shiver}, wife of Peter {Shiver}, resides near Gadsden, and they would all well know what my condition I was when I came out of the service.

I farmed that year on Israel [or James] Weston's place with {James} Mosley, a white man who moved to Texas in 1868.

At Ten Mile Hill I only worked a little for myself in planting peas and potatoes and such like on a piece of land rented by an old lady, {Aushie} Singleton, and I staid with her two or three years. And I next went to live with Henry Gilyard with whom I staid until I came to Charleston. He is a colored man and lives a mile from {Cashil} Singleton. I did farm work for Gilyard. I never worked in the {phelp hole} fields.

When I came out of the army I lived with Mandy Brown though I never was married to her and she resides at Hopkins, Richland County, S.C. and I had three children by her now alive, Simon Goodwin, Eugene Goodwin and Cherry Silas, wife of Houghton Silas. Mandy Brown married Daniel Edwin after I left her and she is now a widow. I married Mollie Washington about fourteen or fifteen years ago, and she lives near Seven Mile Junction with her mother, {Cushile} Singleton. I had ten children by her; one Willie {alive} with his mother, and Irena burned to death.

Those who can bear witness of my condition are: Josh Saunderson, at Seven Mile Junction, S.C. – now known as Josh Washington; John

Goodwin, at Ten Mile Hill, S.C.; and, Thomas Reed, at Reed St., Charleston, S.C.[62]

Molly Goodwin (Wife of the Veteran Soldier)
Date: 16 Nov 1895
Residence: Ten Mile Hill*, Charleston, SC
Occupation: Unemployed

I am 29 years of age. I am the wife of Alfred Goodwin and reside with my mother at the Charleston Mining Company's land. I never knew Alfred Goodwin to go by the name of Richard Adams. I married him when I was 14 years old and it has been fifteen years ago. We lived together until the earthquake in 1886, and after that he deserted me. I knew him when I was a child but I do not recollect anything as to his health before we were married. After we were married he would suffer with pains in his back and chills and fever both in summer and winter and he would be laid up a month at a time and he had these attacks quite often. I never knew anything else ailing him.[63]

---

[62] Deposition of Benjamin Adams, case of Alfred Goodwin alias Benjamin Adams (Charleston, Charleston, SC), dated 28 Oct 1895.

[63] Ibid., Molly Goodwin, dated 16 Nov 1895; * Note: Ten Mile Hill does not appear on most maps of the Charleston metropolitan area today. It lies northwest of Charleston at the location of the Charleston airport. (South Caroliniana Library Archives)

Milledge HANKERSON
alias
Milledge Wimberly

Private, Company K: Born on 04 May 1840, in Barnwell County (now Aiken County), SC; a Slave of Bill Sapp, first, then Edward Wimberly; Enlisted on 07 Mar 1865, at Hilton Head, Beaufort, SC; Honorably Discharged on 10 Oct 1866, at Morris Island, Charleston, SC. 1st Marriage to Jane [MNU] (d. c1881). Children: Mrs. Eliza Davis (b. c1864); Mrs. {Rivana} Garrett (b. c1869); Mrs. Etta Williams (b. c1870); Mrs. Lydia Williams (b. c1872); Mrs. Corinne Williams (b. c1874); Mrs. Fibbie Williams (b. c1878); and John (b. c1881). 2nd Marriage to Rosanna {Seton} (d. Oct 1887), during Apr 1882, Beach Island, Aiken (formerly Edgefield County), SC, by Rev. Sam Hill. **Milledge Hankerson** *died on 07 Apr 1913, at Augusta, Richmond, GA.*[64]

Seaborn Shoemaker (Friend of the Veteran Soldier)
Date: 07 Feb 1905
Residence: Augusta, Richmond, GA

Seaborn Shoemaker states on oath that he is well acquainted with Claimant, Milledge Hankerson, who was formerly called Milledge Wimberly; that he has known Milledge Hankerson from his birth – having gone for the doctor who attended his mother at his birth; that they both belonged, at that time, to Mr. Bill Sapp; that after Mr. Sapp died, Claimant and others were sold, and Claimant was bought by Mr. Ed Wimberly and as it was the custom in that day went in his master's name;

---

[64] Civil War Pension Record of Milledge Hankerson alias Milledge Wimberly, SC No. C-2.469.611, Pvt, Company K, 128th USCI, Records of the VA, RG 15, NARA, WDC; 1910 U.S. Federal Census, Georgia, Richmond County, Augusta Ward 1, ED: 52, Page: 82B, Line: 64 (Roll: T624-210).

That when Milledge joined the army during the late war he was known as Milledge Wimberly; that he, Deponent, has lived in the same settlement within a few miles of Claimant nearly ever since the Civil War; that he, Deponent, knew Claimant's father well and say's that he belonged to a man named Hankerson, and went in his master's name; that Claimant's father was known as Butter Hankerson, both in the days of slavery and after emancipation. He has been dead a long time.

Deponent swears that, to his personal knowledge, Milledge Hankerson, who is now applying for a pension from the United States, is the same and identical man that enlisted and served in the U.S. Army in the name of Milledge Wimberly; that Claimant's residence is on the Georgia side of the Savannah River near the City of Augusta in Richmond County, Georgia, and Claimant lived four or five miles away on the same side of the river; that they have lived this near to each other for the past fourteen years and frequently meet each other.[65]

Robert Hankerson (Friend of the Veteran Soldier)
Date: 07 Feb 1905
Residence: Augusta, Richmond, GA

Robert Hankerson states on oath that he has known Milledge Hankerson from their early years; that they live near each other on opposite sides of the Savannah River, he on the Georgia side and Hankerson on the South Carolina side of the river; that he knew Milledge as belonging to Mr. Wimberly and that he was known as and called Milledge Wimberly; that Deponent, Robert Hankerson, served in the U.S. Army with Milledge and belonged to the same regiment, to wit 128th U.S. Colored Volunteers; that Milledge belonged to Company K and Deponent, Robert Hankerson, belonged to Company C; that Milledge waited on him while in the army sick with the mumps; that they were mustered out of the army at the same time;

That they were personal friends before and during their services in the U.S. Army and have been ever since; that he, Robert Hankerson has

---

[65] Affidavit for General Purpose of Seaborn Shoemaker (Augusta, Richmond, GA), dated 07 Feb 1905.

resided in the City of Augusta since May 1872 and Milledge Wimberly, now known as Milledge Hankerson, has lived a few miles away across the river in Beach Island, S.C.; that he knows that Milledge Wimberly took for himself the name of Milledge Hankerson soon after leaving the U.S. Army because his father who had belonged to a man named Hankerson and continued to go in the name of Hankerson; that he knows from his own knowledge that Milledge Hankerson, who is now an applicant for a pension from the U.S. is the identical man that served with him in the army; and that he was enrolled as Milledge Wimberly and was mustered out of the army as Milledge Wimberly.[66]

Milledge Hankerson (Veteran Soldier)
Date: 01 Jul 1910
Residence: #619, Sibley St., Augusta, Richmond, GA

Personally appeared before me Mr. J. White, Notary Public, duly authorized to administer oath in and for the County of Richmond and State of Georgia, Milledge Hankerson alias Milledge Wimberly late Corporal of Company K, 128th Regt U.S. Colored Volunteer Infantry holding Pension Certificate #1.159.037 who being duly sworn deposed and says he was born May 4th 1840 and was therefore seventy years of age on the 4th day of May in 1910 and he herewith and herein files his affidavit for an increase of pension from eight dollars a month to fifteen dollars as provided by Act of Congress, February 1907.[67]

Andrew Garrett, et al (Minor Children of the Veteran Soldier)
Date: 12 Apr 1913
Residence: Clearwater, Aiken, SC

Before me, a duly {approved} {Notary Public for said County personally appeared Andrew Garrett, {Rivan} A. Garrett and Corina Garrett {all} {full} {person} of Clearwater, Aiken County, South Carolina who after

---

[66] Ibid. Robert Hankerson.
[67] General Affidavit of Milledge Hankerson, in the case of Milledge Hankerson (Augusta, Richmond, GA), dated 01 Jul 1910.

Milledge Hankerson alias Milledge Wimberly

being duly say that Andrew Garrett is a son-in-law of the late Milledge Hankerson who held pension Certificate no 1159037 and that {Rivnna} A. Garrett and Corina Garrett are the daughters of the said Milledge Hankerson;

And that the said Milledge Hankerson died in Clearwater, Aiken County, S.C., on April 7th 1913, where he had been living for a few months with his aforesaid daughters and who was buried on the 9th day of April 1913 in the {Storm} {Branch} Baptist Church Cemetery (Colored) near Clearwater, South Carolina; and that the Milledge Hankerson was pensioned by the United States for service in Company K, 128th U.S. Colored Infantry and held Certificate no 1159037 for pension at the rate of fifteen dollars per month; and that he was last paid on the 4th of February 1913; and that pension is due the said Milledge Hankerson for the 4th of February last to the date of his death, April 7th 1913;

And that for the last two or three years the said Milledge Hankerson has been very feeble {headish} unable to do anything worth talking about for himself and died in destitute circumstances without sufficient means to meet his funeral expenses and {have} the affidavit make this application for the accrued pension so that they applicants may use it in paying a part of that debt.[68]

---

[68] General Affidavit of Andrew Garrett, {Rivan} A. Garrett and Corina Garrett, in the case of Milledge Hankerson (Clearwater, Aiken, SC), dated 12 Apr 1913.

Thomas HARRISON
alias
Thomas Wade

Corporal, Company K: Born on 27 Jan c1839, in Montmorenci, Aiken, SC; a Slave of Drayton Wade; Enlisted on 07 Mar 1865, at Beaufort, Beaufort, SC; Honorably Discharged on 10 Oct 1866, at Morris Island, SC. 1st Marriage to Jane Clayton (d. Aug 1874). Children: Mrs. Mary Glover (b. 1864); and Mrs. Judie Hatcher (b. Aug 1865). 2nd Marriage to Nancy Page, c1879, by Rev. W.H. Mosley. 3rd Marriage to Mary Medlock. 4th Marriage to Carrie Jackson, on 06 Jan 1907, Aiken, Aiken, SC, by Rev. Albany, Pastor – Cumberland AME Church. **Thomas Harrison** *died on 27 Feb 1924, at Montmorenci, Aiken, SC.*[69]

Thomas Harrison (Veteran Soldier)
Date: **28 Feb 1899**
Residence: **Montmorenci, Aiken, SC**

Thomas Harrison takes oath that he was born at or near Montmorenci, Aiken County, S.C., (then Barnwell District) and was about 26 years old at the time he enlisted in the army; and that at the time of his enlistment he was a laborer on the railroad; and that he was five feet 5 ½ inches high, of dark or black complexion, black hair, black eyes; and that his owner's name was Drayton Wade, who is now dead; and that the sons of the said Drayton Wade now living at Montmorenici, Aiken County, S.C.

---

[69] Civil War Pension Record for Thomas Harrison alias Thomas Wade, SC No. C-2.554.060, Pvt, Company K, 128th USCI, Records of the VA, RG 15, NARA, WDC; 1910 U.S. Federal Census, South Carolina, Aiken County, Aiken City, ED: 1, Page: 16B, Line: 52 (Roll: T624-1447).

are John Wade and Richard D. Wade – the latter being a magistrate of Aiken County, S.C.[70]

Herbert E. Gyles (Employer of the Veteran Soldier)
Date: 13 Apr 1915
Residence: Montmorenci, Aiken, SC

Dear Sir: In connection with the inclosed* petition of Thomas Harrison, beg to say that the old negro works in our family. He is very old and his recollection of date is most unsatisfactory and the former owner who had his age is dead, and her daughter has evidently forgotten it because she gives it as 1859 and he is easily between seventy three and seventy eight years of age. Mrs. Laura Woodward, Tom's (Veteran Soldier) "young mistress" is said by him to be seventy six years of age and he says that they were born the same year and are the same age. It is impossible to reach her at this time on account of distance that she is from Aiken.

I regret that I cannot give more complete information about Uncle Tom, and if you can suggest anything further I shall be glad to help him out. Yours very truly, Herbert E. Gyles.[71]

---

[70] Claimant's Testimony in the matter of Thomas Harrison alias Thomas Wade (Aiken County, SC), dated 28 Feb 1899.

[71] Letter from Herbert E. Gyles, Currier & Gyles, Attoneys & Counselors at Law, Aiken, S.C to the Honorable the Commissioner, Bureau of Pensions, Department of Interior, WDC, dated 13 Apr 1915. * No petition is enclosed with this entry.

Daniel HEDDLESTON
alias
Daniel Henderson

Private, Company B: Born c1844, at Charleston, Charleston, SC; a Slave of Dr. Francis Parker; Enlisted on 08 Mar 1865, at Hilton Head, Beaufort, SC; Honorably Discharged on 10 Oct 1866, at Morris Island, Charleston, SC. 1st Marriage to Amelia Chisholm (d. Oct 1887), Dec 1865, Charleston, SC. Children: Mrs. Rose Simmons (b. c1870); and Daniel (b. c1874). 2nd Marriage to Phoebe Brown (d. c1895), on 10 Jul 1890, at Beaufort, SC, by Rev. R.F. Bythewood. **Daniel Heddleston** *died on 06 Nov 1913, at Port Royal, Beaufort, SC.*[72]

Daniel Heddleston (Veteran Soldier)
Date: 11 Mar 1904
Residence: Beaufort, Beaufort, SC
Occupation: Unemployed

My age is about 60. I am the Daniel Heddleston who claim pension under service of Company B, 128th U.S. Colored Troops.

Before the war I was owned by Dr. Francis Parker who had a place near Georgetown, S.C., and also a house in Charleston, S.C. He and his wife are both dead. I was born in Charleston but was sent up to Georgetown when quite small and lived there until I went in the army. I don't know that I told them where I was born, but I told them in the army that I came from Georgetown. I enlisted at Georgetown, and was taken by boat to Charleston and then by boat to Hilton Head where I was put in Com-

---

[72] Civil War Pension Record for Daniel Heddleston alias Daniel Henderson, SC No. C-2.519.031, Pvt, Company B, 128th USCI, Records of the VA, RG 15, NARA, WDC.

pany B, 128th U.S. Colored Infantry. I think that was in March, and the next year, in October, I was mustered out at Morris Island, S.C.

My father was Daniel Heddleston. He died during the war, and that has been my name all my life. I have never had any other name, but I can't say it plain, and I find that white people here call me Henderson. I don't know where my father got the name from. I was never in the U.S. services but that one time.

John Monday and William Davis were in the same company with me. I met them in service. Mark Cashion was in Company D. I knew him before the war. He came from Georgetown and was owned by Mr. Izzard. Jack Hasel, Alonzo Griffin and January Mitchell tented with me. I don't know where they are.

I had a discharge certificate that was given to me when I was mustered out. I sent it to the Pension Office in Washington, D.C., about ten years ago and got $384 for back pay and clothing money, and I sent it to the Pension Office sometime after the 1893 storm about 7 or 8 years ago (See page 38).

As soon as I was mustered out I came here and have lived here ever since. I don't know that any member of my family is living. I had a brother name Charles and a sister name Mary. She was here about 12 years ago and said she was living in Charleston. Soon after that I heard she was married and I have not heard from her since. I don't know the name of the man she married and I don't know that she is still living.

I came here when I was mustered out and in about 2 months married Amelia Chisholm. She bought some land about 1883 and our son, Daniel Heddleston, sold it to Mt. Christensen, about 1894. I don't know whether the land was in the name of Heddleston or Henderson. Our son, Daniel, left here about ten years ago and I don't know where he is.

I was next married to Phoebe Brown and she died about 1895. I have no wife now. My daughter, Rose Heddleston-Simmons is in {Casled}, Fla. I had no children by my last wife.[73]

---

[73] Deposition of Daniel Heddlestron, case of Daniel Heddleston (Beaufort, Beaufort, SC), dated 11 Mar 1904.

July HERIOT
alias
July Harrison

Private, Company F: Born on 20 Oct 1841, at Sandy Island, Georgetown, SC; a Slave of Benjamin Allston; Enlisted on 27 Mar 1865, at Georgetown, Georgetown, SC; Honorably Discharged on 10 Oct 1866, at Morris Island, Charleston, SC. 1st Marriage to Phillis [MNU]. Children: Abraham; {Alison}; Wallace; Gabriel; Isaac; Gilbert; and Sarah. 2nd Marriage to Annie Ellis-Washington, on 13 Oct 1900, at Sandy Island, SC, by Rev. Charles S. Green. Children: Eddie (b. 12 Aug 1902). **July Heriot** *died on 03 Mar 1908, at Sandy Island, Georgetown, SC.*[74]

July Heriot (Veteran Soldier)
Date: 12 Oct 1904
Residence: Georgetown County, SC

July Heriot takes oath that he was a member of Company F, 128th U.S. Colored Troops; that he enlisted as July Heriot; that he was called by July Harrison by members of my company; that his Capt. was James Justus, Orderly Sergt. Richard Hannibal, 3rd Sergt. Thomas Wheeling, and Corp. York Wheeling; that he enlisted on the 27th day of March 1865, and was discharged on or about the 10th or 11th of October 1866.

He further states that the record of his birth, which was written in his bible by Mrs. A.P. Allston (his former mistress), was destroyed by fire about ten years ago, and that he has no other means to prove his age, and;

---

[74] Civil War Pension Record for July Heriot alias July Harrison, SC No. XC-2.645.595, Pvt, Company F, 128th USCI, Records of the VA, RG 15, NARA, WDC; 1900 U.S. Federal Census, South Carolina, Georgetown County, #7 Upper Waccamaw Township, ED: 53, Page: 223B, Line: 55 (Roll: T623-1528).

that Mrs. A.P. Allston, who is the only person that could testify to his age, has been dead about 15 years.[75]

Annie Heriot (Widow of the Veteran Soldier)
Date: 15 Jul 1908
Reesidence: Brook Green, Georgetown, SC

<u>Query from Department of Interior</u>: Madam: Relative to your claim for pension, you are advised that it requires your statement, under oath, showing whether either you or the soldier had been previously married, and if so, whether more than once, the names of all former consorts, and how and when such former marriage or marriages terminated.

<u>Response by Annie Heriot (15 Jul 1908)</u>: Sir: This is to state that I and my late husband, July Heriot, were both married once before, and that my first husband died about 12 years ago. My late husband's wife died about 10 years ago. My first husband's name was Jeff Washington and the first wife of my late husband was Phillis (MNU).

<u>Plea to Department of Interior (09 Oct 1908)</u>: Dear Sir: Jeff Washington did not belong to the army or applied for pension of the soldier, July Heriot, but it is so much of trouble and I don't have the means to go through as I am feeble and poor. Concerning the mistake about the certificate. Rev. C. S. Green make the mistake but I and the soldier had been previously married on November the 14th 1900, and the soldier have six head of grown children with his former wife but all is married. Eddie Heriot is the only small child of his last wife and he is six years old. I am sorry I cannot get anything but I cannot do no good. Very Respectfully Annie Heriot.[76]

---

[75] Claimant Affidavit of July Heriot alias July Harrison (Georgetown County, SC), dated 12 Oct 1904; Affidavit of July Heriot (Georgetown County, SC), dated 25 Oct 1907.

[76] Query and response from Department of the Interior; Letter from Annie Heriot, Brook Green, Georgetown County, S.C. to Acting Commissioner, Southern Division, Bureau of Pensions, dated about 15 Jul 1908; Memorandum from Annie Heriot to Acting Commissioner, Southern Division, Bureau of Pensions, dated 09 Oct 1908.

Hannibal HEYWARD
alias
John Nesbit

Private, Company D: Born c1846, at Mt. Pleasant, Charleston, SC; a Slave of William Ball; Enlisted on 07 Mar 1865, at Beaufort, SC; Disability Discharged on 10 May 1866, at Hilton Head, Beaufort, SC. 1st Marriage to Lydia Dallas (d. c1872), c1868/9, at Mt. Pleasant, Charleston, SC. Children: Nelly (b. c1864); and Phillis (b. c1868). 2nd Marriage to Julia Hayward, on 11 Jul 1874, at Awendaw, Charleston, SC, by Rev. {S.K.} or {Ned/Ted} Howard. **Hannibal Heyward** *died on 07 Sep 1896, at Awendaw, Charleston, SC.*[77]

Julia Nesbit (Widow of the Veteran Soldier)
Date: 10 Sep 1906
Residence: Mt. Pleasant, Charleston, SC

I don't know my age but I think I am 60. I claim pension as the widow of John Nesbit who was a soldier. I was born and raised where I now live and have lived all my life. I was owned by Mr. Peter Manigault. My first husband was Charles Heyward. I married him during slavery and lived with him until he died. He died in October [1871 or 1872] and between 2 and 3 years before I married John Nesbit. I did not marry nor live with a man after Charles died until I married John, 32 years ago; the 11th of last July. I am sure of the year. We were married by {Ned/Ted} Howard, a colored preacher, and John and I lived together until he died on Septem-

---

[77] Civil War Pension Record for Julia Heyward, widow of Hannibal Heyward alias John Nesbit, WC No. 617.183, Private, Company D, 128th USCI, Records of the VA, RG 15, NARA, WDC; 1880 U.S. Federal Census, South Carolina, Charleston County, Christ Church Parish, ED: 79, Page: 43B, Line: 47 (Roll: T9-1223).

ber 7th 1896. I have not remarried nor lived with a man since he died. I do not own any property now. I did have 4 acres of land but let it go for taxes.

My first husband was never in any other U.S. Service. I have only been married twice in my life and have only lived with the two men I have married.

I met John Nesbit a year or two before we married. He was widowed then and did not marry till he married me. He said he was born and raised near here, on Cooper River, near Charleston, and had been owned by Mr. Ball. He said he had been married only once before and that his wife was named Lydia and that she was dead. I knew Lydia was dead for I raised her child after I married John and I met members of his family who told me she died before he married me.[78]

Samuel Jackson (Comrade of the Veteran Soldier)
Date: 24 Sep 1906
Residence: Charleston, Charleston, SC

My age is 65. I served in Company D, 128th U.S. Colored Infantry and I am a pensioner. I was born and raised on Cooper River and have lived here all my life. I was owned by Mrs. Jane Shubred. I knew John Nesbit and I knew him before the war. He was owned by Mr. William Ball and lived only three miles from me. He and I went in the army at the same time and served in the same regiment and company but I came home before him. He came home a little while later after I got home. He lived near me after the war when he came home and we worked together.

He was never married but twice in his life. His first wife was Lydia Dallas. She had been owned by Mrs. Shubred also, and John married her on our place where she was still living, and I was present and saw them married. That was the first wife that John ever had and the first woman that he ever lived with. He married her about 1868 or 1869. I think it was about two years after the war and they had two children and then she died. I went to her funeral and saw her buried.

---

[78] Deposition of Julia Nesbit, case of Julia Nesbit (Mt. Pleasant, Charleston, SC), dated 10 Sep 1906.

She did not live long after her last child was born. I think she died in 1872. I had a child born that same year and she died about the time my child was born. About 2 years after Lydia died he married again over near Awendaw and I know positively that Lydia was dead and buried before he married over there, and I also know, by living near him and seeing him nearly every day, that he did not marry after Lydia died until he marry over at Awendaw.

I don't know that Lydia had been married before she married John but she had a child before she married him. She went up in the state with my mistress during the war and when she came home she had a baby. I don't know who the father of the child was.

I knew John Nesbit from the time he was a boy and I will swear that he was never married but twice. The first time to Lydia, and after she died, he was married to the woman who is now his widow. I also know that he never lived with any woman except the two I mentioned.[79]

Elias Ball (Former Owner of the Veteran Soldier)
Date: 11 Oct 1906
Residence: Charleston, Charleston, SC

My father was Mr. William Ball who had the plantation on Cooper River. I lived up there before and after the war. I remember quite well a slave in our family by the name of Hannibal Heyward. He was owned by my father and I think he went off with General [Edward E.] Potter* when he came by there in 1865. And I am sure that he was a soldier in the Union Army for I saw him when he came back and he had on the uniform worn by the colored Union soldiers.

His name was Hannibal Heyward both before and after the war, as well as I can remember, but I did hear some of the hands call him Nesbit after he came back, although I don't know where he got that name from. While I can't recall that I heard him called John Nesbit but I did hear

---

[79] Ibid., Samuel Jackson, dated 24 Sep 1906. *Note: During April 1865, Brig. Gen. Edward E. Potter led a raiding party from Georgetown to Camden and freed slaves along his route.

Hannibal Heyward alias John Nesbit

them call him Nesbit. He was about my place for several years after the war and I lost sight of him a few years before I quit that section in 1882.

The only wife that I knew him to have was Lydia Dallas, who was owned my Mrs. Shubred, my aunt. He married Lydia just after the war and lived with her until she died. I know that Lydia died a few years after the war and before Hannibal went away from there, but I can't recall the date of her death.

When Hannibal went off with the soldiers he must have been about 18 to 20 years old. That is all I can remember about him at this time.[80]

Lazarus White (Comrade of the Veteran Soldier)
    Date: 15 Oct 1906
    Residence: #36 Inspection St., Charleston, Charleston, SC
    Occupation: Not at Work

My age is 61. I served in Company G, 128th U.S. Colored Troops and I am a pensioner. I was born and raised on Cooper River and was owned by Mr. Coming Ball. I knew John Nesbit who served in Company D, 128th U.S. Colored Troops. I knew him in slavery. He was owned by Mr. William Ball and lived near me. He and I went off with the soldiers at the same time and we enlisted and were put in the 128th, and were mustered out at the same time and went home together. His name before and after service was Hannibal Heyward, but in the army he went by the name of John Nesbit.

    John was not married before or during service but soon after we got home he married Lydia Dallas, who was owned by Mrs. Shubred, and he lived with her until she died and then he went over to Awensdaw and married over there.

I don't know her name but after married her he came to this city and lived here awhile and worked here and I met her but don't think he called her name. He just said she was his wife. He never had but those two wives that I ever heard of. He went back to Awensdaw and died there.[81]

---

[80] Ibid., Elias Ball, dated 11 Oct 1906.
[81] Ibid., Lazarus White, dated 15 Oct 1906.

Benjamin HUGER
alias
Benjamin Weston

Private, Company C: Born on 01 Aug 1847, at Georgetown, Georgetown, SC; a Slave of Francis Westonn; Enlisted on 27 Mar 1865, at Georgetown, SC; Honorably Discharged on 10 Oct 1866, on Morris Island, Charleston, SC. 1st Marriage to Isora Weston (d. 1878). Children: Mrs. Susan Nesbit (b. Feb 1868); and Mrs. Eliza Chisholm (b. 20 Sep 1870). 2nd Marriage to Elmira McCloud, during 188{_}, at Savannah, Chatham, GA, by Rev. Robertson. Children: Rosana (b. 1879); 3rd Marriage to Susan Robinson (b. 08 Jun 1873/4), on 15 Jun 1920, at Charleston, SC, by Rev. W.R.A. Felder. **Benjamin Huger** *died on 29 Oct 1926, at Charleston, Charleston, SC.*[82]

Benjamin Huger (Veteran Soldier)
Date: 16 Apr 1901
Residence: #102 Calhoun St., Charleston, Charleston, SC
Occupation: Express Wagoner

I am 54 years old. I was born August 1, 1847, about 15 miles from Georgetown, S.C. I was born a slave of Francis Watson of Georgetown. My father's name was {Beaver} Huger who was also a slave to my master Watson. I do not know where the Watson's got their name. I was known as Benjamin Huger before enlistment and the way I became enlisted a Benjamin Watson was because the recruiting officer asked me my master's name and when I told him it was Watson he put me down as Weston. I was 19 years old when I enlisted at Georgetown, S.C., on March

---

[82] Civil War Pension Record for Benjamin Huger alias Benjamin Weston, SC No. 974.352, Private, Company C, 128th USCI, Records of the VA, RG 15, NARA, WDC.

27, 1865. I do not remember the name of my recruiting officer but I was stripped and examined. I was discharged October 10, 1866, at Morris Island, Charleston, S.C. I never had any other service. I was on detached duty guarding the small pox hospital in Charleston. I have lived in and about Charleston since my discharge from the army.

My regimental officers were Colonel [Charles H.] Howard, Lieutenant Colonel [William M.] Beebe, Major [William H.] Danielson, Captain]Richard L.] Swartz, 1st Lieutenant [James] Sprague. I do not remember the name of 2nd lieutenant. My 1st Sergeant was Benjamin Baker and my tent mates were Sam Bailey, Michael Gallen and John Simmons. I never was in any battles or engagements. I was in the hospital at Beaufort from September 1865 until February 1866, suffering from injury in my right foot caused by being thrown from a quartermaster wagon in the discharge of duty.

My witnesses for my pension application were John {Michboro} and Tom Lastry, and I testified in their application, but did not pay for their doctors Robert {Burst} and {McClellan}. I have a claim pending for an increase on account of my kidney trouble and rupture. My attorneys are E.H. Gilston & Company, Washington, D.C. My vouchers are executed by Laurence Bennett, 145 Calhoun Street, Charleston, S.C., on the 4th day of the month. I keep all my own paper except my vouchers, which is kept at Laurence Bennett's because they have a safe. I am married but have no children under 16 years of age.[83]

---

[83] Deposition of Benjamin Huger alias Weston, case of Benjamin Huger alias Benjamin Weston (Charleston, Charleston, SC), dated 16 Apr 1901.

Peter HUGGINS
alias
Peter Hawkins

Private, Company G: Born c1840, on the Pee Dee River, Georgetown, SC; a Slave of R.S. Izzard; Enlisted on 08 Mar 1865, at Georgetown, Georgetown, SC; Disability Discharged on 23 Sep 1865, at Hilton Head, Beaufort, SC. Married to Linda Brown (b. c1866), May 1863, at Weymouth Plantation, SC, by Rev. Paul Willis. Children: James H. (b. 11 May 1874); Hagar (b. 16 Jul 1879); and Peter (b. 17 Aug 1880). **Peter Huggins** *died on 03 Sep 1910, at Georgetown, Georgetown, SC.*[84]

Peter Huggins (Veteran Soldier)
Date: 26 Sep 1902
Residence: Georgetown, Georgetown, SC
Occupation: Farmer

I am the Peter Huggins who served in Company G, 128th USC Infantry during the War of the Rebellion, but the officers called me Hawkins. I put in a claim for pension nearly five years ago; under the new law. My attorneys in Washington are W.W. Dudley & Company. The reason I did not put in a claim for pension ten or twelve years ago is that I was able to work then as an engineer and could make two dollars a day.

I was born in Georgetown County, S.C. on the plantation of R.S. Izzard on the Pee Dee River about 12 miles North East of Georgetown and belonged to him until I was freed by the U.S. Army. I was his waiting

---

[84] Civil War Pension Record for Linda Huggins (widow of Peter Huggins alias Peter Hawkins), WC No. 727.210, Pvt, Company G, 128th USCI, Records of the VA, RG 15, NARA, WDC; 1910 U.S. Federal Census, South Carolina, Georgetown County, Georgetown Township, ED: 37, Page: 86A, Line: 25 (Roll: T624-1458).

Petrer Huggins alias Peter Hawkins

man and coachman. Just before Georgetown was captured in the last year of the Confederate war I was working on Cat Island near Georgetown as contraband for the Rebel Army. On the approach of the Federal soldiers the Confederates left and the Colored men who were working on the breastworks scattered. When the Federal gunboats captured Georgetown I came to the town and reported to the authority and went back to the plantation to my wife and children.

I returned to Georgetown within a day or two, enlisted and was sent to Beaufort, S.C., where a regiment was organized and drilled. Tony Allston, Company G, Nat Allston, Company C, Charles {Black}, Company C (dead), Hector Green, Company B (dead), Adam {Meat}, Company B, now in Charleston, S.C., Bob Mitchell, Company E or F (dead) and Caesar Cohen, Company A, Georgetown, S.C., were all from the same plantation. Nat Allston lives in Georgetown, S.C., and has been getting his pension for five years.

Coleman Hayes or Haynes, a big mulatto Negro from Charleston, S.C., was Orderly Sergeant of my company. My colonel was [Charles H.] Howard, 1st lieutenant was Lester Hall. 2nd lieutenant [James B.] Berry. Henry Johnson whereabouts unknown was 2nd sergeant. Charles Tizer was a corporal. I do not know where he is. Bradboy Reed, Chubby Benjamin and Tony Allston were my tentmates – Benjamin is dead. There were some others in my regiment but I cannot remember them.

Tony Allston is the only member of my company whose whereabouts I know. Robert {South}, Georgetown, was in Company B. Scipio Singleton was in either Company D, E or F.

I can not tell the month nor the day of the month on which I enlisted nor the number of the year but it was the last year of the war and in the last winter or first spring. I am more certain it was spring of the year. I was a strong healthy man then. We were examined right on this Front St in Georgetown, S.C., in a big house that has now been torn down. They would take a room full of men and strip and washed them one at a time and punch and thump all over us, them make us hop around the room in a circle first on one foot and then on the other and last thing was a {cut} on the body with a leather strap which make us jump. I went to Beaufort with the regiment and was drilled every day with my company. We were

Borrowed Identity: 128th USCT

through drilling and had been inspected by General [Rufus] Saxton and they said we were going to be going to Richmond, Va., to General [Ulysses S.] Grant when on a Sunday where we were at marching the news came that General Robert E.] Lee had surrendered and the war was over.

My regiment staid in Beaufort all the time. I was with them. I did regular guard and drill duty with my company for a good while after Lee surrendered. But in the late summer I got out. Just got {work}, had no appetite, eyes turned yellow, I had a cough and they said I had "yellow jaundice." Then I was reexamined but I do not know what {meant} if it was and Nat Allston, Frazier Washington Company F, and I and others were sent to the hospital at Hilton Head, S.C., where we staid until our discharge came. But I cannot remember what month I was sent to Hilton Head nor what month I was discharged. I was not doing any duty while I was in Hilton Head. I got paid off but {once} as a soldier and that was before I was sent to Hilton Head. I got about $100. I lost my discharge papers after I was discharged.

When I was discharged they said they owed me for three months service and they gave me a piece of writing to show what was due me but I lost it and never got that pay. I do not know how many months of actual service I did. I think I did as much as six months service. The doctor who examined me said I had yellow jaundice. He did not tell me I had the consumption. If he asked me whether I had had a cough before enlistment I do not recollect it.

I am the man who enlisted and served in Company G, 128th U.S. Colored Troops. I gave my name as Peter Huggins. The only way I can account for my name being put on the roll as Peter Hawkins is that the northern white officer could not understand my way of saying my name. My father was named Peter Huggins and my mother Betty both belonged to R.S. Izzard and lived for some time after the war. All my white people are dead except some grand children of my owner.

I did not know my age at enlistment and do not know what they put down as my age. I told the officer I was a grown man and had a wife and my wife had given birth to twins and one other child. I think I was 21 years old when I married. I was married about the 2nd year of the war by

Petrer Huggins alias Peter Hawkins

a colored church leader, Tony Smith (dead), on the Izzard plantation, to my present and only wife, Linda, who belonged to Izzard but her father was a "Brown." My wife is yet living with me. We have never been separated nor divorced. My youngest living child, Hagar, wife of {Friday} {Charles} {Haynes} is now about 22 years old.

I can not remember how long I have been sick at the time I was reexamined. I had never had any cough or sickness before I enlisted. It was over a year after I was discharged before I could half do regular work. Then my health got good and I could do good and regular work in {lid} six or seven years ago I began to have headaches very bad and since then I have not been able to work. But they gave me a job of oiling the machinery at the rice mill which was for half the year and I got fifty cents a day when at work. But nearly half the time I can not work when the mill is running on account of pain and dizziness. I lost my right thumb in the rice mill over twenty years ago. Before I lost my thumb I had learned to write but can half write my name now. My thumb got caught in the machinery of the engine and mashed so badly that it was cut off by Dr. Sparkman – now dead.

I was wiping the machinery with a rag while it was in motion and got my thumb caught and mashed. I was not at the time under the influence of whiskey. I do not drink intoxicating beverages at all. My memory is very poor since I began to have the headache. I lived on the Izzard plantation after my discharge until about 24 years ago when I came to Georgetown, S.C., where I have since lived. I can not go with you to Columbia, S.C., or to Charleston, S.C., to be examined by the doctors because I have no money to pay my way and do not think I could.[85]

---

[85] Deposition of Peter Huggins, case of Peter Huggins alias Peter Hawkins (Georgetown, Georgetown, SC), dated 26 Sep 1902.

* * * * * * * * * * * * *

Alfred JENKINS
alias
Alfred Lastry

Private, Company I: Born on 01 Feb 1842, Wadmalaw, Charleston, SC; a Slave of Edward Lastry; Enlisted on 08 Mar 1865, at Charleston, Charleston, SC; Honorably Discharged on 10 Oct 1866, at Morris Island, Charleston, SC. 1st Marriage to Nancy Wragg (d. 11 May 1886), on 20 Nov 1872. Children: Mary (d. bef Apr 1915); Josephine (d. bef Apr 1915); Martha (d. bef Apr 1915); Betsy; Maggie; and Sara Ann. 2nd Marriage to Daphney Brown (d. Mar 1910), on 21 Jan 1887. 3rd Marriage to Mary Ann Bennett, on 19 Jun 1910, at Red Top near Johns Island, SC, by Rev. William H. Pader. **Alfred Jenkins** *died on 27 Mar 1923, on Johns Island, Charleston, SC.*[86]

Alfred Jenkins (Veteran Soldier)
Date: 14 Aug 1905
Residence: Johns Island, Charleston, SC
Occupation: Farmer

My age is about 63. I am the man who served in Company I, 128th U.S. Colored Infantry regiment as Alfred Lastry. I was born on Wadmalaw Island, S.C., and was raised on Edisto Island. I was owned by Mr. Edward Lastry and my father was Hector Jenkins. I enlisted in the Army at Charleston in 1865 and was mustered out on Morris Island on October 10th 1866. I sent my discharge certificate to William Fletcher & Compa-

---

[86] Civil War Pension Record for Alfred Lastry now known as Alfred Jenkins, SC No. 679.931, Pvt, Company I, 128th USCI, Records of the VA, RG 15, NARA, WDC; 1900 U.S. Federal Census, South Carolina, Charleston County, St. Andrews Parish, ED: 128, Page: 181A, Line: 14 (Roll: T623-1521)/.

Alfred Jenkins alias Alfred Lastry

ny last March or February and have not seen it since. During my service we were in no battles.

We were in Beaufort, S.C., most of the time, but we were also in Gillionsville, Summerville and Sullivans Island. We were also on Hilton Head and Lands End and Charleston. When we mustered out I went to Edisto for a year and then moved to near where I now live on Johns Island and and been thee ever since. Before and during the war I went by the name of Alfred Lastry, but soon after the war I took the name of Jenkins and have gone by that name ever since.

I was first married in 1872 to Nancy Wragg. She died in 1886, and in 1887, I married Dafney Brown. She had a husband by the name of George Brown before she married me. He died about 1882. Dafney and I parted in 1897 and have not lived together since. She and I couldn't agree and she went to cooking and has supported herself. We have never been divorced and I have never heard of her living with any other man.

I have no child under 16 years.[87]

Thomas Jenkins (Brother of the Veteran Soldier)
Date: 14 Aug 1905
Residence: #67 Beaufain St., Charleston, Charleston, SC

My age is about 65. I was born on Edisto and lived on Wadmalaw and Edisto until I went off during the war. I was owned by Mr. Edward Lastry and my father was Hector Jenkins. I served in Company I, 128th U.S. Colored Infantry regiment as Thomas Lastry.

I enlisted at Charleston and was sent to Beaufort and to Hilton Head and then to Charleston, and while there, about August 1866, Corporal Ford took some of us up the neck (an area north of Charleston) to arrest a man he was mad with. The man shot the Corporal in the hip and then we stuck the man with our bayonets. We were arrested and sent to prison and I was in prison at Ft. Macon, N.C., when the regiment was mustered out.

---

[87] Deposition of Alfred Jenkins, case of Alfred Jenkins (Charleston, Charleston, SC), dated 14 Aug 1905.

I know Alfred Jenkins. He is my brother and we were raised together. We went in the army at the same time. He was a soldier and served in the same company under the name of Alfred Lastry. I have lived in this city ever since the war and Alfred has lived at Johns Island, which is near Charleston. I suppose we have seen each other every month since I came here from the army.[88]

Richard Lastry (Comrade of the Veteran Soldier)
Date: 14 Aug 1905
Residence: #34 Lucas St., Charleston, Charleston, SC

My age is about 85 and I am not employed. I was born on Edisto and lived on Edisto and was owned by Mr. Seabrook and was given to Mr. Lastry when he married Mr. Seabrook's daughter before the war.

I served in Company I, 21st U.S. Colored Infantry regiment. I am a pensioner. I know Alfred Jenkins. He was owned by Mr. Lastry and went by the name of Alfred Lastry before and during the war. He was a soldier. I know for I recruited him and some others. I went in the service first and left him home and in 1865 I was here with the recruiting officer and I am the very man who took him to the army. He was sent to Beaufort and put in the 128th. I saw him as soon as he got home after the war. He had on soldier clothes and he told me that he had been in the 128th and was mustered out on Morris Island. He took the name of Jenkins after the war. His father was Hector Jenkins.[89]

---

[88] Ibid., Thomas Jenkins.
[89] Ibid., Richard Lastry.

Definitions

Conscription

Conscription is a general term for involuntary labor demanded by some established authority. It is most often used in the specific sense of government policies that require citizens (often just males) to serve in the armed forces. It is known by various names — for example, the most recent conscription program in the United States was known colloquially as "'the draft.'" Many nations do not maintain conscription forces, instead relying on a volunteer or professional military most of the time, although many of these countries still reserve the possibility of conscription for wartime and during times of crises.

Impressment

Impressment is the act of conscripting people to serve in the military or navy, usually by force and without notice. Beginning in 1664, the Royal Navy impressed many British merchant sailors, as well as some sailors from other nations. People liable to impressment were eligible men of seafaring habits between the ages of 18 and 55 years, though very rarely non-seamen were impressed as well. If they believed that they were impressed unfairly, pressed men were able to submit appeals to the Admiralty, and those appeals were often successful. The navy had little interest in impressing people who were not ordinary or able seamen, since they would be of no use on board a ship.

Source: http://en.wikipedia.org/wiki/Impressment; http://en.wikipedia.org/wiki/Conscription

Alfred JOHNSON
alias
Alfred Ward

Private, Company F: Born c1841, at Georgetown, Georgetown, SC; a Slave of Joshua Ward; Enlisted on 27 Mar 1865, at Georgetown, SC; Honorably Discharged on 10 Oct 1866, at Morris Island, Charleston, SC. Married to Ella Valion (b. c1850, Glynn County, GA; d. 09 Nov 1919 or 1920), during Jul 1872, at Darien, McIntosh, GA, by Rev. Samuel Ross. Children: James R. (b. Apr 1882); Rebecca (b. Sep 1884); Alex (b. Nov 1890); and Nancy (b. Apr 1893). **Alfred Johnson** *died on 16 Nov 1911 or 12, at Darien, McIntosh, GA.*[90]

W.M. Armstrong & W.M Young (Friends of the Veteran Soldier)
Date: 30 Mar 1903
Residence: Darien, McIntosh, GA

I, William M. Armstrong (65), have known Alfred Ward for about 25 years and have known him to suffer with heart disease and debility during the years 1897 to the present date, March 30, 1903. I have during those dates seen him loss his breath almost entirely and only from the best nursing he would get better for a time, but only for a short time. He is weak and, in my opinion, not a strong or healthy man and cannot do manual labor to any great extent;

and

---

[90] Civil War Pension Record for Ella Johnson (widow of Alfred Ward also known as Alfred Johnson), WC No. 745.449, Pvt, Company F, 128th USCI, Records of the VA, RG 15, NARA, WDC; 1910 U.S. Federal Census, Georgia, McIntosh County, Militia District 271, ED: 126, Page: 104B, Line: 78 (Roll: T624-202).

Alfred Johnson alias Alfred Ward

I, W. M. D. Young (50), have known Alford Ward about 30 years and have lived with him in the same county. I have known him to suffer with heart disease since 1897. He suffers often with shortness of breath and at times looks as if he would never recover from these attacks. He has them often and they are severe. He is a weak man and is not healthy. He cannot do manual labor as these attacks takes him if he gets excited or over strains himself.[91]

Ella Johnson (Widow of the Veteran Soldier)
Date: 25 Jun 1912
Residence: Darien, McIntosh, GA

I do not know my right age, but I was about 16 years old when I was married. I am the widow of Alfred Ward who served in the army with the Colored Troops. I do not know the company or regiment he was in. He was a pensioner. He died at Darien, Ga., November 16, 1912.

I am known as Ella Johnson and the soldier was known as Alfred Johnson while I knew him and we were married over 40 years ago. He married me as Alfred Johnson and he and I and our children were always known as Johnson after that. He never called himself Ward, but he told me when I first knew him that he served in the army as Alfred Ward and that his name before he went into the army was Alfred Ward – taken from his master, Joshua Ward, who lived in Georgetown, S.C. where my husband was born and raised. He said he took the name of Johnson after he was discharged – that being his father's name.

My maiden name was Ella Valiant.* I have never been married before and neither has the soldier. I was born in Glynn County, Ga., but came to Darien and lived here ever since. I was married to soldier by Reverend Samuel Ross, a Colored Methodist preacher. Isabella Bryant and J.T. Gibbs are the only people living who were present at the marriage. We lived together as man and wife continuously from the time of our marriage until his death. I have not remarried since his death.

---

[91] General Affidavit of W.M. Armstrong and W.M.D. Young, in the matter of the application for pension of Alfred Ward for pension (McIntosh County, GA), dated 30 Mar 1903.

Isabella Bryant and J.T. Gibbs knew me before my marriage to Alfred Johnson and know that I was never before married. John Baptist of Darien knew the soldier before he enlisted. He was a slave of Joshua Ward with him at Georgetown, S.C.[92]

John Baptist (Friend of the Veteran Soldier)
Date: 25 Jun 1912
Residence: Darien, McIntosh, GA

My age is 87. I knew Alfred Johnson as Alfred from the time he was a child. We were both slaves of Joshua Ward at Georgetown, S.C. I remember well the fact that he left the plantation as an enlisted man in the Union Army in the latter part of the war. I saw him while he was in the army with his company at Hilton Head, S.C. I was not an enlisted man but was employed by the government at Hilton Head as a teamster.

I came to Darien, Ga., right after the close of the war and have lived here ever since. Alfred Johnson came here soon after I did. I know that he was called Alfred Ward before he enlisted and also, sometimes, Alfred Johnson. His father's name was Johnson – Jacob Johnson. I knew his father well. I don't know which name, Ward or Johnson that Alfred went under before the war, but I know that he was called Johnson all the time after he came to Darien.

He was never married before he married Ella, who is now his widow. I remember the fact that he was married to Ella about 40 years ago, by common marriage at the time. I saw them often every year after they were married and know that they lived together as man and wife continually until last fall when he died. I know that after Alfred Ward, who was a slave with me as Joshua Ward at Georgetown, S.C., and Alfred Johnson, who was the husband of Ella Johnson was one and the same person.[93]

---

[92] Deposition of Ella Johnson, case of Ella Ward (Darien, McIntosh, GA), dated 25 Jun 1912. * Note: Ella's maiden name is spelled in several variations (Valliat; Valion; Valliant, etc) throughout the pension record.
[93] Ibid. John Baptist, dated 25 Jun 1912.

Alfred Johnson alias Alfred Ward

James R. Johnson (Son of the Veteran Soldier)
Date: 30 Jan 1936
Residence: 136 Somerset, St., Newark, Essex, NJ

Gentlemen, Dear Sirs: I am asking yours, please to retrace for me the discharge certificate of my father, or rather please to send me a duplicate of his discharge. The original one has been lost since the death of mother in December of 1919. I would like a duplicate for Civil Service purposes. My father was in the Civil War. He was a slave. He volunteered in his master's name – the name of Alfred Ward. He then, after the war, settled in a place name Darien, Ga. There he got his pension until his death and then my mother got it until her death.

There are two boys of us alive. The rest are dead. James (42), and Alex (29). My father's regiment was the 17th or 51st South Carolina Volunteer, Company D or C, or Battery 17th or 51st.* I do not if it was the South Carolina Volunteer. You can retrace it as Alfred Ward. My father, after the war was over, went in his own name afterward – Alfred Johnson. He married to my mother who was then Ella Valion, then Johnson. She died December 1919 in Darien, Ga.

Gentlemen, would you be so kind as to give this your immediate attention please. Answer by return mail and let me know please how I can get a duplicate of his discharge. It was the South Carolina Volunteer Infantry, D Company. I can remember. Please answer at once to me. Thanks Very much,

Jas. R. Johnson
136 Somerset St.
Newark, N.J.[94]

---

[94] Letter from James R. Johnson, son of the Veteran, Alfred Johnson to Pension office (nondescript) (136 Somerset St., Newark, NJ), dated 30 Jan 1936. * Note: His father served in the 128th United States Colored Troops. There were no black or colored Civil War regiments organized in South Carolina by those other designation cited by James Johnson.

* * * * * * * * * * * * *

Samson JOHNSON
alias
Lancey Johnson

Private, Company K: Born c1840, at Ashley River, Charleston, SC; a Slave of William Middleton; Enlisted on 07 Mar 1865, at Beaufort, Beaufort, SC; Honorably Discharged on 10 Oct 1866, at Morris Island, Charleston, SC. Married to Clarinda Oliver (b. 15 Jan 1848, Ashley River, SC; d. 30 Dec 1918, Summerville, Dorchester (formerly Colleton County), SC), on 12 Apr 1867 or 68, at the Dawson Place, Charleston, SC, by Rev. Anthony Allston. Children: Frank (b. 06 Dec 1867; d. 13 May 1896); Samuel (b. 15 Jun 1869); Mrs. Nancy Bailey (b. 14 Feb 1871); Isabella (b. 07 Sep 1873); and Mary Jane (b. 05 Feb 1875; d. 13 Jul 1881). **Samson Johnson** *died on 25 Mar 1880, Summerville, Colleton, SC.*[95]

Clarinda Johnson (Widow of the Veteran Soldier)
Date: 29 Jul 1901
Residence: Pine St., Summerville, Dorchester, SC

I am 53 years of age. I reside in the next house to the First Baptist Church (colored). I am the widow of Samson Johnson and I draw a Widow's Pension of $8 a month under the Act of June 27, 1890 on account of his service in the U.S. Army during the War of the Rebellion and death.

I was born on the Ashley River, Charleston County, S.C. I was born a slave of Isaac Dwight and lived with him on the plantation until free-

---

[95] Civil War Pension Record for Clarinda Johnson, widow of Samson alias Lancey Johnson, WC No. 445.681, Pvt, Company K, 128th USCI, Records of the VA, RG 15, NARA, WDC; 1880 U.S. Federal Census, South Carolina, Colleton County, Collins Township, ED: 104, Page: 366B, Line: 43 (Roll: T9-1226).

Samson Johnson alias Lancey Johnson

dom. My father was named Frank Oliver. He belonged to the same owner with me. I had the name of Oliver before I married. I do not know where my father got his name. I was called Oliver and no other name before I was married. My husband's full name was Samson Johnson. When he was in camp he was sometimes called Lancey. He was never called Lancey before the war. I knew him from my childhood. After he returned out of the army he was sometimes called Lancey but I called him Samson.

My husband served in Company K, 128th U.S. Colored Troops. He had no other U.S. service. He was never in the Confederate Army. I never heard him talk about any other service or of being in the Confederate Army. He was born on Ashley River, Charleston County, S.C. He was a farm hand at enlistment. He was a slave and owned by William Middleton. His father was named Timothy Johnson. I do not know where they got the name Johnson.

He was in no battles and never wounded. I can only name and locate one of his comrades, Ben Edna, who lives about five miles west of here on the Orangeburg Road.

We were married in 1868 at Dorsey Place, Charleston County, S.C., by the Rev. Allston – my minister at the present time. I was not married in the church, but in the society hall. When Allston was fully ordained he married me again. Samson Johnson was my first and only husband. I think he was never married until he married me. I knew him when he was only a large boy. If he had ever had another wife I know I would have heard of it. We lived together as man and wife continually from our marriage to his death.

After my husband died I lived in that neighborhood for nine years. I only had my children in my house then. I then moved to Stallsville, S.C., three miles out from here, and lived there eight years. I lived only with my children at Stallsville. I then built this house and have lived here three years.

My daughter is now married to Edward Bailey and they with one of his children by a former wife live here with me in this house now. The Rev. Singleton and his wife also occupy a room in my house. They have only been here five months.

My husband died March 25, 1880, at Dawson, S.C., of Apoplexy. There were only three children alive when Samson died: Frank, born December 6, 1867, and died May 13, 1896; and Mary Jane was born February 5th 1875 and died July 13th 1881. She was my youngest child. Nancy was born February 14th 1871 and is my only living child.

I have a record of my children's births, as you all, in my family bible which I wrote in there about three weeks ago and which I took from a little book in which I had written the dates of births of my children at time of birth. Someone wrote them for me. This book has been nearly destroyed by the rats.

The midwives who attended me at the births of my children are both dead and there are no public records kept in my locality of births and deaths or of my marriage.

My husband's owner was William Middleton and he was raised on the plantation known the "Middleton's Flower Gardens" on the Ashley River and formerly as the "Ashley Barony." His father was Timothy Johnson and his mother Nancy (both dead). He had two sisters (now deceased) - Susana Laurence, wife of Hercules Laurence (dead) and Juliana Brown, wife of Abram Brown (dead). Susana left the following children – Elina Rogers, widow of Mark Rogers, resides in Summerville, S.C.; Susana Rogers, wife of Israel Rogers, on the Shaw Place on Ashley River, six miles from Summerville; Robert Laurence, who is about 50 years old, lives on Red Top, Charleston County, S.C.; Sam Laurence, about 38 years old, lives on the Dawson Place; and Nelson Brown, about 38 years old, resides in Summerville. Paris Salters, who resides at 6 mile bridge, is a first cousin of my husband and he is over fifty years old. Mary Mitchell, an old settled lady, is also his first cousin and resides here in Summerville. And that is all of his first cousins alive.

He was always known at home as Sampson Johnson and I never heard him called by any other name than Sampson. He told me that he served in the army as Lancey Johnson and gave me the reason why they called him that and it was because there were two other men by the name of Sam Johnson and the captain said that he would call him Lancey to distinguish him from the others.

Samson Johnson alias Lancey Johnson

I own one acre of land with two small houses on it. I paid $20 for the land. It cost $175 to build both houses. I value the whole property at $300. I only get $1.50 a month from both houses. I have paid all the mortgage on that property but $16. I own the house and lot where I now live. I paid $75 for the lot and $485 to have the house built. There is a mortgage to the Building and Loan Association of about $100. That is the extent of all my property.

Doctor Ellington, now dead, attended my husband in his last illness. My husband never put in for a pension. When I was married to my husband he was a sound and healthy man. I never claimed that my husband died from any disease he got in the army. He did not. He came home well and healthy. I have never applied under the old law if I understand it. Ben Edna, Elias Johnson and Prince Grant were all my original witnesses. Ben Edna was a tent mate of my husband. Elias Johnson was born and raised with my husband and knew him all his life. Prince Grant knew him before the war. All of them knew me well.[96]

---

[96] Deposition of Clarinda Johnson, case of Clarinda Johnson (Summerville, Colleton, SC), dated 06 Oct 1896; Deposition of Clarinda Johnson, case of Clarinda Johnson (Summerville, Dorchester, SC), dated 29 Jul 1901. Note: In 1897, Dorchester County was split-off from Colleton County.

Scipio JOHNSON
alias
Sippy Johnson

Private, Company F: Born 03 Feb 1840, at Georgetown, Georgetown, SC; a Slave of Dr. Francis Parker; Enlisted on 27 Mar 1865, at Georgetown, Georgetown, SC; Honorably Discharged on 10 Oct 1866, at Morris Island, Charleston, SC. 1st Marriage to Maria [MNU], c1870-75. 2nd Marriage to Kate Watson (b. Mar 1852), during 1897, Charleston, Charleston, SC, by Rev. Crosby. Step-Children:* Susanna (Watson) (b. Aug 1886) and Martha (Watson) (b. Jul 1888). **Scipio Johnson** *died on 24 Jun 1920, at Charleston, Charleston, SC.*[97]

Scipio Johnson (Veteran Soldier)
Date: 03 Apr 1901
Residence: #147 Comings St., Charleston, Charleston, SC
Occupation: Carpenter

I was born 03 February 1840. I am unable to work now, but I used to be a carpenter. I was born a slave of Francis Parker of Georgetown, S.C. My father's name was John Johnson. I could not tell where he got the name. He was also born a slave of Francis Parker. Francis Parker remained my master up to the time I enlisted in the army.

In the war I was called Sippy Johnson and also Scipio Anson, but my real name is Scipio Johnson. I enlisted at Georgetown, S.C., at the age of

---

[97] Civil War Pension Record for Scipio Johnson alias Sippy Johnson, SC No. 925.090, Pvt, Company F, 128th USCI, Records of the VA, RG 15, NARA, WDC; 1900 Federal Census Record, South Carolina, Charleston County, Charleston – Ward 8, ED: 97, Page: 316A, Line: 97 (Roll: T623-1520). *Note: Scipio Johnson has two step-daughters from his 2nd marriage.

Scipio Johnson alias Sippy Johnson

about 18 or 20. I think Captain Stone enlisted me, but I could not swear to it. I was examined, stripped, etc at enlistment. I was sworn in to the U.S. service at Hilton Head, S.C. I enlisted March 1865.

I was discharged at Morris Island, S.C., on October 10, 1866. I had no other service in the army or navy, Federal or Confederate. The only time I was detailed away from my company was in the spring of 1866 when I was detailed to do garrison duty at Ladies Island, S.C. I was there about 5 months. Since my discharge I have lived continuously here in Charleston, S.C.

Witnesses for my pension claim, as near as I can recall, were Paul Blunt and William Gallant. I have also witnessed for them. They testified that I had the measles in Beaufort, S.C., in 1865-66. I cannot recall what I testified for them. I have made several affidavits for them. I did not pay for their affidavits and did not receive any pay for testimony for them.

I have not been examined by a board of doctors since 1892 when I was examined by the board of doctors in Charleston. I have a claim pending under the general law on account of results of measles viz paralysis. My attorney is George P. McClay. I have not paid him anything. I have promised to pay him what the law allows when I get my pension.

I go to Mr. Bennett with my vouchers. I carry my certificate with me and swear to any vouchers. I show my certificate every time. I never pawned my certificate for any purpose whatsoever.

I have been married twice. My first wife was Maria. I cannot recall her other name. I married her between 1870 and 1875 and lived with her up to 1882 when she left me and married a man in Mt. Pleasant, S.C. I cannot recall his name, but I might find it out if it was necessary. I married Kate Johnson in 1897 in August or September Reverend Crosby of Charleston, S.C., married us. I never had any children.[98]

Benjamin Huger alias Weston (Comrade of the Veteran Soldier)
 Date: **13 May 1901**

---

[98] Deposition of Scipio Johnson, case of Scipio Johnson alias Sippy Johnson (Charleston, Charleston, SC), dated 03 Apr 1901; Ibid., dated 13 May 1901

Borrowed Identity: 128th USCT

My name is Benjamin Huger. The name of Weston was the name of my master before the war. I am a pensioner and my pension certificate is number 974352, and I receive $6.00 per month. I was a member of Company C, 128th Regiment, U.S. Colored Infantry. I was discharged at Morris Island on October 10, 1866. I cannot recall any such man as Scipio Johnson as serving in any company of the 128th Regiment, neither can I recall to mind Cipio Anson or Cipio Inson.

About three years ago I met on Calhoun Street, between Smith and Pitt Streets, this man Cipio Johnson. We talked a while and I told him that I heard he was drawing a pension. He said yes, since George (meaning George P. McClay) is doing so well for the boys I had him get one for me. Then I asked him how long he was a member of the Grand Army as I noticed he wore a button, and he said not long. I asked him this question because I did not think the Grand Army would take a man who had been in the penitentiary or a man who did not have a good moral character. Then I asked him what company he belonged to and he said Company F, 128th Regiment, but I never knew him as a member of that company, and I used to visit that company often but never saw this man there, and I never knew anybody in the war who looked like him. Then he told me that when he got his pension money he gave George McClay $50.00, but that McClay wasn't satisfied.

As I said, I do not recall this man as a member of any company of the 128th U.S. Colored Infantry, and I never knew him until about three years ago and I cannot refer you to anyone who ever knew him as a member of any regiment. I cannot tell just what he was in the penitentiary for, but earlier he shot a man and I know that his reputation is not good.[99]

---

[99] Ibid., Benjamin Huger alias Weston. Editor's Note: Based on this narrative, it appears that Scipio Johnson may have been and imposter. However, there was a soldier by the name of Sippy Jonson (or Johnson) carried on the rolls of the 128th Regiment.

Scipio Johnson alias Sippy Johnson

Photograph of Private Scipio Johnson (c1900), formerly a member of Company F, 128th United States Colored Infantry regiment.

Courtesy of the U.S. National Archives, Washington, DC.

James JONES
alias
James Kilpatrick

Private, Company C: Born c1830, on the W.L. Kilpatrick Plantation, Burke, GA; a Slave W.L. Kilpatrick; Enlisted on 03 Mar 1865, at Beaufort, Beaufort, SC; Honorably Discharged on 10 Oct 1866, at Morris Island, Charleston, SC. Married to Sarah Williams (d. 01 Jan 1939, Munnerlyn, Burke, GA), during June 1872, in Burke County, GA, by J.C. Hickman. Children: Arrington. **James Jones** *died during 1887, at Waynesboro, Burke, GA.*[100]

Sarah Jones (Widow of the Veteran Soldier)
Date: 12 Mar 1931
Residence: Route #3, Waynesboro, Burke, GA

I do not know my age but I was a good sized girl and big enough to work at the time of the Civil War. I live here with my son, Arrington Jones. I have no occupation and I am supported by him. I am the same Sarah Jones who is applying for pension as the widow of Jim Jones who served in the U.S. Army in the Civil War. He died near where I am now living many years ago but I do not know the date of his death. I was living with him at the time of he died.

I was born on the Jones place just a short distance from here and I belonged to the Jones family in slavery. I have lived here in this neigh-

---

[100] Civil War Pension Record for Sarah Jones, widow of James Jones alias James Kilpatrick, WC No. 1.603.924, Pvt, Company C, 128th USCI, Records of the VA, RG 15, NARA, WDC; 1920 U.S. Federal Census, Georgia, Burke County, Munnerlyn Parish, ED: 25, Page: 57A, Line: 20 (Roll: T625-239). Note: The W.L. Kilpatrick Plantation is located about ten miles Southwest of Waynesboro in Burke County, GA

borhood all my life except during late years when I have been visiting my grandchildren in Savannah part of the time. My father was Joe Williams and my mother Julia Ann McCoy. My parents are dead long ago and I have no living brothers or sisters. I went by the name of Sarah Williams up to the time of my marriage.

I have never had but the one husband and that was Jim Jones. We were married at the home of my mother near here and the ceremony was performed by a preacher named J.C. Hickman who is now dead. There is no one now living who was present at the marriage as far as I know. We had a license which we got at Waynesboro. I lived with Jim Jones until he died and was standing over his bed at the time he died. We were never separated or divorced.

Jim Jones was raised on the Kilpatrick place in this county and I had not known him very long before we were married. I have often heard him say that he was in the army and he often talked about his army service. Ben Walker knew about his army service but he died some time ago. I do not know of anyone else who would know. Jim had some army papers but the rats destroyed them. He always went by the name of James Kilpatrick Jones. He belonged to the Kilpatrick family. All of the family is dead now and the last one was Mr. George Kilpatrick who died about three years ago. Jim had one brother but he died.

I have borne 7 children, all by Jim Jones. Only one of them is now living and that is Arrington Jones with whom I live. I have not remarried or lived with any man in a marital relationship since Jim Jones died. "I have dipped about a little bit with men but ain't lived with any man but Jim Jones and never had a child by any other man."

My son started to put in a claim for me for pension years ago but did not because we found that rats had cut up the papers and we thought we couldn't get it. Lately we were told that a claim could be filed without having the discharge paper so we put in for it.[101]

---

[101] Deposition of Sarah Jones, case of Sarah Jones (Waynesboro, Burke, GA), dated 12 Mar 1931.

Calvin KILPATRICK
alias
Thomas Jones

Corporal, Company C: Born c1840, in Burke County, GA; a Slave of J.H. Kilpatrick; Enlisted on 03 Mar 1865, at Savannah, GA; Honorably Discharged on 10 Oct 1866, at Morris Island, Charleston, SC. 1st Marriage to Phyllis [MNU] (b. c1846; d. c1874, Greene County, GA). Children: Andrew (b. c1869); James (b. c1871); and Elizabeth (b. c1872). 2nd Marriage to Sarah Giles (b. c1848), on 21 Aug 1881, in Hancock County, GA, by Rev. Arnold Howell. **Calvin Kilpatrick** *died on 26 Sep 1904, at Crawfordville, Taliaferro, GA.*[102]

Calvin Kilpatrick (Veteran Soldier)
Date: 03 Sep 1900
Residence: White Plains, Greene, GA
Occupation: Disabled

Thomas Jones declares that he is the claimant named in this affidavit and; that he has been informed that the Board of Surgeons by whom he was examined discovered that he is afflicted with hernia of right side, a disability not alleged in his original declaration; that he therefore, now, makes claim for pension on account of said disability to be considered in connection with the disabilities claimed for in his declaration and that he be rated on this and all others found and claimed for in his declaration and medical reports, and he requests that this statement be accepted as a

---

[102] Civil War Pension Record for Calvin Kilpatrick alias Thomas Jones, SC No. C-2.511.875, Pvt, Company C, 128th USCI, Records of the VA, RG 15, NARA, WDC; 1900 U.S. Federal Census, Georgia, White Plains – Militia District, ED: 37, Page: 226B, Line: 60 (Roll: T623-201).

part of his original declaration under the Act of June 27, 1890, and considered in connection therewith;

He further states that said disability is not in any way due to vicious habit and is to the best of his knowledge and belief of a permanent character and that he first felt the effect of same on or about 15 years ago, and he said the rupture was caused by straining in rolling logs. He, hereby, appoints, with full powers of substitution and revocations Mr. V. Tierney & Company of Washington, DC.[103]

J.F. Kilpatrick & J. Howard (Acquaintances of Veteran Soldier)
Date: 06 Jan 1900
Residence: White Plains, Green, GA

J.F. Kilpatrick (46) declares that he has known Thomas Jones (alias Calvin Kilpatrick) from a child up to the present date – having lived with him on the same farm for a long time and in the same neighborhood all the time and; that he knows from his own personal knowledge that the said Thomas Jones (alias Calvin Kilpatrick) is of good habit, and further testifies; that the said Thomas Jones (alias Calvin Kilpatrick) is broken down from hard labor and old age and suffers from rheumatism, to some extent;

and

John Howard (46) declares; that he lives in the same neighborhood and that he is a neighbor of the said Thomas Jones (alias Calvin Kilpatrick) and a member of the same church and the said Thomas Jones (alias Calvin Kilpatrick) habits are good, and further states that the said Thomas Jones (alias Calvin Kilpatrick) is in destitute circumstances and in need of help from some quarters, and the said J.F. Kilpatrick and John Howell each further declares that they have no interest in said case and is not concerned in its prosecution.[104]

---

[103] General Affidavit for Thomas Jones, in the matter of a Pension Claim #1090614 of Thomas Jones, Company C – 128 Regt USC Inf (Greene County, GA), dated 03 Sep 1900.
[104] General Affidavit for J.F. Kilpatrick and John Howell, in the matter of a claim for pension for Thomas Jones (Greene County, GA), dated 06 Jan 1900.

J.H. Kilpatrick & J. Johnson (Acquaintances of Veteran Soldier)
Date: 25 May 1900
Residence: White Plains, Greene, GA

J.H. Kilpatrick (66) testifies that I am well acquainted with Calvin Kilpatrick and have been for more than fifty years. I know that he joined the Federal Army under the name of Thomas Jones and that during the time of his service he sometimes sent to me part of his monthly pay for me to hand to his wife who was living with me during the time of his service in the army. The said Calvin Kilpatrick, or Thomas Jones, was my slave at the time of his joining the army;

and

John Johnson (61) testifies that I have been knowing Calvin since before the War and that I have had him working for me several years now.[105]

J.H. Kilpatrick (Acquaintance of Veteran Soldier)
Date: 02 Jun 1900
Residence: White Plains, Greene, GA

J.H. Kilpatrick (66) declare that I have known Calvin Kilpatrick (or Thomas Jones, his army name) for more than fifty years, he having been born the slave of my father, from whom I received him by gift in the year 1856. My reason for believing that Calvin joined the Federal Army is that he ran away from me during the war, and that after Lee's Surrender, and before Calvin could get his discharge from the army he would sometimes send part of his monthly pay to me to give to his wife who lived with me during the time of his service in the army. His letter purported to come from a soldier in the Federal Army and he seemed quite anxious to come back home but was unable to obtain a discharge from service. After returning, he freely talks of his army experiences.[106]

---

[105] General Affidavit for J.H. Kilpatrick and John Johnson, in the matter of Thos Jones, also called Calvin Kilpatrick (Taliaferro County, GA), dated 25 May 1900.

[106] Ibid., J.H. Kilpatrick, (Taliaferro County, GA), dated 02 Jun 1900.

Calvin Kilpatrick alias Thomas Jones

John Jones & Frank Lewis (Acquaintances of Veteran Soldier)
Date: 12 Feb 1903
Residence: Burke County, GA

John Jones (62) and Frank Lewis (55) declares that they are well and intimately acquainted with the claimant Calvin Kilpatrick alias Thomas Jones, as they served in the same company and regiment with him during the War. While in the service he was known by the name of Thomas Jones and since his discharge therefrom he is known and goes by the name of Calvin Kilpatrick. We know this fact by having served with him and knew him under the name of Thomas Jones of Company C, 128th Regiment, U.S. Colored Infantry, and have known him continuously from the date of his discharge up to the present time, see and converse with him quite often and have seen and talked with him this day and since the date of his discharge, he is known by the name of Calvin Kilpatrick. We know him and call him such as others do and know from our long acquaintance and personal knowledge that Calvin Kilpatrick is the same man who served with us in Company C, 128th Regiment under the name of Thomas Jones.[107]

---

[107] Ibid., John Jones and Frank Lewis, (Burke County, GA), dated 12 Feb 1903.

Napoleon B. KINLOCH
alias
Napoleon Skenlore

Private, Company A: Born on 07 Oct 1845, at (Balldam Plantation) St. Stephen, Charleston,*SC; a Slave of Dr. John S. Palmer; Enlisted on 07 Mar 1865, at Beaufort, SC; Honorably Discharged on 10 Oct 1866, at Morris Island, Charleston, SC. 1st Marriage to Annie Jenkins (d. Oct 1869, St. Stephen Parish), on 26 Dec 1866. 2nd Marriage to Emma Bash, on 07 Feb 1871, in Charleston County, SC, by Reverend Harry Taylor (Colored AME). Children: Mrs. Sarah Ramsey (b. 24 Oct 1870); Mrs. Elizabeth Brunson (b. 11 Feb 1872); Mrs. Margaret Wright (b. Sep 1876); Paris (b. 31 Jul 1879); Ester (b. May 1885); and Andrew (b. 10 Apr 1891; d. 30 Mar 1915). **Napoleon Kinloch** *died on 24 Apr 1917, at Alvin, Berkeley, SC.*[108]

Napoleon Kinloch (Veteran Soldier)
Date: 20 Sep 1905
Residence: St. Stephens, Berkeley, SC

Napoleon B. Kinloch (60) swears that he is the same person who enlisted in Company A, 128th Regiment U.S. Colored Troops at Beaufort S.C., on the 9th day of March A.D. 1865, but that his name was written by the enrolling officer as Napoleon Skenlore; that he was at that time unable to read or write and did not know that his name had not been enrolled as

---

[108] Civil War Pension Record for Emma Kinloch (widow of Napoleon Skenlore now known as Napoleon B. Kinloch), WC No. 853.175, Pvt, Company A, 128th USCI, Records of the VA, RG 15, NARA, WDC; 1910 U.S. Federal Census, South Carolina, Berkeley County, St. Stephen Township, ED: 14, Page: 212A, Line: 45 (Roll: T624-1451). * Note: Berkeley County was established in 1882 from a portion of Charleston County.

Napoleon B. Kinloch alias Napoleon Skenlore

Kinloch but as Skenlore and that he never signed his name. That he was allowed the net sum of ten dollars and eighty two cents $10.82 in the year 1892 when he applied {change} John & Duffie as attorney in Washington, D.C. In Bounty due: and which can be proved by a document he has now and which is forwarded along with the affidavit; that he received from the Treasury Department – the amount of three dollars and eighty to him for clothing and pay due {**grantor**} the he was disbanded at Morris Island, S.C. on the 10th day of October 1866.[109]

Napoleon Kinloch (Veteran Soldier)
Date: 26 Jun 1908
Residence: St. Stephens, Berkeley, SC

Napoleon B. Kinloch (63) further states that he is unable to obtain or furnish any record of his birth; either from public records or of Baptismal or family records for reasons as follows; that there is no record of marriages or births kept in the State of South Carolina, and that among slaves, there were no record of Baptismal - if any were ever made and the family of slaves could not read and write and kept no record except that of memory, but that the farm owners usually a kept record of all birth and seldom, if ever, recorded the day or the month of the year of which children of slaves were born and the year being usually given, that he {**suffer**} with this record of slaves of his former owner, Dr. John S. Palmer of Berkeley County (now), formerly Charleston County, of South Carolina which record is {**knolly**} leave by this son of Dr. John S. Palmer, and in which book it will be {**ohmn**} at no. 94 that he was born in or about A.D. 1845 – but that his mother, Caty, told him that he was born on the Seventh day of October AD 1845; that he is the son of Andrew no. 90, written as Driver Andrew, his father being the Driver or Foreman for his owner, Dr. James S. Palmer.[110]

---

[109] General Affidavit for Napoleon B. Kinloch (St. Stephen, Berkeley, SC), dated 20 Sep 1905.

[110] Affidavit by Napoleon B. Kinloch, in the matter of Napoleon Skenlore now known as Napoleon B. Kinloch (Berkeley County, SC), dated 26 Jun 1908.

Hector Kooger
alias
Hector Tracy

Private, Company A: Born during Aug 1840, at Round, Colleton, SC; a Slave of the Tracy Family; Enlisted on 07 Mar 1865, at Beaufort, Beaufort, SC; Honorably Discharged on 10 Oct 1866, at Morris Island, Charleston, SC. Married to Georgiana Martin (d. Feb 1914, Williams, Colleton, SC), on 07 or 08 Mar 1867, at Walterboro, Colleton, SC, by Ben Stokes, Notary Public. Children: Sarah (b. 26 May 1868); Armarita (b. 05 May 1870); Joseph (b. 09 Aug 1872); Arthur (b. 12 Jun 1880); and Hector (b. 01 Jul 1884; d. bef 07 Apr 1915). **Hector Kooger** *died 30 or 31 May 1917, at Williams, Colleton, SC.*[111]

Hector Kooger (Veteran Soldier)
Date: 13 Aug 1901
Residence: near Williams, Colleton, SC
Occupation: Farmer

I am about 61 years of age. I am known under the name of Hector Kooger. Most people call me that way and I used that name from the time I was discharged until I applied for pension. They told me that I would have to apply under the name I used in the service. Now all the people know that I draw Pension as Hector Tracy. I was at the battle of Honey Hill. I got a shell wound there. There were people killed in piles at that battle. I was not in the regular battle but I was wounded in a skirmish

---

[111] Civil War Pension Record for Hector Tracy alias Hector Kooger, SC No. 631.305, Pvt, Company A, 128th USCI, Records of the VA, RG 15, NARA, WDC; 1900 U.S. Federal Census, South Carolina, Warren Township, ED: 51, Page: 378A, Line: 15 (Roll: T623-1525), This family is listed in the census records as "Heckter & Georgian Coger."

near the battle and on the same day that the battle was fought. I was on the battlefield of Honey Hill and I saw them killed laying on the field by the hundreds.

I had enlisted in Company A of the 1st South Carolina Colored Volunteer Infantry. About 6 months before the battle of Honey Hill. I could not exactly tell when I joined the company. It was a full regiment of U.S. Troops. The regimental commander was Colonel Beecher. I went under the name of Hector Kooger. I was at Pocotaligo and Hardeeville and Port Royal. I was in all those battles, but I did not do any fighting I got that shell wound at Honey Hill.

At the battle of Pocotaligo they used dogs. We had U.S. uniforms on. I got wounded in the hip. I was sent to Beaufort Hospital and discharged from them as near as I can remember. I was in the hospital about one month. When I left the hospital I went right and enlisted at Beaufort, S.C. in Company A, 128th U.S. Colored Volunteers.

I was never in any other company or regiment than the 1st South Carolina and Company A, 128th U.S. Colored Volunteer Infantry. I cannot tell why I did not remember this service before. I had a discharge from the 128th but nothing to show for the other service.[112]

Response from the Bureau of Pensions
    Date: 17 Oct 1901
    Location: Washington, DC
    Agent: Chief of Law Division

Sir: I forward herewith the original papers pertaining to the claim of Hector Tracy, late of Company A, 128th U.S. Colored Infantry, Certificate No. 631.305, together with a deposition of the pensioner taken by Special Examiner D.K. Doe under the general letter of instructions of February 2, 1901, relative to South Carolina cases.

The soldier is pensioned for shell wound of left hip under the provisions of the Act of June 27, 1890, and says that he got that wound at the battle of Honey Hill, which was fought on November 30, 1864. He en-

---

[112] Deposition of Hector Tracy, case of Hector Tracy (Williams, Colleton, SC), dated 13 Aug 1901.

listed in the 128th Colored Infantry, on March 8, 1865; four months after the wound incurred, and says that he served in Company A, 1st South Carolina Colored Infantry, under Colonel Beecher. Colonel Beecher commanded the 35th Colored Infantry, and the petitioner's name has not been found upon the rolls thereof or upon the rolls of any regiment which is shown by the records of the War Department to have participated in the battle of Honey Hill. There does not exist any apparent reason for questioning the pensioner's identity as the Hector Tracy who served in Company A, 128th U.S. Colored Infantry, but it is apparent that he must have served in some other organization if, as he alleges, he was a soldier and wounded at the battle of Honey Hill.

You are requested to forward the papers to Special Examiner W.L. Harris at Charleston, S.C., with instructions to take such testimony as may be available to show the correct designation of the organization in which the prior service was performed and the name under which the soldier served.

This letter should appear as an exhibit in the examiner's report.[113]

Hector Kooger (Veteran Soldier)
    Date: 02 May 1902
    Residence: near Williams, Colleton, SC
    Occupation: Farmer

After all our talk now I will tell you the whole truth:

I did tell the pensioner examiner that that I was in the 1st South Carolina, that I was wounded at Honey Hill and that Colonel Beecher was my colonel. I told him I was in the battle of Pocotaligo, Port Royal, Hardeeville and Honey Hill. It is all false. I never saw Colonel Beecher. I was not in the 1st South Carolina. I was never in a battle in my life. I put it in my first papers that I got a shell wound in the army and I told Mr. Doe I got shell wound in the army. I never got a shell wound anywhere. That scar I passed off for a shell wound was incurred in the following

---

[113] Letter from Chief of Law Division, Department of the Interior, Bureau of Pensions, Washington, DC to Chief of the Special Examination Division, Department of the Interior, dated 05 Nov 1901.

Hector Kooger alias Hector Tracy

manner: While we were stationed in Charleston, while I was in the army, I went out one night to a dance. There came up a big row and when the shooting commenced, I quit the dance and started to my quarters. Just as I got outside a policeman came up and arrested me and beat me over the head and carried me to the guard house. I was so badly hurt from the beaten that I was out of my head the next day and they carried me to the government hospital. I can't tell how long I was in the hospital but as near as I can recollect, it was about one month. While there, a bad sore came on my hip and it got so bad that it had maggots in it. After I got well it left a scar which I told was caused by a shell wound.

This is the whole truth. I was never in but one company and that was Company A, 128th U.S. Colored Infantry. Captain Field was Provost Marshall when I was in the hospital. He was a captain in my regiment. I had but the one bed sore on me. John Owens was the hospital steward who nursed me. He was also in my regiment. He now lives about four miles from [the town of] Williams – about due east. I am sure he will remember me. I do not remember what doctor had charge of the hospital. Jesse Folk, who now lives in Charleston, was a sergeant in my company – he will know me.[114]

---

[114] Deposition of Hector Tracy, case of Hector Tracy (Williams, Colleton, SC), dated 13 Aug 1901.

* * * * * * * * * * * * * *

John LAWRENCE
alias
John Trappier

Private, Company F: Born c1847, at Georgetown, Georgetown, SC; a Slave of William Trappier; Enlisted on 27 Mar 1865, at Georgetown, Georgetown, SC; Honorably Discharged on 10 Oct 1866, at Hilton Head, Beaufort, SC. Married to Caroline Rutledge (d. c1894). Children: Sue (b. c1892/3). **John Lawrence** *died on 30 Jun 1911, at Savannah, Chatham, GA.*[115]

John Lawrence (Veteran Soldier)
    Date: 11 May 1903
    Residence: Savannah, Chatham, GA
    Occupation: Farmer

I am in receipt of a pension of six dollars a month under the Act of June 27, 1890 having served during the War of the Rebellion in Company F, 128th U.S. Colored Infantry.

    I was born in Georgetown, S.C., and was a slave. I was owned by William Trappin or Trappier. My father was Adam Lawrence. General [Milton S.] Littlefield enlisted me under the name of John Trappier. Before the war I was called John Lawrence but ever since I enlisted in the army I have been called John Trappier.

    I enlisted in Georgetown, S.C., but I cannot recollect the year. I was in the army just one year and eight months. After enlistment at Georgetown we came to Hilton Head and from there we went to Beaufort and then to Morris Island and we were mustered out there. We were never in any battles.

---

[115] Civil War Pension Record for John Lawrence alias John Trappier, SC No. 790.468, Pvt, Company F, 128th USCI, Records of the VA, RG 15, NARA, WDC.

John Lawrence alias John Trappier

Emory Steadman was a corporal. He is the only corporal whose name I can recollect. Frank Duncan ate and slept with me in service. He is dead. Francis Ward is somewhere in this city and Bill Emory, who was 1st Sgt. till he was reduced because he could not read and write and who now lives here were friends of mine in service. Snow Flag was friend of mine in service but I have not seen him in years and do not know what became of him.

At Hilton Head I was in the hospital for two weeks. I had pneumonia there. That was the only time and place that I was ever sick in service.

I put in for pension under the old law under a man named Toomer, but never got it through. I do not recollect what ailment I claimed pension for. I now suffer with and infection of my knees. My knee first began to trouble me between five and ten years ago. Fifteen or sixteen years ago I had my hand and knee knocked out of place. I was working on a brick kiln and fell off.

I do not recollect who my attorney in Washington when I got my claim allowed. Renty Green was my local attorney and I paid him fifty cents for every paper that he wrote for me. I paid him nothing else.

After my discharge from the army I lived for six months in Charleston and then I came to Savannah and have been here and on {Willimon} Island ever since. Some people call me John Lawrence still, but my army name is John Trappier.

I have only been married once; I married Caroline Rutledge, but she died about nine or ten years ago on the Rutledge Plantation near this city. I have a girl named Sue who is now about fifteen years of age. I don't know her exact age but she was four months old when the great storm came. My brother Abraham Trappier lives at Coosawhatchie, South Carolina. He is the only relative whom I know that is alive. My mother and father are both dead.[116]

---

[116] Deposition of John Trappin, case of John Trappin (Savannah, Chatham, GA), dated 11 May 1903.

John LUCAS
alias
John Smith

Private, Company I: Born on c1847, at Strawberry Ferry, Charleston District (now Berkeley County), SC; a Slave of John Warren; Enlisted on 01 Feb 1865, at Beaufort, Beaufort, SC; Honorably Discharged on 10 Oct 1866, at Morris Island, Charleston, SC. Married to Sarah Rivers, during 1869, at Strawberry, Charleston, SC, by Rev. Thomas Evans. Children: Catherine (b. c1875); Mary Jane (b. 1877); Benjamin (b. 1879); Sallie (b. 1890); and Henry (d. 1894). **John Lucas** *died on 20 Aug 1925, Foxbank Plantation, Moncks Corner, Berkeley, SC.*[117]

John Lucas (Veteran Soldier)
Date: 08 Feb 1890
Residence: Strawberry, Berkeley, SC

My age is 52. I am the John Smith who served in Company I, 128th U.S. Colored Troops. I enlisted in Beaufort, S.C., in 1865 and was mustered out at Sullivans Island, S.C., in 1866. I was in service about a year and eight months. I was not grown I went in service. I was owned by Dr. Warren (dead) before the war and raised at Strawberry Ferry (now Berkeley County). I came back here to Strawberry as soon as I was mustered out of service and have lived near here ever since.

After muster out, I injured my left hand in the following way. I was minding the Dean Hall rice field with Aaron Gillard one September and

---

[117] Civil War Pension Record for John Lucas alias John Smith, SC No. C-2.528.918, Pvt, Company I, 128th USCI; Records of the VA, RG 15, NARA, WDC, 1900 U.S. Federal Census, South Carolina, Berkeley County, St. James – Goose Creek Parish, ED: 19, Page: 46B, Line: 80 (Roll: T623-1519).

started to draw the load out of my gun. I took out the ball and while I was trying to knock the power out with my hand over the gun, it went off and the power tore my hand badly. I cannot give you the date but it was about twenty years ago. I know that for I shot my hand a few days before my daughter, Mary Jane, was born and she is about twenty.

I was sober at the time. I do not drink and was not in a fuss with anybody, but shot myself just as I have stated. That is all I can tell you about it.[118]

March Washington (Comrade of the Veteran Soldier)
Date: 08 Feb 1890
Residence: Mount Holly, Berkeley, SC

I am 56 years of age. I have known John Smith twenty five or thirty years. I know that he shot himself in the left hand accidentally in September 1879 while minding the Dean Hall rice field and I know the date and year he was shot because I was living in one room of the same house with him at the time and saw him in twenty minutes after he was shot and know that he was minding the rice field that day and heard him tell how he had draw out the shot and how the gun went off and the power tore his left hand.

I dressed his hand for him until it healed. I know the date because I know he was shot five days before his daughter, Mary Jane, was born and I wrote the date of her birth in my bible at the time and I have it written that she was born September 19th 1879.

I know that John Smith is a man of good habits and that he was not drinking nor in a fuss the day he shot himself.[119]

---

[118] Deposition of John Smith, case of John Smith (Mount Holly, Berkeley, SC), dated 08 Feb 1890.
[119] Ibid. March Washington.

Cain MAYHAMS
alias
Cain Mayhew

Private, Company D: Born c1846, on Rosemont Plantation, near Georgetown, Georgetown, SC; a Slave of John S. Pyatt; Enlisted on 08 Mar 1865, at Beaufort, SC; Honorably Discharged on 10 Oct 1866, at Morris Island, Charleston, SC. Married to Lucretia Shubrick (d. 18 Mar 1891), on 03 Jan 1867, on Rosemont Plantation, near Georgetown, SC, by Augustus T. Carr. Children: Alice (b. 17 Dec 1870); Norridge (b. Aug 1874); Mrs. Delilah Walker (b. 23 May 1877); Eugenia (b. 17 Jul 1879: d. 13 Feb 1905); and Mrs. Sarah Rebecca Moultrie (b. 10 March 1882). **Cain Mayhams** *died on 14 Aug Oct 1884, near Georgetown, Georgetown, SC.*[120]

Frederick G. Mayhams (Brother of the Veteran Soldier)
Date: **09 Aug 1905**
Residence: **#420 Orange St., Georgetown, Georgetown, SC**

My age is 56. I am blind now and cannot see to write or work. Cain Mayhams was my brother. We were born and raised in Georgetown, County, S.C., about 3 miles from town. We were owned by John S. Pyatt. We were on his place until the war broke out and then were taken up in Marion and came back in October 1864.

This town was captured the next February and Cain and I went to enlist soon after that. I was only 16 and they would not take me, but Cain

---

[120] Civil War Pension Record for Delilah & Eugenia & Sarah Mayhams, minors of Cain Mayhams alias Cain Mahew, MC No. 596.808, Private, Company D, 128th USCI, Records of the VA, RG 15, NARA, WDC. Note:* Frederick was the Guardian of his brother's minor children.

was 19 and they took him. I know he was a soldier because 2 months after he enlisted I went to Beaufort to see him and he was a member of Company D, 128th U.S. Colored Infantry. I was with him there for 3 weeks.

As soon as he was mustered out he came right here and lived here until he died in October 1884. He was never married and never lived with a woman up to the time he went in the army. I know for I was with him all the time and he did not marry while in the service for he did not bring a wife home with him. The first wife he ever had, and she was the only one, was Lucretia Shubrick. He married her in Jan. 1867. I was present and saw them married. They were married by a colored man by the name of Augustus Carr. They were married on Mr. Pyatt plantation, Rosemont, about 3 miles from town, and they lived together and were known as man and wife from that time until Cain died.

I knew Lucretia from the time she was a child. She was also owned by Mr. Pyatt and I know that she was never married and never lived with a man until she married my brother. She did not remarry nor lived with a man after my brother died and she died on March 18th 1891.

She and Cain had about 10 children. Six were living when Cain died, and five were living when Lucretia died, and four are living now. Those living when Lucretia died were: Alice, Norridge, Delilah, Eugenia and Sarah. They are all living now except Eugenia. She died on February 13th 1905 and left a husband and two children.

I don't know when they were born but I have our bible and their births were recorded in there by Cain Himself –

(Bible record shows – Alice, born December 17th 1870; Norridge, born August 1874; Dililah, born May 23, 1877; Eugenia, born July 17th 1880; Sarah, born March 10th 1883, but the 3 has been recently added in pencil. The balance of the record is old and genuine. Bible also shows marriage of "Cain Mayhams & Lucretia Shubrick" on January 3rd 1867, and death of Lucretia on March 18th 1891. All of wording except death of mother said to be that of soldiers. The records all appear genuine except the 3 in date of birth of Sarah – e.h.j.)[121]

Norridge Mayhams (Daughter of the Veteran Soldier)
Date: 10 Aug 1905
Residence: Georgetown, Georgetown, SC

My age is 31. Cain Mayhams was my father and Lucretia was my mother. I was born on August 15th 1874. I know the date of my birth by seeing it in our bible and by hearing my father tell me when I was born.

My father made all of the bible record and up to his death and I have made them since. My father died in October 1884, and my mother in March 1891. I have 3 sisters living – Alice, who is older than I and Delila, who is younger. I don't know when any of them were born except by seeing the record in the bible.

I know the record was made by my father except the 3 in date of Sarah's birth. I don't know who did that. My father and mother were living together when my father died. They were known and recognized as man and wife. My mother buried him. My sister Eugenia was next to Sarah. She died in February 1905. There are no other children of my father living except for the four just mentioned.[122]

Frederick Allston (Comrade of Veteran Soldier)
Date: 11 Aug 1905
Residence: Georgetown, Georgetown, SC

My age is 69. I served in Company C, 104th U.S. Colored Infantry as Doctor Allston. I knew Cain Mayhams before the war. He was owned by Mr. John Pyatt and by Governor Allston. I lived 15 miles from him but would meet him in Georgetown.

I know that Cain was a soldier for he and I and Nat Allston and Tony Allston and others all went at the same time from here during the war.

---

[121] Deposition of F.G Mayhams, case of F.G. Mayhams (Georgetown, Georgetown, SC), dated 09 Aug 1905. Note: The initials of E.H.J is that of E.H. Jennings, Special Examiners of the Bureau of Pensions.
[122] Ibid. Norridge Mayhams, dated 10 Aug 1905

Cain Mayhams alias Cain Mayhew

We were sent to Beaufort, where I was put in the 104th and Cain in the 128th. I saw him there while he was soldier. The 104th and 128th was camped there at the same time. I came home first and Cain came as soon as he was mustered out. He was not married up to that time but soon after he came home he married Lucretia. I did not see them married, but I knew about it at the time and I know they lived together as man and wife from that time until Cain died – which was a year or two before the earthquake. I know he never had but that one wife in his life. I did not know Lucretia until he married her. Lucretia did not marry again and died some 12 or 15 year ago

Lucretia left 5 children: Alice, Norridge, Delia, Eugenia and Sarah – born in that order. Eugenia died a few months ago. I know these children were the children Cain Mayhams who served in the 128th. I don't know when they were born nor how old they are. I know that Sarah and Delila are young married girls.[123]

---

[123] Ibid. Frederick Allston, dated 11 Aug 1905.

* * * * * * * * * * * * *

Henry MCCREARY
alias
Henry McCrea

Musician, Company K: Born c1842, in Barnwell County (now Colleton), SC; a Slave of Robert McCreary; Enlisted on 07 Mar 1865, at Beaufort, Beaufort, SC; Honorably Discharged on 10 Oct 1866, at Morris Island, Charleston, SC. Married to Ella Hickson, 01 Jan 1868, at Winsdor, Aiken, SC, by Cyrus Keadder, Justice of the Peace or Magistrate. Children: Neal (b. 15 Sep 1870); J.H. (b. 14 Jan 1872); Clara (b. 09 May 1874); Marchel (b. 10 Aug 1876); Cora (b. 10 Sep 1878); J. (b. 15 Oct 1880); Stella (05 Dec 1882); and Lillie (b. 09 Jun 1895). **Henry McCreary** *died on 30 Jan 1914, at White Pond, Aiken, SC.*[124]

Henry McCreary (Veteran Soldier)
Date: **21 Jan 1891**
Residence: **White Pond, Aiken, SC**
Occupation: **Farmer**

Henry McCreary declares that he has resided at White Pond, S.C., all the time since his discharge from the army; that his occupation has been farming; that his disability was caused by rheumatism in right leg which has continued three fourths of his time till the present; that he has never employed a physician not being able to pay them, but; that he has used Patient Medicines Recommended for Rheumatism; that he used Dr. Hopkins medicine which he thinks has done some good but has not cured him; that Dr. Hopkins lives in Atlanta, Ga.; that Dr. Hopkins is now liv-

---

[124] Civil War Pension Record for Ella McCreary (widow of Henry McCreary alias Henry McCrea), WC No. 781.726, Pvt, Company K, 128th USCI, Records of the VA, RG 15, NARA, WDC: 1910 U.S. Federal Census, South Carolina, Aiken County, Winsdor Township, ED: 24, Page: 169A, Line: 9 (Roll: T624-1447).

ing; that he can't give any definite dates of time lost in consequence of his disease, but; that he will average three quarters of his time.[125]

Ella McCreary (Widow of the Veteran Soldier)
Date: 25 Feb 1914
Residence: White Pond, Aiken, SC

When I was a small child my father and mother were owned by Hickson. My next master was Staley and at freedom my master was Holman. So I was known by all of these names – Ella Hickson, Ella Staley and Ella Holman which was very common among slaves of that time, but being owned by Staley and Holman after I was I was grown I held to the name of Ella Holman-Staley; the masters whom I had always known and loved. Being owned by Hickson when a child, it was natural for me to want to keep the names of those who owned me when I was older. There are many people of the old slaves who were known after freedom by more than one name from the above cause.[126]

Mrs. Dora Carley (Acquaintance of the Veteran Soldier)
Date: 20 Feb 1914
Residence: White Pond, Aiken, SC

Mrs. Dora Carley (70) declares that she was well acquainted with the soldier, Henry McCreary, and with his wife, Ella McCreary, whose maiden name was Holman, from the time they were old enough to be married and knows that neither was married until they married to each other in 1867; that she also knows that they lived together without divorce from marriage until the soldier died; that the soldier, Henry McCreary, belong to her father before freedom; that they were living at her father's place when they were married; that they went to Cyrus Keadder – a Justice of the Peace or Magistrate for South Carolina; that they were married by him; that she did not see the marriage, and; they have lived together

---

[125] General Affidavit for Henry McCreary (Aiken County, SC), dated 21 Jan 1891.
[126] General Affidavit for Ella McCreary, in the matter of Ella McCreary, widow of Henry McCreary alias McCrea (White Pond, Aiken, SC), dated 25 Feb 1914.

ever since and to the death of Henry McCreary, on Jan 30, 1914. She further declares that she has no interest in the case, and is not concerned in its prosecution.[127]

Henry Carley (Acquaintance of the Veteran Soldier)
Date: 07 Mar 1914
Residence: White Pond, Aiken, SC

Henry Carley (66) declares that he has known Henry McCreary and his wife Ella McCreary all of his life; that the said Ella McCreary, who was Ella Holman before she was married to Henry McCreary, in 1867; that he did not see the marriage himself, but knew of it at the time, and; that he knows that they have lived together continuously up to January 30, 1914; the day of the said Henry McCreary's death;

That they were never separated during said time, and; that neither one of them were ever married before they were married to each other; that they were married by Cyrus Keadder, a Justice of the Peace of South Carolina; that he has no interest in her claim for pension; that he is sixty six years old and, that he has lived around White Pond, S.C., all his life.[128]

Ella McCreary (Widow of the Veteran Soldier)
Date: 05 Aug 1914
Residence: White Pond, Aiken, SC

Ella McCreary declares that she was married to Henry McCreary, on January 1, 1868. She further states that their daughter, Lillie McCreary, was born on June 9, 1895, which makes her over sixteen years of age.[129]

---

[127] Ibid., Mrs. Dora Carley, dated 21 Feb 1914.
[128] Ibid., Henry Carley, dated 07 Mar 1914.
[129] Ibid., Ella McCreary, dated 05 Aug 1914.

Definitions

Affidavit

Definition:

A sworn, written statement made in the presence of a notary public or a person who is authorized to administer an oath. Affidavits are used in legal proceedings and may be submitted in lieu of having a person appear in court.

Possible Use:

To allow evidence to be gathered from witnesses or participants who may not be available to testify in person before the court, or who may otherwise fear for their safety if their true identities are revealed in court.

Deposition

Definition:

A sworn testimony of a witness taken before trial held out of court with no judge present. The witness is placed under oath to tell the truth and lawyers for each party may ask questions. The questions and answers are recorded. When a person is unavailable to testify at trial, the deposition of that person may be used.

Possible Use

The testimony of a deponent or witness reduced to writing in due form of law, taken by virtue of a commission or other authority of a competent tribunal.

Source: http://en.wikipedia.org/wiki/Affidavit; http://en.wikipedia.org/wiki/ Deposition_(law)

Isaac MCCREARY
alias
Isaac McCrea

Private, Company K: Born on during Nov 1848, at Barnwell County, SC; a Slave of Robert McCreary; Enlisted on 07 Mar 1865, at Beaufort, Beaufort, SC; Honorably Discharged on 10 Oct 1866, at Morris Island, Charleston, SC. 1st Marriage to Viney Bonnet (d. c1875, near Williston, Barnwell, SC), during 1869, at Williston, SC. 2nd Marriage to Susanna Butler (d. 10 Jan 1904, near Jefferson, Jefferson, AK), during 1889, near Williston, SC. Children: Emma (b. 12 Mar 1892); Henry (b. 12 Jan 1895); Rosie (b. 27 Jun 1897); Effie (b. 07 Apr 1900); and Samuel (b. 01 Jun 1904). **Isaac McCreary** *died on 12 Sep 1912, near Madison, St. Francis, AK.*[130]

Isaac McCreary (Veteran Soldier)
Date: 03 Aug 1909
Residence: Widener, St. Francis, AK
Occupation: Unknown

I am 62 or 63 years of age. I am the identical Isaac McCreary who served during the late civil war in Company K, 128th U.S. Colored Volunteer Infantry. I served about one year and ten months and was mustered out with the regiment. I was never in other service in the United States Service. I was 17 years old when I enlisted near Williston, Barnwell County, S.C. I was owned by Bob McCreary. He has children still living in that old neighborhood named Paul McCreary and Robert McCreary.

---

[130] Civil War Pension Record for Isaac McCreary alias Isaac McCrea, SC No. C-2.466.085, Pvt, Company K, 128th USCI, Records of the VA, RG 15, NARA, WDC.

Isaac McCreary alias Isaac McCrea

Some of my old fellow slaves are Henry McCreary, Sam McCreary (dead), John McCreary (dead), Sam Ryan and Marshall Ryan. They lived near White Pond, Aiken County, S.C. Seventeen years ago when I left there. I have one brother, Henry McCreary, living near or in White Pond, S.C. I have always been known as Isaac McCreary. I have no record of my birth but I think Robert McCreary has the old McCreary family record. He lives in Aiken City, Aiken County, S.C. If he has no record maybe one of his brothers has the record.

Nearly all of our service was in Beaufort, S.C., then to Charleston, S.C., then to Morris Island, S.C. We were mustered out at Morris Island. I was in no battle. I was in a hospital at Charleston on account of a blow across my head from my right eye almost back to my ear. A policeman was trying to arrest a man. The man got in a boat I was in and the policeman was after him. They fought and the policeman hit me by accident. I was in the hospital a month or more and was treated by Dr. Rector. I was in a hospital another time, in Beaufort, with a fever. This time I was treated by Dr. [Henry K.] Durrant.

During the first year I was in service, while unloading coal from a vessel at Parris Island near Beaufort, I was pushing a wheelbarrow load of coal off the plank and I lost my balance someway. The wheelbarrow turned and fell in the water and I fell on the side of the wharf and somehow the handle of the wheelbarrow struck me in the right side of my groin and I found right away that I had a rupture in my right groin. A rupture developed in the left side after the war.

To prove the origin of my rupture while in service and in the line of duty I will refer you to my brother Henry McCreary and Thomas Wade, in Aiken, S.C.; Benjamin Edney and John Baker, in Savannah, Ga.; and Millege Wimley, at Beach Island, Aiken County, S.C.

I lived at White Pond until 17 years ago. The only comrade there is my brother Henry McCreary. Thomas Harrison or Wade, at Aiken, saw me a good many times after the war and he knew my first wife Viney and my children – Chester and Edward McCreary. All other comrades who knew me after the war are dead. There was Emery and Henry Stedman and Boston Sexton (both dead). They used to live near White Pond. My brother Henry McCreary used to have my picture. If he still has it I believe he will lend it to the Pension Bureau in order to help establish my claim for pension.

I have been married only twice. My first wife was Viney Bonnet. I married her in Williston, S.C., the 3rd year after I was mustered out of service. She died near Williston about 34 years ago. I next married Susannah Butler near Williston, Barnwell, S.C. She died near Jefferson, Jefferson County, Ark., during April 1904. I never had any other wife.

While I was a slave I lived with Becky Johnson. We were not married. We lived together for a while but had parted before I enlisted. We had no children and I don't consider she was my wife. I don't know where she lives now. I have 4 children under the age of 16 years of age. They are named Henry, Rosetta, Effie and Samuel McCreary.[131]

Robert W. McCreary (Acquaintance of the Veteran Soldier)
    Date: 14 April 1910
    Residence: Aiken, Aiken, SC
    Occupation: Merchant

My age is 59 years. I well remember a negro named Isaac McCreary who was a slave for my father Robert McCreary on his plantation near White Pond, S.C. He was about my age and we played together as boys. I know that he and his brother, Henry McCrery, who now lives near White Pond, and is a pensioner who enlisted in the U.S. Services. I saw Isaac with his uniform on just after his discharge from service. I don't know in what regiment or what company he served in, but he and his brother Henry went in at the same time, and I think they were both in the same regiment and company.

After his discharge Isaac stayed near this part of the county for a number of years, until about 20 years ago – possibly a little less than that. He left here and went west somewhere. I have no doubt whatever that this Isaac McCreary who resides at Widener, St. Francis, Arkansas is the same Isaac McCreary who was slave of my father, Robert McCreary, and

---

[131] Deposition of Isaac McCreary, case of Isaac McCreary (Forest City, St. Francis, AK), dated 03 Aug 1909.

Isaac McCreary alias Isaac McCrea

who, with his brother Henry McCreary, served in the U.S. Army during the Civil War.

I recollect well that my brother Isaac had a rupture before he left here. He had this rupture a great many years before he left here and that was 17 years ago. Dr. Brooks (now dead) examined him and gave him a truss for this rupture. I saw the rupture many times and know that Isaac long before he left here and went to Arkansas.[132]

Henry McCreary (Brother and Comrade of the Veteran Soldier)
    Date: 15 April 1910
    Residence: White Pond, Aiken, SC
    Occupation: Farmer

My age is 67 years. I served in Company K, 128th U.S. Colored Volunteer Infantry. I am a pensioner of the United States. Isaac McCreary of Widener, St. Francis, Arkansas, who left this vicinity about 17 years ago, is my brother. He served with me in the same regiment and company. We enlisted together and were discharged at the same time. We were both slaves for Robert McCreary (now dead), near White Pond, Aiken County, S.C. There is no possible doubt that my brother, now in Arkansas, is the Isaac McCreary who served in Company K, 128th U.S. Colored Volunteer Infantry.

I recollect well that my brother Isaac had a rupture before he left here. He had this rupture a great many years before he left here and that was 17 years ago. Dr. Brooks (now dead) examined him and gave him a truss for this rupture. I saw the rupture many times and know that Isaac long before he left here and went to Arkansas.[133]

---

[132] Ibid., Robert W. McCrary, (near White Pond, Aiken, SC), dated 14 Apr 1910.
[133] Ibid., Henry McCrary, dated 15 Apr 1910.

Nero MCFARLAN
alias
Nero Rogers

Private, Company A: Born during 1835, at Cashs Depot (near Cheraw), Chesterfield, SC; a Slave of Allen McFarlan; Enlisted on 06 Mar 1865, at Beaufort, Beaufort, SC; Honorably Discharged on 10 Oct 1866, at Morris Island, Charleston, SC. Married to Adeline Austin (b. c1851; d. 14 Feb 1910, Society Hill, Darlington, SC), on 18 Aug 1883, at Cheraw, SC, by Rev. A.J. Wilson. Children: Mrs. Della Willson (b. 03 Dec 1884). ***Nero McFarlan*** *died on 27 Jun 1905, at Cheraw, Chesterfield, SC.*[134]

Nero McFarlan (Veteran Soldier)
Date: 11 Oct 1904
Residence: Cashs (near Cheraw), Chesterfield, SC
Occupation: Farmer

I don't know my age, but I think I am between 60 and 70. I was born near here and was owned by Colonel Allen McFarlan (now dead) and lived on his place near where I now live up to the time Sherman's Army came by here. Some of his soldiers took me with them and made me cook. They were Christian soldiers and I would sing and pray every night. They made me go with them and cook for them. They took me to some place near Wilmington, N.C., and then put a lot of us on a boat and took us to Edisto Island just below Charleston and there they enlisted us, but we did not know what we were doing. Their they took us to Hilton

---

[134] Civil War Pension Record for Adeline McFarlan (widow of Nero McFarlan alias Nero Rogers), WC No. C-2.520.776, Pvt, Company A, 128th USCI, Records of the VA, RG 15, NARA, WDC.

Nero McFarlan alias Nero Rogers

Head and then to Beaufort where they made us all strip and wash in the sea and put on soldier clothes and threw the others away. We were camped at Beaufort a long time and {boarded} to drill and do guard duty and then we went to the islands about Charleston and were mustered out on Morris Island.

Robert McFarlan is my brother. He was taken from here about the time I was but I did not see him until we met in Beaufort and were put in the same company.

I served in Company A, 128th U.S. Colored Troops as Nero McFarlan. I am known as McFarlan and Rogers. My father was Rogers. I am called by one as much as the other. I knew other McFarlans who served in the army. Roman and Lewis McFarlan were in the army with me. Roman is dead – he left some children . I think Della was one , but I don't know where she is. Lewis is living but he is over in Darlington County now. Jet McFarlan went with us to Beaufort, but he was very young and I don't know whether he was made a soldier or not. I think they said he was too young but they let him stay with us and wear soldier clothe. Jet has been dead a long time. I think he died a year or so after the war. I never knew him to have a wife.

I was never married up to the time I enlisted in the army, but soon after I came home I married Sylvia McBride. She died before the shake and then in about 3 years I married Adeline Austin and she still live with me. I married her about a year before the shake (Page 136). I have only one child living. Her name is Della. She was a young lady at the time of the shake. I have one other child. I don't know its name and never saw it. It's mother is a woman by the name of Sarah. I staid with her some when I was down in Barnwell working while my first wife was living and after I left I heard she had a baby by me. I never lived with her and she was never my wife.

Adeline was never married until she married me, but she had one child before she married me. I don't know who the father was. I don't think she lived with my name.[135]

---

[135] Deposition of Isaac McCreary, case of Isaac McCreary (Forest City, St. Francis, AK), dated 03 Aug 1909.

Geoffrey Broughton (Comrade of the Veteran Soldier)
Date: 14 Oct 1904
Residence: Meeting St., Charleston, Charleston, SC
Occupation: Not at Work

My age is 59 years. I served in Company A, 128th U.S. Colored Troops. I am a pensioner. I was born and raised on Cooper River and went back there after muster out and was there for 7 years and then came here and have been here ever since.

I remember Nero McFarlan who served in my company. He had a brother by the name of Robert who was also in my company and there were several other McFarlans in Company I. They all came from the same place – somewhere up in the state. I don't know just where. I have not seen Nero since we were mustered out.[136]

Janie Purcell (Friend of the Widow)
Date: 28 Jul 1910
Residence: Society Hill, Darlington, SC

I am 42 years of age. My age is 67 years. I am the wife of William J. Purcell. I was well acquainted with Adaline McFarlan (the claimant) during her lifetime. I was not related to her, nor have I any interest in this claim for pension. She belonged to an insurance society here for which I am a local agent. My record shows that she died February 14, 1910. Her funeral expenses were paid by the society. She left but one child, Della Wilson, aged 24. I have her name and age in my books. Adaline left no property.[137]

---

[136] Deposition of Geoffrey Broughton, case of Nero McFarlan Charleston, Charleston SC, dated 14 Oct 1904.
[137] Ibid., Janie Purcell, dated 28 Jul 1910.

Pawning Pension Certificates
Arrest of A Pawn Broker for his Dealings with a Pensioner

Philadelphia, September 4. – Moses Hamburg, a pawnbroker, had a hearing before United States Commissioner Edmunds today on the charge of loaning money on a pension certificate in violation of the law. James Lafferty, of Second and Oxford streets, a hunchback and a cripple from rheumatism, said he was in receipt of $24.00 a month pension, and was in the habit of pawning the certificate frequently with Hamberg & Co. He pawned it June 7 for $2.50; received $10.00 on June 9, and $5.00 on August 31, and when he drew his money he was handed $12.00. This made the interest on the loans, aggregating $17.50, $42.50.

On several occasions when the pawnbroker could not accompany him to the pension office to draw his money he left his daughter, a girl of 15, as security and she was released when he brought back the certificate. This fact the witness spoke of as if it were the usual routine of business. The daughter, Ellen Eugene Lafferty, a bright girl, said that her father and mother always spent the pension money for drink, and she been used as security several times and did not seem to look upon it as a hardship. Once when her father handed her over to Hamburg to be locked up until he returned, he said "Now you are in prison, you know." Hamburg was held in $500.00 bail to answer at the next term of court, and care will be taken to prevent the disappearance of the witnesses.

Source: The New York Times, Published: September 5, 1883: Copyright - The New York Times (http://query.nytimes.com/gst/abstract.html?res=9501E0DB13 3BE033A25756C0A96F9C94629FD7CF)

Frank MCNEILL
alias
Frank Gray

Private, Company G: Born on 04 Dec 1848, at Charleston, SC; a Slave of Benjamin Gary; Enlisted on 08 Mar 1865, at Charleston, Charleston, SC; Honorable Discharge on 10 Oct 1866, at Morris Island, Charleston, SC. 1st Marriage to Elizabeth (MNU) (d. 26 Jun 1886). Children: Mrs. Leonora Carter (b. 08 Feb 1871); Edward (b. 12 Sep 1879). 2nd Marriage to Jane Anna (MNU) (d. 21 May 1888). Children: 3rd Marriage to Mahala Williams (b. Barnwell, SC; d. 11 Feb 1908, Charleston, SC), on 11 Jan 1891, at the Wesley Church, Charleston, SC by Reverend E.M. Pinckney. Children: Frank (b. 04 Mar 1893); Fred (b. 04 Sep 1894); Magdaline (b. 14 Mar 1896), and; Beatrice (b. 04 Nov 1900). **Frank McNeill** *died on 30 Jun 1914, at Charleston, Charleston, SC.*[138]

Frank McNeill (Veteran Soldier)
Date: 25 Jun 1896
Residence: Charleston, Charleston, SC

I was born in Charleston, S.C., and my age was 18 at enlistment. The name that I now bear, Frank McNeil, is from my father. My master's name was Benjamin Gary. I enlisted under the name of Gary, but it seems that the recording officer wrote it as Gray, so I answered at roll call as Gary. I was a member of Lieutenant Lester Hall's Company – Company G, 128th U.S. Colored Troops and served under the name of Frank Gray – answering to that name at roll call. My present name of

---

[138] Civil War Pension Record for minor children of Frank Gray known as Frank McNeill (Under the Guardianship of Leonora Carter), MC No. 799.967, Pvt, Company G, 128th USCI, Records of the VA, RG 15, NARA, WDC.

Frank McNeill alias Frank Gray

Frank McNeill is my father's name and I gave the name of my owner at enlistment which accounts for the difference.[139]

Eliza Finley (Friend of the Veteran Soldier)
Date: 06 Sep 1915
Residence: Charleston County, SC

I am well acquainted with Frank McNeill and his family and have been so acquainted with them all her life. I know that the child Beatrice McNeill was born in November before the opening of the Charleston Exposition, but I don't know the exact day of her birth. She was born the early part of the month, about the first week in the month. I do not remember the year in which the Exposition was held, but believe it was opened in the Fall of 1901. I visited Mahala McNeil during her confinement and spent much time with her and in this way know a great deal of the circumstances surrounding the infancy of this child.

The name of the mid-wife is {Silbina} Deas (now dead) and before the parents named the child, the mid-wife reported its birth to the Health officer and gave her the name of "Emma McNeill," but as the child grew older, she was named "Beatrice" and continued to be known by that name. I positively declare that "Beatrice" is the only minor child of Frank McNeill and Mahala McNeill, and that "Emma McNeill" and "Beatrice McNeill" is one and the same child. I further declare that I gained the knowledge of these facts from personal intimate and long acquaintance with the family of Frank McNeill and Mahala, his wife. Further, I knew Mahala when she was the wife of George Williams and has never heard that George Williams ever served in the Army or Navy of the United States.[140]

---

[139] General Affidavit for Frank McNeill, in the matter of Frank McNeill alias Frank Gray (Charleston, Charleston, SC), dated 06 Feb 1896. Ibid. dated 25 Jun 1896
[140] Ibid., Eliza Finley, dated 06 Sep 1915.

Stephen MILLER
alias
Simon Poosa

Sergeant, Company K: Born c1847, at Walterboro, Colleton, SC; a Slave of John Poosa; Enlisted on 08 Mar 1865, at Beaufort, SC; Disability Discharge on 23 Sep 1865, at Hilton Head, Beaufort, SC. Married to Matilda Cobb, on 25 Dec 1869 or 1871, at Colleton County, SC, by Reverend July Maggett. Children: Laney (b. 01 Oct 1874; dead); Adam (b. 10 Sep 1876); Rosy (b. 02 Dec 1878); Stephen (04 Aug 1880; dead); Octavia (b. 29 Oct 1882; dead); Zilla (b. 03 Aug 1885); Misher (b. 03 Aug 1885); Esau (b. 04 Aug 1889); Isaac (b. 01 Mar 1889; dead); Goull (aka Guarantee) (b. 07 Aug 1891); Priestly (b. 09 Nov 1893), and; Cicero (b. 29 Jun 1897). **Stephen Miller** *died on 13 Feb 1907, at St. Stephen, Berkeley, SC.*[141]

Stephen Miller (Veteran Soldier)
Date: 02 Jan 1902
Residence: Georges Station, Dorchester, SC
Occupation: Farmer

I was born within 3½ miles of Ridgeville, S.C., about 64 years ago. My owner was John Poosa of that place. My father was Adam Wetzel; owned by John Wetzel. I was about 21 years of age when I enlisted at Charleston, S.C., in Company K, 128th U.S. Colored Volunteer Infantry. I enlisted in the spring and was discharged at Parris Island about the fall.

---

[141] Civil War Pension Record for Matilda Miller (widow of Stephen Miller alias Simon Poosa), WC No. 660.008, Pvt, Company K, 128th USCI, Records of the VA, RG 15, NARA, WDC; 1900 U.S. Federal Census, South Carolina, Dorchester County, Koger Township, ED: 73, Page: 168A, Line: 37 (Roll: T623-1526).

Stephen Miller alias Simon Poosa

The first 2 or 3 years after my discharge I lived in Ridgeville, S.C. Since then I have lived within 4 to 5 miles of where I now live.

After the war when I came up to Ridgeville where I now live I found my father had taken the name of Miller. He called himself Adam Miller. He told me that my name was Stephen Miller and I have gone under that name ever after.[142]

Matilda Miller (Widow of the Veteran Soldier)
Date: 15 Sep 1908
Residence: Grover, Dorchester, SC

I am the widow of Stephen Miller who served in the U.S. Army and who was a pensioner. I claim pension as a widow.

I was born and raised here and have lived here all of my life. My maiden name is Matilda Cobb. I was never married and never lived with a man and never had a child until I married Stephen Miller. Stephen and I were married right here (this place used to be called Murrays Cross Roads) by Reverend July Maggett. I do not know the date and there is no record of it, but it was about three years after freedom. We were never parted but lived together from marriage until he died on February 13th last year. He died on Wednesday before day.

My husband left 40 acres of land that cost him one hundred and twenty dollars, but it is not worth that for it is on the river and the water overflows nearly every year.

We had fourteen head of children, eight are living. The youngest one is Cicero. He is about 11 or 12. I don't know the year that he was born but I know it was on the 29th of June. The next youngest that is living is Guarantee. He is about 16 or 17. I don't know the year he was born but it was on August 4th.

Stephen Miller was born a few miles from Ridgeville, and was owned by Mr. Poosa. He came up here to live as soon as he got out of the army. I knew his father before freedom – he was owned by Mrs. Wetzel and later went to her daughter, Mrs. Johnson. His father was Adam Mil-

---

[142] Deposition of Simon Poosa, case of Simon Poosa (Waltersboro, Colleton, SC), dated 23 Apr 1901.

ler. Adam came up here from near Ridgeville before the war. I think his wife down here was owned by the Poosa's and that is the way Stephen came to be owned by them.[143]

Isaac Brown (Comrade of the Veteran Soldier)
Date: 15 Sep 1908
Residence: Grover, Dorchester, SC

My age is about 66. I was born and raised here and lived here all my life.

I have known Matilda ever since she was born. Her maiden name is Cobb. She was never married and never lived with a man until she married Stephen Miller. I lived right at them and know what I am saying. She was nothing but a child when she married Stephen. I was present at her father's house about two years after the war and saw Reverend July Maggett marry them, and I know that they lived together as man and wife from that time until Stephen died last February. I live in hearing distance of Matilda and know that she was not remarried nor lived with a man since Stephen died.

I knew Stephen's father, Adam Miller, before the war, and when I ran away towards the last of the war and went to Charleston, Stephen came there also and I met him. At that time he was then going by the name of Simon Poosa.

I tried to be a soldier but they would not take me but they took Stephen and sent him to Beaufort. I came home as soon as freedom come but I did not see Stephen again until after he got out of the army and came here. That was immediately after the war. He was not married when I met him at Charleston, and he did not have a wife when he came here, and he did not marry nor live with a woman until he married Matilda Cobb.

He and I lived on the same place before he married Matilda Cobb and we worked for Judge Carroll. Stephen left two young boys when he died. One is half crazy and always has been so. His name is Guarantee. The other is only a baby and his name was Cicero. I don't know when

---

[143] Deposition of Matilda Miller, case of Matilda Miller (Grover, Dorchester, SC), dated 15 Sep 1908.

they were born, but I think Cicero is about ten or eleven and Guarantee is about sixteen or seventeen.[144]

Witty Simmons (Friend of the Widow)
Date: 29 Jun 1901
Residence: Wando, Berkeley, SC
Occupation: Farmer

I am 77 years of age. I never knew Simon Poosa before he came out of the army but I knew his wife before the war. We belonged to the same owner, Dr. {I}.K. Farmer of Sumter, S.C., and he took all of his slaves down to Daniels Island 20 years before the war and Poosa's wife was among them. When she was brought down she had a baby in her arms and said that she was married to Simon Poosa, who belonged to Dr. John Harriet of Sumter, S.C.

She remained on Daniels Island, S.C., up to after freedom. She used to go about with other men a good deal, but she had no children from them and when Simon Poosa came down their first year after freedom, she went back to him and they lived together until his death – some 6 or 7 years after freedom. The first two years after freedom he was planting under me. I am sure he is dead. He died on his own land on St. Stephens about 7 miles from where I live. I was at his funeral and helped to bury him.[145]

---

[144] Ibid., Isaac Brown.
[145] Ibid., Witty Simmons, dated 29 Jun 1901.

Jonas MITCHELL
alias
June Mashaw

Private, Company D: Born c1840, in Georgetown, Georgetown SC; a Slave of the Izzard Family; Enlisted on 08 Mar 1865, at Georgetown, SC; Honorably Discharged on 10 Oct 1866, at Morris Island, Charleston, SC. 1st Marriage to Catherine Green (d. May 1895, at Charleston, Charleston, SC), during 1864/5, at Georgetown, SC, by Rev. Tony Izzard. Children: George (b. 1870); Mrs. Rebecca Washington (b. 1872); Jane (b. 1874); and Eloise (b. 1876; d. Sep 1914). 2nd Marriage to Anita Welton, during Oct 1901, Charleston, SC. **Jonas Mitchell** *died on 12 Apr 1925, at Charleston, Charleston, SC.*[146]

Jonas Mitchell (Veteran Soldier)
Date: 21 Jan 1890
Residence: #4 Motts Ln., Charleston, Charleston, SC
Occupation: Laborer

I am 60 years of age and I am the man who served in Company D, 128th U.S. Colored Infantry as June Mashaw. I was born and raised near Georgetown, S.C. and was owned by Mr. Izard. I enlisted into service at Georgetown in March 1865 at the same time with my brother Robert Izzard (now dead) and Aaron West and we were sent to Beaufort and mustered into the 128th.

Before the war I was called June and when I went in service I told them my name was June Mitchell but not being able to talk plain they did

---

[146] Civil War Pension Record for Jonas Mitchell alias June Mashaw, SC No. 997.291, Pvt, Company D, 128th USCI, Records of the VA, RG 15, NARA, WDC. [Note: Could not locate a listing for this family on the 1900 U.S. Federal Census Records].

Jonas Mitchell alias June Mashaw

not understand me and wrote it as June Mashaw as they thought I gave that name.

After the war I took my uncles name of Jonas but I am called both June and Jonas Mitchell. I was mustered out in October 1866 at Morris Island just in front of this city. After muster out I went back to Georgetown and about a month after I got there we heard of land to be sold near Charleston and several of us came here and settled. That was up where James Polite now lives. I lived there until last year and now I am here with my daughter.

I had the knee of my right leg mashed in the spring of 1890 by being thrown out of my ox cart and bouncing the cart wheel {here} over the leg. James Polite happened to be near and helped me up in the cart again and I went home and was laid up over a month with it and have suffered with it ever since.

I was in the Post Hospital here in Charleston in the summer of 1866 when I had small pox. After enlistment we did garrison duty in Beaufort and then came to Charleston where my company guarded the jail and then we went to Morris Island and mustered out.[147]

Aaron West (Comrade of the Veteran Soldier)
Date: 22 Jan 1890
Residence: #192 Wentworth St., Chas, Charleston, SC

I am 51 years of age. I served in Company B, 128th U.S. Colored Infantry. I was born and raised near Georgetown, S.C. and was owned by Mr. Izzard. I knew Jonas Mitchell before the war He was owned by the same man who owned me. He and I went in service at the same time. His brother, Robert Izzard, went with us. We all enlisted at Georgetown and were sent to Beaufort, S.C., and mustered in there. We were put in the same regiment but in different companies.

Jonas was put in Company A and took the name of Mashaw. He was only called June before the war. We all went by our masters name and

---

[147] Deposition of Jonas Mitchell, case of Jonas Mitchell (Charleston, Charleston, SC), dated 21 Jan 1890.

were only given first names. Jonas' father was called George Mitchell because his father had been owned by the Mitchells. After the war June took his father's name and has called himself Jonas Mitchell ever since.

Robert Izzard, who went with us, was Jonas' brother, and he went by the name of Mitchell after the war also. He died about two months ago.[148]

James Polite (Comrade of the Veteran Soldier)
Date: 26 Jan 1890
Residence: #91 Concord St., Charleston, Charleston, SC

I am 58 years of age. I met Jonas Mitchell in 1865 during the war. I served in Company C, 33rd U.S. Colored Troops. In 1865 I went to Beaufort, S.C., on furlough and there I met Jonas Mitchell. The 128th was camped there I went out to see them and was introduced to Jonas but he went by the name of June then. He was a member of the 128th U.S. Colored Troops and he was called June but I don't recall the last name.

I went to where Izzard lived as soon as mustered out and he came up there after he was mustered out; that same year, and we have lived as neighbor ever since and that he s staying in town at present.

He has always been a man of good habits. About two years ago I saw him fall out of his ox cart and the cart ran over his leg. I helped him up. His right knee was busted and he has suffered with it ever since.[149]

Annie Mitchell (Daughter of the Veteran Soldier)
Date: 26 Jan 1890
Residence: #4 Motts Ln., Charleston, Charleston, SC

I am 22 years of age. Jonas Mitchell is my father. I was at home about ten years ago when he came home with his leg hurt. He had fallen on his cart and the wheel had run over his right knee. He was laid up over a month with it and has suffered with it ever since.[150]

---

[148] Ibid., Aaron West, dated 22 Jan 1890.
[149] Ibid., James Polite, dated 26 Jan 1890.
[150] Ibid., Janie Mitchell.

The Great Earthquake of 1886

On September 01, 1886 (evening of August 31, 1886), the most damaging earthquake to occur in the Southeast United States and one of the largest historic shocks in Eastern North America rattled Charleston and the surrounding areas. It damaged or destroyed many buildings in the old city of Charleston and killed 60 people. Hardly a structure there was undamaged, and only a few escaped serious damage. Property damage was estimated at $5-$6 million. Structural damage was reported several hundred kilometers from Charleston (including central Alabama, central Ohio, eastern Kentucky, southern Virginia, and western West Virginia), and long-period effects were observed at distances exceeding 1,000 kilometers.

At Summerville, a small town of 2,000 population, 25 kilometers northwest of Charleston, many houses settled in an inclined position or were displaced as much as 5 centimeters. Chimneys constructed independently of the houses commonly had the part above the roofline thrown to the ground. Many chimneys were crushed at their bases, allowing the whole chimney to sink down through the floors. The absence of overturning in piered structures and the nature of the damage to chimneys have been interpreted as evidence that the predominant motion was vertical.

Source: Excerpted from - Abridged from Seismicity of the United States, 1568-1989 (Revised), by Carl W. Stover and Jerry L. Coffman, U.S. Geological Survey Professional Paper 1527, United States Government Printing Office, Washington: 1993; Richard N. Côté. City of Heroes: The Great Charleston Earthquake of 1886, Mount Pleasant, SC: Corinthian Books, 2006, p.542.

* * * * * * * * * * * * *

Humphrey MOULTRIE
alias
Holfus Mushree

Private, Company D: Born on 24 Feb 1844, at City Hill Plantation, near Wando, Charleston District, SC; a Slave of W. J. Ball; Enlisted on 08 Mar 1865, at Georgetown, Georgetown, SC; Honorably Discharged on 10 Oct 1866, at Morris Island, Charleston, SC. 1st Marriage to Rebecca Ingram or Gibbs (d. 1892), on 02 Jan 1868, at Longwood Plantation, SC, by Rev. Collins. Children: Peter (b. 08 Aug 1868); Levi (b. 15 Jul 1870); Humphrey (b. 10 Apr 1871); Susan (b. 10 Mar 1872); Anna Retta (b. 12 Sep 1875); Mrs. Rachel Kinloch (b. 10 Feb 1878); Sukey (b. 19 Feb 1880); Mamie (b. 09 Mar 1882); Rebecca (b. 08 Mar 1886); and Christina (b. 03 Apr 1890). 2nd Marriage to Hagar Jones, on 27 Dec 1894. **Humphrey Moultrie** *died on 05 May 1927, at Wando, Berkeley, SC.*[151]

Humphrey Moultrie (Veteran Soldier)
Date: 25 Nov 1905
Residence: Wando, Berkeley, SC

Claimant (62) declares that he is known now by the name of Humphrey Moultrie, which was the name of his father; that when he went in the army and served in Company D, 128th U.S. Colored Infantry, that he was known as Holfus Mushree, by which name he was generally called by men in service; that the name of Ohomfest Musaree as well as Helfus Mushree are really corruptions of the correct name Humphrey Moultrie,

---

[151] Civil War Pension Record for Jonas Mitchell alias June Mashaw, SC No. 997.291, Pvt, Company D, 128th USCI, Records of the VA, RG 15, NARA, WDC. [Note: Could not locate a listing for this family on the 1900 U.S. Federal Census Records].

Humphrey Moultrie alias Holfus Mushree

as there was a family living on St. Thomas Parish by the name of Humphrey and another by the name of Moultrie, which name his father went by which was Humphrey; that on entering the army he gave, as he thought, the said name but the enrolling officer misspelled it, and the comrades miscalled it; that since being out of the army he has been known by the name of Humphrey Moultrie, which name he now carries.[152]

Lazarus White (Comrade of the Veteran Soldier)
Date: 07 Feb 1905
Residence: #36 March St., Charleston, Charleston, SC

Affiant, Lazarus White, (68) declares that he is personally acquainted with Claimant, Humphrey Moultrie, and knew him in slavery times as they lived near each other and belonged to the Ball family; that Claimant enlisted in Company D, 128th U.S. Colored Volunteers while Affiant enlisted in Company G, 128th U.S. Colored Volunteers and is a pensioner under certificate #920.628 as Lazarus White; that he knew Claimant in the service as Holfus Mushree but that after leaving the service he has been known by the name of Humphrey Moultrie; that they have known each other before and since discharge and have been friends and neighbors; that they were together on St. Thomas Parish, Wando, Berkeley, S.C., and were fellow servants.[153]

---

[152] General Affidavit of Humphrey Moultrie, in the Pension Claim of Ohamfest Mushree (Wando, Berkeley, SC), dated 25 Nov 1895.
[153] General Affidavit of Lazarus White, in the Pension Claim of Humphrey Moultrie alias Holfus Mushree (Charleston County, SC), dated 07 Feb 1906.

Henry MUNGEN
alias
Henry H. Way

Private, Company A: Born on 09 Aug 1837, on the Way Plantation, Liberty County, GA; a Slave of Dr. Samuel Way / Henry H. Way; Enlisted on 27 Feb 1865, at Hilton Head, Beaufort, SC; Disability Discharged on 21 Sep 1865, at Hilton Head, SC. Married to Ella [MNU], on 01 Mar 1881, at Darien, McIntosh, GA, by Rev. Harris. Children: Sarah D. (b. c1885); Martha (b. c1887); Catherine (b. c1890); Naome (b. 1892); and Wyatt (b. c1894). **Henry Mungen** *died on 15 July 1915, at Poughkeepsie, Dutchess, NY.*[154]

Henry Mungen (Veteran Soldier)
Date: 22 Jan 1904
Residence: Darien, McIntosh, GA

I was born a slave on the plantation of Henry H. Way in Liberty County, Ga., and was a waiter or house boy until the last of 1863, and sometime during the first of 1864* General Sherman Army took me as a slave near Savannah, Ga., and I joined his army and was placed in Company A, 128th U.S. Colored Troops in 1864* and served until discharged in 1865.

I was called by my owner's name which was Henry H. Way. My father's name was Stephen Mungen, mother Sarah Latson, and after I was made free I took my father's name or Mungen and also my owner's first name of Henry and was soon known as Henry Mungen in place of

---

[154] Civil War Pension Record for Ella Mungen (widow of Henry H. Way now known as Henry Mungen), WC No. 800.858, Private, Company A, 128th USCI, Records of the VA, RG 15, NARA, WDC. *Note: Sherman Army passed through Savannah during 1865.

Henry Mungen alias Henry H. Way

Henry H. Way, my former owner's name. My height is 5 feet 10 inches; complexion dark; eyes dark and a scar on my right leg from a bullet wound.[155]

Willie J. Way (Acquaintance of Veteran Soldier)
Date: 22 Jun 1913
Residence: #1026 Stonewall St., Brunswick, Glynn, GA

I am called Willie Way and I was 68 years old in April of this year and I know that Henry H. Way, known as Henry Mungen, the pensioner in this case, is older than I am.

My recollection of his early history is this:

He had belonged to my uncle Henry Way and, to satisfy an indebtedness of Uncle Henry's to my father, Dr. Samuel Way, he, the pensioner, was with other slaves, turned over to my father, in this way he became my father's property when I was about eleven years old, as I remember, and that he continued to be my father's property and that he was employed on fathers place from that time until he became free. He we went off with the Federal Troops when Sherman passed through the state and I did not again see him until he made himself known to me in this city when I made an affidavit for him at his pension case a few years ago.

My father had over a hundred slaves and many of the others I didn't know. At the time this pensioner came to me here in Brunswick, I did not recognize him, but, after he told me who he was I remembered him.

To the best of my recollection, this Henry was about 19 years old at the time he came into my father's possession. I remember, also, that father in, in conversation with him me afterward concerning the {pensioner} in which he acquired Henry, he told me the date of Henry's birth, and I think he stated that he was born in 1837.[156]

---

[155] General Affidavit for Henry H. Way, in claim of No. 674.543 of Henry H. Way of Company A of 128 Regt. Of U.S.C.I. Vols (Darien, McIntosh, GA), dated 22 Jan 1904.

[156] Deposition of W. J. Way, case of Henry H. Way now known as Henry Mungen (Brunswick, Glynn, GA), dated 22 Jun 1913.

Samuel C. MURPHY
alias
Samuel Charles

Private, Company D: Born on 25 Dec 1845/9, at Walker Plantation, Charleston District (now Berkeley County), SC; Enlisted on 08 Mar 1865, at Beaufort, SC; Disability Discharge on 23 Sep 1865, at Hilton Head, Beaufort, SC. Married to Margaret Haynes (b. c1853), during Oct 1870, at St. Stephen, Charleston, SC, by Magistrate S.D. Russell. Children: Mary (b. 1875); Rebecca (b. 1878); Flora (b. 1880); Agnes (b. 1882); Rachel (b. 1884) and Steven (b. 1886). **Samuel Murphy** *died on 14 May 1914, at St. Stephen, Berkeley, SC.*[157]

Samuel Murphy (Veteran Soldier)
    Date: 02 Jan 1902
    Residence: St. Stephen, Berkeley, SC
    Occupation: Farmer

I served in Company D, 128th Regiment U.S. Colored Infantry, under the name of Samuel Charles. My father belonged to Theodore Freeman and before the war he was called Robert Freemen, but his right name was Robert Murphy and that is where I got the name of Samuel Murphy.

I am generally known as Samuel Murphy, but my full name is Samuel Charles Murphy. I gave them the name of Samuel Charles and not my right name and I was known by that name in the army. I was between 18 and 19 when I enlisted. I was born in St. Stephen Parish, S.C., about

---

[157] Civil War Pension Record Margaret Murphy (widow of Samuel Murphy alias Samuel Charles), WC No. 770.061, Pvt, Company D, 128th USCI, Records of the VA, RG 15, NARA, WDC.

Samuel C. Murphy alias Samuel Charles

four miles from this place. I came back here after I was discharged from the army and have lived here ever since.

Brutus Butler, Ephraim Bragg and John Snipe were in my regiment. Bragg was a corporal in my company. Julius Tingman, who lives about five miles this side of Bonneau, was also in my regiment. {Hilton} {Bordech} now lives in Georgia. I think he was in my Company.[158]

F.N. Shipman & J. Milligan (Comrades of the Veteran Soldier)
Date: 12 Mar 1900
Residence: St. Stephens, Berkeley, SC

F.N. Shipman (50) and John Milligan (47) make oath that they are personally known by the Claimant, Samuel Charles, and have been acquainted with him for thirty years, and have resided in the same parish with him and have seen him two or three times each week, and saw him when he was laid up with a broken leg, which happened to him while working as a laborer on the railroad. He was laid up for five to six months. He is now not able to do any hard or laborious work, and is in very destitute circumstances having no property nor any income from any source. We were present when he got his leg broken by a piece of lumber (12 x 12) fell on it and we helped to get him up.

We have known the Claimant for thirty years and he is a sober and peaceable person and of good behavior and not addicted to any vicious habits.[159]

---

[158] Deposition of Samuel Murphy alias Samuel Charles, Case of Samuel Murphy alias Samuel Charles (St. Stephen, Berkeley, SC), dated 02 Jan 1902.

[159] General Affidavit of F.N. Schipman and John Milligan, in the matter of Samuel Charles (St. Stephen, Berkeley, SC), dated 12 Mar 1900.

Simon MYERS
alias
Samuel or Simon Miles

Private, Company A: Born during 1842, at Robertsville, Beaufort, SC; a Slave of William J. Lawton; Enlisted on 02 Mar 1865, at Beaufort, SC; Disability Discharged on 21 Sep 1865, at Hilton Head, Beaufort, SC. 1st Marriage to Hager Lawton (d. 1900, Duck Bush, Hampton, SC), on 15 Oct 1864, in Barnwell County, SC, by Rev. Daniel Frost. Children: Tamah (b. 20 Jul 1865); Edie (b. 20 Jul 1867); Ben (b. 01 Jun 1870); Margaret (b. 01 Dec 1872); Patsy (b. 01 Jan 1874); Rebecca (b. 01 Apr 1876); Caroline (b. 03 Aug 1878); Rena (b. 10 Aug 1882); and, Alice (b. 15 Feb 1892). 2nd Marriage to Molsie Hampton, during 1906, in Beaufort County, SC, by Rev. J. Myers. **Simon Myers** *died after 04 Aug 1891, in Hampton County, SC.*[160]

Simon Myers (Veteran Soldier)
 Date: 04 Aug 1891
 Residence: Brunson, Hampton, SC
 Occupation: Farmer

I am 57 years old. I have not lived over 7 miles from my present place of residence at any time since my discharge from the army. I was a member of Company A, 128th U.S. Colored Infantry. I enlisted in March; I think, in 1865. It was the year before the slaves were actually free. The slaves were free in January and I enlisted in March of the same year. I was mustered out the same year I enlisted during October. I could not do anything

---

[160] Civil War Pension Record for Samuel Myers now known as Simon Miles, SC No. 657.874, Private, Company A, 128th USCI, Records of the VA, RG 15, NARA, WDC; 1880 U.S. Federal Census, South Carolina, Hampton County, Peeples Township, ED: 120, Page: 131A, Line: 31 (Roll: T9-1231).

Simon Myers alias Samuel or Simon Miles

on account of my rheumatism and heart disease and was mustered out on that account.

I enlisted for 3 years on Beaufort Island, S.C., and was discharged at Hilton Head, S.C. I enlisted under the name of Simon Miles and my father's name was Ben Miles. William J. Lawton was my master's name. When I enlisted I did so by my father's name and have never changed that name since and have always called myself that and if they at anytime called me Myers or got my name in the papers as Myers it has been without my knowledge or consent.

I claim a pension for heart disease and rheumatism contracted in the U.S. services. All the time I was in service we lay on and around Beaufort Island, S.C. First, I took a cold by laying on the wet ground and from rain, and then soon felt the rheumatism in my left knee and it worked up my leg to my hip. I never had any sever sickness before I enlisted. I never had any chill and fever, but I had some spells of light fever before I enlisted but never doctored for it. These fevers were a couple of years apart generally, and I generally took it from eating green fruits or watermelons, but I never had rheumatism or heart disease before I enlisted.

I can prove by the following named men who knew me before service, were with me in service and who have known me ever since service that I was a sound man at enlistment and that I got rheumatism and heart disease in service and that I have been afflicted with these diseases ever since my discharge. They are Henry Johnson; Seabron Blake; Loby Price; Daniel Samuel and Stephen Snyder.[161]

---

[161] Deposition of Simon Myers alias Miles, cases of Simon Myers alias Miles (Clutes House, Hampton, SC), dated 04 Aug 1891.

Cain NESBIT
alias
Cain Piatt

Private, Company B: Born during 1845, in Georgetown County, SC; a Slave of John Piatt; Enlisted on 27 Mar 1865, at Hilton Head, Beaufort, SC; Honorary Discharge on 10 Oct 1866, Morris Island, Charleston, SC. 1st Marriage to Mary [MNU] (d. c1869/70, Georgetown County, SC). Children: Maria; 2nd Marriage to Lydia Jaunt. Children: Rose (b. c1898). **Cain Nesbit** *died on 24 Apr 1915, at Edisto Island, Charleston, SC.*[162]

Cain Nesbit (Veteran Soldier)
    Date: 01 May 1908
    Residence: Charleston, Charleston, SC
    Occupation: Unknown

I am now known as Cain Nesbit but I am the man who served in Company B, 128th U.S. Colored Infantry Regiment as Cain Piatt. I was born and raised at Georgetown, S.C., and was owned by Mr. John Piatt.* My father was Caesar Nesbit and he was also owned by Mr. Piatt. I was just about grown when the Yankees took me out of our place at Georgetown and carried me off. The soldiers took me at Georgetown and brought me to Charleston on a steamer and then took me to Hilton Head, S.C., on a steamer. There we got with the other soldiers, and then we were taken to Beaufort, S.C., and made up into companies.

---

[162] Civil War Pension Record for Lydia Nesbit, gdn (widow of Cain Nesbit alias Cain Piatt or Pyatt), WC No. 938.695, Pvt, Company B, 128th USCI, Records of the VA, RG 15, NARA, WDC: 1910 U.S. Federal Census, South Carolina, Charleston County, Edisto Island, ED: 69, Page: 220B, Line: 91 (Roll: T624-1453). *Note: A contradiction exists between this statement and data provided in the serviceman's record. His military service name was Kane Nesbit.

Cain Nesbit alias Cain Piatt

When I enlisted I told them my name was Nesbit and that I was owned by Mr. Piatt. I went by the name of Cain Nesbit before and ever since the war. Several other men around here knew me in service and who were in my regiment; they are Stephen Vermin, Ben Huger, Clarence Palmer, Hercules Wins, Jonas Mitchell, Lazarus White, Joseph Johnson, Daniel Frazier and Brass Ward. Brass Ward was in my company and he and I ran on a boat together after the war.

I have a sister, Harriet, in this city who belonged to my owner. She knew I went off with the soldiers and she came to Beaufort while I was in service and washed my clothes. When I mustered out I went back to Georgetown and was there five or six years and then came back here and was in this city until I moved across the river to Edisto Island.

My first wife was Mary. I married her during slavery and went back to her when I got out of the army and was with her until she died in Georgetown about four or five years after the war. I did not marry after Mary died until I married Lydia Jaunt about ten years ago. I have only two children living – Maria and Rose. Maria is grown and married and Rose, the daughter of Lydia, is about ten years old.[163]

Stephen Ward (Comrade of the Veteran Soldier)
    Date: 09 May 1908
    Residence: #17 Queen St., Georgetown, Georgetown, SC
    Occupation: Laborer

My age is 62. I served in Company B, 128th U.S. Colored Infantry Regiment. I was born and raised in Georgetown County, S.C., and was there until I enlisted. I have lived here ever since muster out. I knew a man in service by the name of Cain Nesbit but did not know him before. He was in the 128th, but I don't recall the company. He lived in Charleston for many years and at one time he ran on the Planter. I know positively that he is the Cain Nesbit who served in the 128th Regiment.[164]

---

[163] Deposition of Cain Nesbit, case of Cain Nesbit (Charleston, Charleston, SC), dated 01 May 1908.
[164] Ibid., Stephen Ward alias Verrin, dated 09 May 1908.

****

Richard NOVILLE
alias
Richard Boyd

Private, Company C: Born during 1849, at Boyd's Neck, Beaufort (now Jasper County), SC; a Slave of Benjamin Boyd; Enlisted on 08 Mar 1865, at Beaufort, Beaufort, SC. Disability Discharged on 23 Sep 1865, at Hilton Head, Beaufort, SC. 1st Marriage to Laura Nelson (d. Jul 1912, Ridgeland, Jasper, SC), on 14 Oct 1869, at Grahamville, Beaufort, SC, by W.S. Lance. Children: Charlotte (b. 29 May 1874; d. 1904); James (b. 01 Jan 1877); Dillard. 30 Oct 1886); Grace (b. 05 Jan 1889; d. 1907); and Alexander (b. 20 Aug 1893). 2nd Marriage to Elizabeth Norton, on 27 Feb 1913, at Coosawatchie, Jasper, SC. **Richard Noville** *died on 06 May 1916, at Coosawatchie, Jasper, SC.*[165]

Richard Noville (Veteran Soldier)
Date: 16 Apr 1901
Residence: Grahamville, Jasper, SC
Occupation: Carpenter

I am 52 years of age. I was born of slave parents near Grahamville, S.C., in 1849. My father's name was Isaac Noville and my mother's name was Phoebe Noville – both slaves of Benjamin Boyd, a planter living in Grahamville, S.C. I was born a slave of Benjamin Boyd. I don't know how my parents got the name of Noville, but I took my name from my master when I enlisted in the army, but was called Noville before I enlisted.

---

[165] Civil War Pension Record for Richard Noville alias Richard Boyd, SC No. 746.382, Private, Company C, 128th USCI, Records of the VA, RG 15, NARA, WDC; 1900 U.S. Federal Census, South Carolina, Beaufort County, Coosawatchie, ED: 7, Page: 141A, Line: 1 (Roll: T623-1518).

Richard Noville alias Richard Boyd

My correct name is Richard Noville and that is the name I am known by when I sign any papers, but I am called Richard Boyd by the people here and about. I enlisted at Beaufort, S.C., in 1865 and was 16 years old. I was a private of Company B, 128th U.S. Colored Volunteer Infantry and have never been in any other military or naval service of the United States and not in the Confederate Service. I was never away from my company on detached duty.

I have lived where I do now ever since my discharge from the army. I sent my discharge to a white man by the name of Waterhouse in Beaufort, S.C., 25 years ago and have not seen it since. My tent mates were William and Moses Boyd. Moses Boyd is in Florida somewhere. I was never in any battles or engagements and was not injured in the army. I was discharged because I was too young for the service.

I first got a pension of $70.00 all at once. I don't know what year. I now get $6.00 per month for a {Userv} in the left side and hip and a head ache all of the time. My witnesses were Benjamin Baker and Renty Jenkins, both living near Grahamville. They know me and know that I complained of my side and was unable to work. I did not pay them anything and I did not testify for them. I was examined one year ago in Beaufort by the Board of Surgeons. I have no other pension claim pending. Mr. Wright of Washington, D.C., was my attorney. I did not pay him anything and do not know whether he got anything or not.

I have been married but once. I married Laura Nelson (maiden name) in Grahamville, S.C., in 1867. We were married by a Trial Justice; a white man. We had a marriage certificate but it has "worn out." My wife lives with me now and has always lived with me. I have three children under 16 years of age. The oldest one is Paul. I don't know what year he was born in but he is 15 years old; Grace is 12 years old; and Alexander is about 7 years old.[166]

---

[166] Deposition of Benjamin Huger alias Weston, case of Benjamin Huger alias Benjamin Weston (Charleston, Charleston, SC), dated 16 Apr 1901.

Ellis OWENS
alias
Ellis King

Private, Company G: Born on 15 Dec 1842, near White Oaks, Camden, GA; a Slave of Stephen Clay King; Enlisted on 22 Mar 1865, at Beaufort, Beaufort, SC; Honorably Discharged on 10 Oct 1866, at Morris Island, Charleston, SC. Married Priscilla Williams (d. 27 Jun 1930, Philadelphia, PA), c1867, by Thomas Harrison, J.D. Children: Minnie (b. 20 Dec 1872); Amos (b. 25 May 1872); William (b. 19 Jul 1878); James (b. 16 Oct 1880); Henry (b. 15 Feb 1882); Mrs. Luella Seymour (b. Dec 1882); and Rosa (b. 07 Apr 1884). **Ellis Owens** *died on 30 Sep 1939, at Philadelphia, PA.*[167]

Ellis Owens (Veteran Soldier)
Date: 04 Feb 1903
Residence: Camden County, GA

Ellis Owens declares that prior to the abolition of slavery, he belonged to Mr. Stephen Clay King of Camden County, Ga; that when he enlisted in Company G, 128th U.S. Colored Troops, in accordance with general custom, then prevailing in the south, he assumed his master's name and enlisted under the name of Ellis King; that his father's name was Ned Owens; that after the war, when he was mustered out and free; he resumed his father's name, and called himself Ellis Owens and has since been known under that name; that he is the same person who enlisted as

---

[167] Civil War Pension Record for Ellis Owens alias Ellis King, SC No. C-2.498.565, Pvt, Company G, 128th USCI, Records of the VA, RG 15, NARA, WDC; 1900 U.S. Federal Census, Georgia, Camden County, Taraboro, ED: 13, Page: 179A, Line: 14 (Roll: T623-183).

aforesaid, in Company G, 128th U.S. Colored Troops, under the name of Ellis King, under the circumstances above stated.[168]

John & Anthony Green (Acquaintances of the Veteran Soldier)
Date: 14 Aug 1907
Residence: Camden County, GA

John A. Green (55) and Anthony Green (64) declare that they are well acquainted with Ellis Owens, alias King, and that they have known him from early boyhood, all having belonged to the same master before the abolition of slavery; that they and Ellis Owens enlisted together and at the same time in Company G, 128th U.S. Colored Troops and served together during the Civil War; that Ellis Owens is the same man who enlisted and served with them under the name of "Ellis King" in "Company G"; that they belonged to Mr. Stephen Clay King and that following a not uncommon custom in those days, they understood that Ellis Owens assumed his masters name; that after the soldier, as Ellis King, was discharged and returned to Camden County, Georgia, he resumed his own name of Ellis Owens, and has since been known by that name.[169]

Ellis Owens (Veteran Soldier)
Date: 14 Aug 1907
Residence: Camden County, GA

Ellis Owens declares that he was born on the 15th day of Dec. A.D. 1842. He says that according to the traditions of his father, Ned Owens, now deceased, that no record of the births of colored people were commonly kept in this section of the country – neither baptismal records nor public records, that his birth was on December 15th 1842, as stated above, is the true and correct to the best of his knowledge and belief.[170]

---

[168] General Affidavit of Ellis Owens, in the matter of Pension Claim # 1.075.028 of Ellis Owens alias Ellis King (Camden County, GA), dated 04 Feb 1903.

[169] Ibid. John A. Green and Anthony Green.

[170] Sworn Statement by Ellis Owens (Camden County, GA), dated 14 Aug 1907.

****

Carolina PEGLER
alias
Carolina Sumter

Private, Company H: Born c1833, St. Stephens, Charleston, SC; a Slave of David or Daniel Preagler; Enlisted on 07 Mar 1865, at Charleston, Charleston, SC. Died on Active Duty from Small Pox. 1st Marriage to Emma Small (b. St. Stephens, Charleston, SC; d. 12 May 1865, St. Stephens, SC), on 20 Aug 1852. Children: Simon (b. 20 Sep 1853); Samuel (b. 26 Aug 1855); Mrs. Emma Johnson (b. 15 Aug 1859); Mrs. Tisby Jones (b. 17 Jul 1861); Mary (Twin) (b 08 May 1863; d. 06 Jun 1866) and Martha (Twin) (b. 08 May 1863; d. 10 Aug 1866). 2nd Marriage to Louisa Houston. **Carolina Pegler** *died on 26 Mar 1866, at Sullivans Island, Charleston, SC.*[171]

Simon Preagler (Son of the Veteran Soldier)
Date: 26 Sep 1889
Residence: Walker Swamp, Berkeley, SC

I am about 35 years of age. I live on my own place. I married Mary Davis on December 9, 1889. I have seven children; "Phobe" is 18, "Rosalie" is 15, "Frank" (dead) would be 10 or 11, "Harriet" is about 7, "Scipio" aged 8 years, "Jane" aged 2 years, and a baby girl who died 2 years back while a baby. I have one brother, "Samuel," and two sisters, "Emma," now know as Emma Johnson, wife of Henry Johnson, and "Tisby," now known as Tisby Jones. I know my brother Samuel is about 27, "Emma," is about 22, and "Tishby," is about 19 or 20.

---

[171] Civil War Pension Record for Simon Pregler, et al (minors of Carolina Pregler alias Carolina Sumter), Minor's Certificate No. 260.767, Company H, 128th USCI; Records of the VA, RG 15, NARA, WDC. Note: The surnames of Pegler, Pragler, Pregler and Preagler are mentioned interchangeably throughout this pension record.

Carolina Pegler alias Carolina Sumter

I claim pension as one of the children of Carolina Sumter or Pragler and his wife, my mother, "Emma." She was known as "Emma Small" and she belonged to James Pragler who lives at Pleasant Hall in Berkeley County, S.C. – about 3½ miles from St. Stephen. My brother, Samuel, and my sisters, Emma and Tisby" and myself belonged to James Pragler, and my father belonged to Daniel Pragler, a brother of James Pragler.

Us children lived with our mother. My father did not lived on the James Pragler place – he only visited her on Saturday nights and stayed with her until on Mondays when he would return to his master's place known as the {Hopten} place.

Julius Smith, a colored preacher who belonged to Mr. Press Smith, married my father and mother on the Preagler place - with the consent of both masters. My mother had her own house when she lived in the slave quarters when my father visited her and where I myself and brother and 2 sisters were born.

My father was known as Carolina Sumter, but he was also called by his master's name, of Preagler. In the early part of 1865, General Potter, a Federal officer, made a raid through this country and he carried a great deal of the slaves into Charleston and he took my father and mother and we 6 children with him. After we got to Charleston, I think about one week, my father went in the Federal Army.[172]

Mrs. Emma Johnson (Daughter of the Veteran Soldier)
Date: 26 Sep 1889
Residence: Walker Swamp, Berkeley, SC

My name is Emma Johnson. I am the wife of John Henry Johnson. I live in a rented place. I have had 8 children, the four living ones are "Elizabeth," aged about 14, "Susan," about 12, "John," about 7 and "Roxanna," about 2 years of age.

My husband died one year ago this month. I am supporting myself and children with their assistance. My husband left no property. I am the oldest daughter of my father, Carolina Sumter Pragler, who was owned by David Preagler, and my mother, Emma, who was owned by James Preagler. I have one sister living now "Tisby" Jones and two brothers, Simon and Samuel Pregler. We were all raised on the James Preagler

---

[172] Deposition of Simon Sumter Pragler, case of Simon Sumter Pragler & Others, request for Accrued Pension Benefits (St. Stephen, Berkeley, SC), dated 26 Sep 1889.

place near here. My mother's name before she married my father was Small. She was a brown woman. My father was a black man. We all have our father's complexion except "Simon" who resembles our mother in complexion.

I was small when my father went in the army. During the "Genl. Potter Raid", our family went with other slaves with General Potter to Charleston, S.C. and my father left us at the 6 mile house and he went on to the city with some other men. We stayed at the 6 mile house for a short while. I can't state exactly how long. There my mother took us all to Charleston and we lived on Middle Street.

My mother took sick with the small-pox and died, and we children were taken by our grandmother Small and put in the orphan house where we stayed about a year when Mr. {Hereford'}, a white man, took us in his wagon and brought us to the old plantation of Mr. James Peagler.

In a year of so Laura Butler [formerly Laura Peagler], who told us she had married our father while he was a soldier at Beaufort, came to us, said she was with our father when he died and he told her to come up to Berkeley County and take care of us. She lived with us for a couple of years then she married Brutus Butler. She died a few years ago. I can't give the year, the date or the month. Maybe her husband, Brutus Butler, can fix the date.

My step mother Laura Peagler-Butler came here to us from Charleston with Uncle Peter Vergen. Hammond Brown, a colored man, came in the wagon with us and Mr. Peter {Hereford}.[173]

Hilton Shipman (Comrade of the Veteran Soldier)
Date: 28 Sep 1889
Residence: St. Stephens, Berkeley, SC

I am about 40 years of age, and married with a family. I live in the same place with my brother, Ephraim Bragg. I took my master's name when I went in the army and Ephraim took the name of General Bragg, a big general in the Rebel Army. As a slave, I belonged to Harman Shipman, and was a neighbor to and well knew the man Carolina Sumter, who was in the army in Company H, 128th U.S. Colored Troops as Carolina Pregler. I enlisted in Company D in March 1865* and was mustered out in

---

[173] Ibid., Emma Johnson, dated 28 Sep 1889.

Carolina Pegler alias Carolina Sumter

December on Morris Island, S.C. I was not in Charleston when Carolina Sumter died, but I heard all about his death from comrades. I was guarding the jail with Capt. [Frederick] Field of my company at the time of his death.

Peter Vergen told he was going back home, and Louisa was going to go with him and take care of Carolina Sumter's children {in whe late we of} Carolina Sumter and how his wife, Louisa, had gone to Sulliivans Island having received a letter from him that when she got to the regiment Surgeon [Henry K.] Durrant had a talk with her and told her that Carolina Sumter, just before his death, asked him to say to Louisa, his wife, to go to St. Stephen and take of the children and it has amount to what he asked for, that {shed} {was} going with Peter Vergen.

I know Louisa to be his {new} wife for in company with all the soldiers in our regiment {who} came from St. Stephens. I was present with them when he was married to her by Chaplain Noble under the flag at Beaufort the same year we join the army. I knew his first wife, Emma, who was a {small} before he married her and knew that they lived together on the {Jurus} Pregler place as man and wife for I visited them a good many times on Sunday and I went to St. Stephens Church that was built by {weditsh} King. Our owner belonged to that church, they were Protestants. He had to sit in the slave gallery.

Carolina had 5 or 6 children by Emma. Only four of them are now living – Simon, Samuel, Emma and Tisby. I can't tell you their ages. Emma, the first wife, died of small pox soon after we had all gone to Charleston with General Potter. I know of her death for my wife told me of it when she came to {wed} at Beaufort. Carolina had no other wife that I ever heard of or any children by any other woman but Emma.

I can remember him well. The oldest son, Simon, resembles the mother, Emma, in color, but is the same height as the father. The other children have their color from Carolina.[174]

---

[174] Ibid., Hilton Shipman.

Canning PINCKNEY
alias
Canning Finnick

Private, Company E: Born c1845, at Johnsonboro (**or Jacksonboro, Colleton SC**), *SC; Enlisted on 03 Mar 1865, at Charleston, Charleston, SC; Honorably Discharged on 10 Oct 1866, at Morris Island, Charleston, SC. Married to Rosanna McPherson, on 15 Jan 1869, at Mt. Pleasant, Charleston, SC, by Rev. John Graham. Children: Johnson (b. 20 Oct 1874); Edward (b. 21 Mar 1878); Mary (b. 06 Mar 1884); Richard (b. 19 Aug 1886); Sara Ann (b. 11 Mar 1888); and Teana (b. 11 Jan 1892).* **Canning Pinckney** *died on 27 Dec 1893, Stono, Charleston, SC.*[175]

Rosanna F. Ford (Former Spouse & Guardian of Minors)
Date: 21 Jan 1902
Residence: Johns Island, Charleston, SC

I am about 50 years of age. I am the wife of George Ford, a farmer. I am a claimant for pension as the guardian of the minor children of Canning Finick, my former husband. Canning Finick was the name under which he enlisted, but his correct name was Canning Pinckney, and our children go by the name of Pinckney.

I am the mother of the children for whom I claim pension, but I do not know their exact age. I did have such a record in my bible, but the bible was destroyed in the big storm of 1893 (see Page 38).

Isaiah Pinckney was three years of age the 11th of April following my husband's death and he died on the 27th of December 1893 the same

---

[175] Civil War Pension Record for Sarah A., guardian of minor children of Canning Pinckney alias Canning Finnick, MC No. 528.996, Private, Company E, 128th USCI, Records of the VA, RG 15, NARA, WDC; 1900 U.S. Federal Census, South Carolina, Charleston County, Johns Island Parish, ED: 123, Page: 99B, Line: 55 (Roll: T623-1521).

Canning Pinckney alias Canning Finnick

year of the big storm. Sarah was born on the 11th of March, just a few months before the earthquake (see Page 136) and I remember that she was only a small baby at the time of the earthquake. Richard was born on the 8th of August and was just about four years of age at the time of the earthquake. I had one child by the name of Henry and who was between the ages of Sarah and Richard but he died before my husband did. Mary was born on the 16th of August about two years before Richard was born. Richard, Sarah and Isaiah are now living with me. They are the only children that I had under 16 years of age when I asked for pension for them.

I had no physician when any of my children were born. The nurse who was with me when Sarah was born is dead. Della Brown was with me when Isaiah was born, but not when any of the others above named were born. My mother was with me when Richard was born, and she is dead. Sarah is the only one of the above named whom I have ever had christened.[176]

Rosanna further stated that: the late soldier, Canning Finick, died on December 27th 1893 at Johns Island. There is no public record of his death neither can I furnish affidavit of any physician because Dr. Beckett is dead also. I was married to the soldier on August 15, 1869 on Johns Island, by Rev. John Graham. He died several years ago. There are very few people alive who knew when I married the soldier or knew when the soldier died. My husband, the said soldier, was born and raised at Johnsonboro, S.C. I met him when I was quite a girl on Johns Island after he mustered out of the army and I am certain he has never married before though he was quite a man.

My last husband, George Ford, died on Johns Island, S.C., on June 20th 1906. I was married to him on December 31st 1894.[177]

---

[176] Deposition of Rosanna F. Ford, case of Rosanna F. Ford (gdn) (Stono, Charleston, SC), date 21 Jan 1902.

[177] General Affidavit of Rosanna Ford (Johns Island, Charleston, SC), dated [unintelligible].

Lymas POWELL
alias
Lymas Pease

Private, Company G: Born c1837, at Darien, McIntosh, GA; a Slave of James True; Enlisted on 22 Mar 1865, at Beaufort, Beaufort, SC; Honorably Discharged on 10 Oct 1866, at Morris Island, Charleston, SC. 1st Marriage to Charlotte [MNU] (d. 12 Jan 1868). 2nd Marriage to Phyllis [MNU] (d. Apr 1882), Children : James (b. Oct 1870); Eliza (b. Nov 1872); Isaiah (b. Nov 1875); Flora (b. 26 Dec 1880); and Lymas II (b. 1882). 3rd Marriage to Julia Dennis, on 18 Aug 1892, at Baker Plantation, near Burton, Beaufort, SC, by Rev. Jolly Middleton. Children: Wellington (b. 27 Aug 1892); and Elizabeth (b. 12 May 1896). **Lymas Powell** *died on 08 Dec 1911, Burton (Rose Hill), Beaufort, SC.*[178]

Lymas Powell (Veteran Soldier)
  Date: 20 Jul 1903
  Residence: Burton, Beaufort, SC
  Occupation: Farmer

I am 85 years of age.* My full and correct name is Lymas Powell. My father's name was Hector Powell and my mother's name was Jannie Powell. My owner was James True. I was born about six miles from Darien, McIntosh County, Ga., and resided there until March 1865 when Benjamin March, Major Margood, {Jeremiah} {Wenger} and myself

---

[178] Civil War Pension Record for Lymas Powell alias Lymas Pease, SC No. C-2.505.316, Pvt, Company G, 128th USCI, Records of the VA, RG 15, NARA, WDC; 1900 U.S. Federal Census, South Carolina, Beaufort County, Beaufort, ED: 1, Page: 53, Line: 53 (Roll: T623-1518). * Note: His age, in this instance, is exaggerated. According to other documentation, he was born about 1837.

Lymas Powell alias Lymas Pease

took a catboat and came here to Beaufort, S.C., where the soldiers were. We stopped first at Hilton Head Island, where we enlisted in the 128th U.S. Colored Infantry. We were stripped and examined at Hilton Head and again right here in Beaufort. We were given uniforms and gears here in Beaufort, and enlisted in Company G; all four of us.

I enlisted under the name of Lymas Pease, because I was generally known, before the war, as Lymas Pease. I was given the name Pease simply because I was fond of "peas," a vegetable, and all the plantation people called me "Peas." It was a nickname but it stuck to me and I was generally known as "Pease."

We were in camp here in Beaufort about nine months and then went to Charleston, S.C., and the different companies were scattered about the Charleston vicinity. Company G was on Folly Island most of the time. The regiment was mustered out on Morris Island and I was mustered out with it in November 1866. I received $16.00 per month. We were never in any battle.

[Charles H.] Howard was colonel. [William M.] Beebe was lieutenant colonel. [William H.] Danielson was major. Dexter Howard was captain, but he was not with us when we mustered out. Lieutenant [Lester] Hall was in command. Joe Pino was our [first]/ordnance sergeant. Jackson Ford was corporal. March, Margood, and {Wagoner} and I tented together. William Davis and John Monday served in my regiment. Jackson Ford is the only member of my company I can think of who reside near Beaufort or in this county.

I received $100 bounty in May 1866 and another hundred at muster out. I was married to my present wife, Julia, on August 18, 1892, by Rev. Jolly Middleton. I had two former wives; Charlotte and Phyllis, both of whom were dead at the time of my marriage to Julia.[179]

---

[179] Deposition of Lymas Powell, case of Lymas Powell alias Lymas Pease (Beaufort, Beaufort, SC), dated 20 Jul 1903.

Henry REED
alias
Henry Reeves

Corporal, Company G: Born c1844, at Savannah, Chatham, GA; a Slave of Stephen Elliott; Enlisted on 08 Mar 1865, at Savannah, GA; Honorably Discharged on 10 Oct 1866, at Morris Island, Charleston, SC. Married to Harriett Barnett (b. c1846), on 16 Oct 1871, at John Hill Plantation, Beaufort, SC, by Reverend Murchison. Children: Jestine (b. Sep 1879); and Clara (b. Feb 1881). **Henry Reed** *died on 06 Jul 1892, at Levy, Beaufort, SC.*[180]

Harriet Reed (Widow)
Date: 27 May 1901
Residence: Taylor's Plantation, near Levy, Beaufort, SC

I am about 70 years of age. I am the widow of Henry Reed who was a soldier and is now dead. He went by Henry Reeves when he was getting up his pension, but his right name was Reed.

I was born in Beaufort County, S.C., and was the slave of Stephen Elliott. I was first married to Charles Robinson right after the war by a white doctor that came from the North named Zacharias. Charlie and I lived together for about three years. I had two children by him but both died. He went away to work and that is the last I saw of him. I have never seen anybody that saw him or heard from him since he went away. I

---

[180] Civil War Pension Record for Harriett Reeves (widow of Henry Reed alias Henry Reeves), WC No. 390.541, Corporal, Company G, 128th USCI, Records of the VA, RG 15, NARA, WDC; 1880 U.S. Federal Census, South Carolina, Beaufort County, Yemassee Township, ED: 51, Page: 315A, Line: 26 (Roll: T9-1454).

waited five or six years for Charlie to come back and I never did hear from him and then I and Henry were married.

Henry told me he had had a wife "up the country" but she was dead. I do not know exactly what he meant by "up the country" but I know it means "away off." When Charlie and I were married we had "a little time." My friends and his friends were all there and we had some shouting. They are pretty much all died out now and I can't tell where anyone lives who saw Charlie and me married.

My husband Henry Reed was a light colored man and somewhat taller than the average man. Mike Bush, who lives up in the "Pine Lands" now, but who did live here then, was one of my original witnesses. Mike was on the place and help bury my husband. Pleasant Johnson was another of my original witnesses. He knew the same as Mike did. I had no witnesses who knew me when I lived with Charlie Robinson. My husband died of consumption. He was sound and in good health when I married him.

I think I got $130 the first draw. I do not know my attorney in Washington, but Renty Reeves was my attorney in Beaufort. I execute my vouchers before Mr. A.R. Greene; Postmaster at Levy. I only take the voucher. I keep my certificate here all the time. You see, I am old and crippled up and don't write and she keeps the paper and sends me my money. I never go to Levy. I have not been to Levy for about four years. I saw Mrs. Greene once on my way to church. She sends me my full $24 and charges me nothing for my papers. She sends me $24 each time and I send her back $1.00.[181]

C. R. Greene (Acquaintance of the Widow)
      Date: 28 May 1901
      Residence: Levy, Beaufort, SC
      Occupation: Postmaster

I am about 40 years of age. I am the Postmaster at Levy, S.C., and the wife of A. R. Greene. I execute a few pension vouchers. Harriet Reed has

---

[181] General Affidavit of Harriet Reed, case of Harriet Reed (Levy, Beaufort, SC), dated 27 May 1901.

her vouchers executed by me. She lives a long distance out of town and she sends her voucher to me by the foreman who has seen her sign the paper and I then execute it just as if she were present in person. I do this on account of her ill health and to accommodate her.

I execute other vouchers, but I make all others comply with the law in every particular. I insist on seeing the certificate each time and my strictness with them has driven them to other persons to execute their quarterly vouchers.

I have been doing Harriet Reed's business I this land ever since her pension was granted. The agent of hers who brings me her papers is a way reliable man. He is not the owner of the plantation where she lives but he is a preacher and acts as her agent in her pension matters. This agent of hers {such} they other witness sign. Of course I do not swear her or any of her witnesses. It would be impossible for me to tell when she was present at the execution of her voucher or when she was not.

I see her every three months, I think. She sent her last voucher up by her agent, J. H. Johnson. His post office is here. He lives within a mile of this place. I have not executed the vouchers of John Washington for a long time – nearly a year. I assure again that the Harriet Reed case is the claim or case wherein, and the only one where I have been irregular.[182]

Thomas Chisholm (Comrade and Friend of Veteran the Soldier)
Date: 18 May 1892
Residence: Mingo Plantation, Beaufort, SC

Thomas Chisholm (42) declares that he knew Henry Reed intimately while in the army; that the Claimant, Henry Reed, was known as Henry Reeves while in the service; that he has seen the Claimant almost daily since his discharge from the army; that he personally know the Claimant to be the identical man who served in his regiment and in Company Gas Henry Reeves; that the Claimant was a corporal but most times he acted

---

[182] Ibid., C.R. Greene, dated 28 May 1901.

as Sergeant; that his knowledge is from years of personal acquaintance.[183]

Dick Phoenix (Friend of the Veteran Soldier)
Date: 23 May 1892
Residence: Taylor Plantation, Beaufort, SC

Dick Phoenix (26) declares That he is personally acquainted with Henry Reed and live only a few hundred yards from him and sees him daily; that the claimant was taken sick last year in the spring or fall and has been unable since to do any work or even to leave his house; that the claimant has no one to care for him and most of the time suffer for want of something to eat; that he cannot help himself in any way and is in a pitiful condition; that he also suffer greatly for the want of money to provide medical treatment; that just three weeks ago this affiant bought for the claimant a bottle of cod liver oil; that the claimant life has only been spared by the charity of the people on the plantation who give him everything he eats, but the claimant is also greatly in need of means to procure the proper nourishment.

This affiant pray that the pensioner commissioner will take such step as to make this case special as it may be the means of saving the life of the claimant. Affiant is no relation to the claimant and gains his knowledge from personal and daily observation of claimant.[184]

---

[183] Ibid., Thomas Chisholm, dated 18 May 1892.
[184] Ibid., Dick Phoenix (Taylor Plantation, Beaufort, SC), dated 23 May 1892.

* * * * * * * * * * * * *

Brass RICHARDSON
alias
Brass Ward

Private, Company B: Born during May 1837, at Brook Green, Georgetown, SC; a Slave of Joshua J. Ward; Enlisted on 08 Mar 1865, at Georgetown, Georgetown, SC; Medically Discharged on 14 Jun 1865, at Morris Island, Charleston, SC. 1st Marriage to Eliza Gainey (d. Georgetown, SC). Children: Johnnie; Henry; Mary (d. bef Apr 1915) and Rosa (d. bef Apr 1915). 2nd Marriage to Francis Hasel, on 03 Dec 1900, at Georgetown, SC, by Rev. Bruce H. Williams. **Brass Richardson** *died on 10 Nov 1917, at Georgetown, Georgetown, SC.*[185]

Brass Richardson (Veteran Soldier)
Date: 02 May 1904
Residence: #911 Church St., Georgetown, Georgetown, SC
Occupation: Fireman (on Steamer Boats)

I think I am between 60 or 65. I was born and raised near here on the Waccamaw River and was owned by Mr. Joshua Ward (dead). I lived on his place until March 1865 when I came to Georgetown and enlisted in the army and was sent to Beaufort, S.C., where I was put in Company B, 128th U.S. Colored Troops and served as Brass Ward.

My father was John Richardson and, during slavery, and ever since the war, my name has been Brass Richardson, but when we enlisted they asked the name of my owner and put me down as Ward. All the boys

---

[185] Civil War Pension Record for Brass Richardson alias Brass Ward, SC No. C-2.516-246, Pvt, Company B, 128th USCI, Records of the VA, RG 15, NARA, WDC; 1910 U.S. Federal Census, South Carolina, Georgetown County, Georgetown City, ED: 37, Page: 99A, Line: 28 (Roll: T624-1458).

from my place, except Israel Carr went by the name of Ward in service. Stephen Virene of Charleston also went as Ward. In a short time after muster in I was taken sick with a pain in my side and I had a cough and was sent to the sick tent and was sick quite a while and never did get strong any more while in the service. But when I felt somewhat better I tried to do duty and one day I was shooting at a target after coming off of picket and something move the gun and it kicked me in the left eye.

Just after that I was drilling one day and I fell over a stump and cut the skin on my right leg in front on the bone between the ankle and knee. It did not hurt much but at times since the war it has gotten sore. It has a small sore about the size of a button on it now. When a number of the boys were reexamined I was still sick and was sent to Hilton Head with them where I was reexamined. The doctors said I had something the matter with my lung and as I could not talk plain and they could not understand me so they said I would leave to be mustered out.

Me, Nat Alston, Peter Huggins and {Leon} Pinckney (dead) were mustered out at the same time and we came home together. We came from Charleston here on a three-mast schooner which ran aground at the Georgetown bar and the captain tried to shoot the pilot.

I was here for 2 or 3 years and then went to Charleston and lived at 105 Howard St., but during that time I was a fireman on the *Planter* and ran from Charleston to Georgetown, so I was here as much as in Charleston, and just after the big shake (see Page 136) I came back over here to live. The old *Planter* was lost and I was working on the *Louisa* and she ran from here to Charleston – then laid over here.

My colonel was [William] Beebe and [Benjamin] Manning was my captain and his brother was my lieutenant and [James] Justus was also one of my lieutenants, and [Charles] Lewis was our first sergeant.

My first wife was Eliza. She died in Charleston ten years ago and I was married here five years ago. I married my present wife, Francis. I have one child living, Sam, who is 20 years old.[186]

---

[186] Deposition of Brass Richardson, case of Brass Richardson (Georgetown, Georgetown, SC), dated 02 May 1904.

Sarah Mandora (Comrade of the Veteran Soldier)
Date: 11 Jan 1910
Residence: #105 Hanover St., Charleston, Charleston, SC
Occupation: Fireman (on Steamer Boats)

My age is about 60, and I am the widow of Robert Mandora. I was born and raised in Georgetown but married and came here before the war. I know Brass Richardson; he married my sister Eliza at Georgetown just after the war and they came here and lived in this house for years and then went back to Georgetown, but Eliza came back and she died here about ten years ago and was taken to Georgetown and buried.[187]

Nathaniel and Tony Allston (Comrade of the Veteran Soldier)
Date: 11 Jan 1910
Residence: Georgetown, Georgetown, SC

I, Nathaniel Allston (64), do certify that I have resided in this county all of my life. I have known Brass alias Brant Ward for the past 36 years and know him to be the identical person who enlisted in the army in Company B, 128th U.S Colored Infantry, under the name of Brass Ward. We were enlisted here at Georgetown, S.C., in March 1865, and went from Charleston to Beaufort, S.C. I have known him intimately ever since then to the present day and know him to be the identical person {known} in the application for pension to be Brass alias "Brant" Ward.

I, Tony Allston (55), do certify that I am a native of Georgetown County, S.C., and have resided here all of my life. I became acquainted with Brass Ward while we were in service during the year 1865 at Beaufort, S.C. He was in Company B, 128th U.S. Colored Troops and I was in Company G, of the 128th and I saw him daily. I have known him intimately and personally ever since then to the present time and know him to be the identical person who enlisted as Brass Ward.[188]

---

[187] Ibid., Sarah Mandora, dated 11 Jan 1910.
[188] General Affidavit of Nathaniel Allston and Tony Allston, in the matter of claim# 1.248.956, Brass Alias Brant Ward, Company "B" 128th USCT (Georgetown, Georgetown, SC), dated 11 Jan 1901.

Black Man's "Bill of Rights" in the United States of America

The Emancipation Proclamation was a landmark event in the history of the United States. However, at best, afforded limited freedom for African Descendants, but in order to receive citizenship it took three Constitutional Amendments: abolition of slavery (13th); citizenship in the United States (14th); and, the right to vote (15th).

13th Amendment
06 Dec 1865

Section 1. Neither slavery nor involuntary servitude, except as a punishment for crime whereof the party shall have been duly convicted, shall exist within the United States, or any place subject to their jurisdiction.

14th Amendment
09 Jul 1868

Section 1. All persons born or naturalized in the United States, and subject to the jurisdiction thereof, are citizens of the United States and of the State wherein they reside. ...

15th Amendment
17 Feb 1870

Section 1. The right of citizens of the United States to vote shall not be denied or abridged by the United States or by any State on account of race, color, or previous condition of servitude.

Source: Funk & Wagnalls New Encyclopedia (MCMLXXXVI), Volume 7, Colorado-Daly City, Constitution of the United States.

* * * * * * * * * * * * * *

Archie ROBINSON
alias
Archie Ward

Musician, Company D: Born on 04 Feb 1837, at Brook Green, Georgetown, Georgetown, SC; a Slave of Joshua Ward; Enlisted on 27 Mar 1865, at Beaufort, SC. Disability Discharged on 21 Sep 1865, at Hilton Head, Beaufort, SC. 1st Marriage to Ameritta Right (d. 1870), during 1867. Children: Hester (b. 1868); and Archie (b. 1870). 2nd Marriage to Yanekey Daise (d. June 1882), during 1872, at Brook Green, SC. Children: Susie (b. 1873); and Andrew (b. 1875). 3rd Marriage to Elvira Varene-Gourdine, on 12 Sep 1890, at Brook Green, SC, by Rev. J. Turner Harrison. Step-Children (Gourdine): Jack (b. Nov 1882); Joshua (b. Dec 1883) and Joseph (b. Dec 1886). **Archie Robinson** *died on 12 Jan 1918, at Brook Green, Georgetown, SC.*[189]

Archie Robinson (Veteran Soldier)
Date: 25 Mar 1901
Residence: Brook Green, Georgetown, SC
Occupation: Laborer

I am 60 years of age. I am the Archie Ward who served as a private in Company D, 128th U.S. Colored Infantry. I am pensioned at $12 a month under the Act of June 27, 1890. I was born on this plantation and have never been any place else except when I was in the army. I was born the slave of Joshua Ward and remained in the Ward family until freedom.

---

[189] Civil War Pension Record for Elvira Ward (widow of Archie Ward known as Archie Robinson), WC No. 882.864, Musician, Company D, 128th USCI, Records of the VA, RG 15, NARA, WDC; 1900 U.S. Federal Census, South Carolina, Georgetown County, Waccamaw, ED: 53, Page: 209A, Line: 14 (Roll: T623-1528).

Archie Robinson alias Archie Ward

My master lived on this plantation. My father was named Leonard Robinson. He belonged to the Wards also. I was known as Archie Robinson before the war but they put me down as Ward and when I came back I went by the name Archie Robinson again. I am called Robinson now but I am the same man who served as Archie Ward in Company D, 128th U.S. Colored Infantry. These two names are all I have ever been known by.

I enlisted at Beaufort, S.C. The doctor stripped me and thumped me and made me hop up and down and bent me over and looked at me. I was discharged at Beaufort, S.C. I think I served about three quarters of a year in service, then was discharged due to disability. I was not in any Confederate Army in any capacity. I never was on detached duty. I was in the Company area all the time except that time I was in the hospital. I was sick three months and never went back on duty.

Peter White was our [first]/ordnance sergeant. He was a short black man. Israel Carr and Randall Ward were my tentmates. I was in no battle. When I put in papers for pension I had Israel Carr and Randall Ward for two of my witnesses. They both knew me before the war, were in the war with me and know me well since the war. I was a witness for both of them in their claims for pension.

I have been married three times. My first two wives were dead before I married my present wife. My present wife was Elvira Gourdine. She had been married but once before I married her. I was married this last time by a colored minister named Harrison. We were married in the church. That preacher is dead now. I do not know how old my wife is but she is too old to have children. I think I have had this woman about fifteen years.[190]

---

[190] Deposition for Archie Ward, case of Archie Ward (Brook Green, Georgetown, SC, dated 25 Mar 1901.

John ROBINSON
alias
John Cashion

Corporal, Company D: Born c1844, at Camden, Kershaw, SC; a Slave of the Cashion family; Enlisted on 08 Mar 1865, at Charleston, Charleston, SC; Honorably Discharged on 10 Oct 1866, at Morris Island, Charleston, SC. Married to Charlotte Bellinger (b. 1850, Round, Colleton, SC; d. 27 Jul 1908, Round, SC), on 03 Jan 1870, at John {Sleen} Place, Sheridan Township, Colleton, SC, by S.A. Jacoby, Trial Justice or Magistrate. Children: James (b. 17 {Feb} 1870); Isabella (b. 15 Jun {1872}); Hector (b. 01 Aug {1874}); {Samuel} (b. 22 Mar 1877); John (b. 16 May 1880); Lizzie (b. {16 Apr} 1882); Irene (b. 27 {Jun} 1884); Emmaline (b. 25 Aug 1889)/?{(b. {01} May 1886)}; Annie Lois (b. 25 Apr 1893); and Rosa Pearl (b. 02 Sep 1894). **John Robinson** *died 07 Jul 1904, at Round, Colleton, SC.*[191]

Charlotte Robinson (Widow of the Veteran Soldier)
Date: 12 Oct 1906
Residence: Round, Colleton, SC
Occupation: Unemployed

I think I am 56 years old. I claim pension as the widow of John Robinson who served in the army as John Cashion. I was born and raised near here and have lived here all my life. I was owned by Mr. John {Kee}. I was never married and never lived with a man and never had a child until I married John Robinson. I married him here about a year after the war

---

[191] Civil War Pension Record for Rosa P. Robinson ,minor of John Cashion afterward known as John Robinson, MC No. 721.881, Pvt, Company D, 128th USCI, Records of the VA, RG 15, NARA, WDC; 1900 U.S. Federal Census, South Carolina, Colleton County, Sheridan Township, ED: 47, Page: ?, Line: ? (Roll: T623-1524).

John Robinson alias John Cashion

was over. We were married by Mr. S.A. Jacoby (dead) in my father's house on the {Slee} place and we lived together from that time until he died on July 7th 1904. I have not remarried nor lived with a man since my husband died. I had 13 children for John Robinson. The three youngest living are Emmaline, Annie and Rosa – born in the order named. Emmaline was born in August during the year of the earthquake (see Page 138). Annie was born in almost exactly two years after Emmaline. Rosa was born on the 2nd of Sept after the big storm (see Page 28).

I met my husband a year or two before we were married. He was then going by the name of John Robinson and he told me he had been a soldier and had served under the name of John Cashion. He got a pension under that name. He said he was born and raised near Camden, S.C., in the Columbia District/vicinity and that his owner was named Mr. Cashion. He said he ran away and joined the army.

I don't remember when he joined nor where he was mustered out. I am sure he was a soldier for he always said so. I don't know of anyone who was in with him.

He came home right after he got out of the army. He did not bring a wife with him and did not marry nor live with a woman after he came home until he married me.

My husband went by both names of Robinson and Cashion but most people called him Jack and John Robinson.[192]

James Robinson (Son of the Veteran Soldier)
    Date: 12 Oct 1906
    Residence: Round, Colleton, SC
    Occupation: Farmer

I am 33 years of age. Charlotte Robinson is my mother and John Robinson is my father. My mother's youngest living children are Emmaline, Annie and Rosa – born in the order named. I know when Rosa was born for I was married my mother was in bed with her and could not come to my marriage. I was married on September 13th 1894 and Rosa was born

---

[192] Deposition of Charlotte Robinson, case of Charlotte Robinson (near Round, Colleton, SC), dated 12 Oct 1906.

on September 2nd 1894 – just 11 days before I was married. I don't know the dates of birth of Emmaline and Annie but I know Emmaline was born about three years before the earthquake (see Page 136) and Annie - about a year and a half later.

My father told me he had been a soldier and that he served under the name of Cashion.[193]

John Bellinger (Brother of the Widow)
Date: 12 Oct 1906
Residence: Round, Colleton, SC
Occupation: Farmer

I am 40 years of age. I was born and raised here and have lived here all of my life. I know Charlotte Robinson and have known her since I was born. She is my sister. I know her children and know when they were born but don't know the dates. I have no record of their births and none of the birth dates of my own children.

I know that I was married in 1881 or 1882 and Annie was born about that time and so was Emmaline, but she was born before I was married. Rosa was born at the time James Robinson married but I don't know the date of his marriage. I hear him say he was married on September 13th 1894 and I think that is right.[194]

Edward Tucker and Thomas Chisholm (Friends of the Widow)
Date: 26 Jul 1904
Residence: Round, Colleton, SC

Edward Tucker (54) and Thomas Chisholm (52) declares that they have been well acquainted with John Robinson alias Cashion, for a number of years, also his wife, Charlotte, whose maiden name was Bellinger; that Charlotte Bellinger was married to John Robinson, or Cashion; his army name, by S.A. Jacoby, who was the Trial Justice or Magistrate for Sheridan Township in this county; that affiants were both present when the

---
[193] Ibid. James Robinson.
[194] Ibid. John Bellinger.

John Robinson alias John Cashion

Trial Justice married the couple (Charlotte Bellinger & John Robinson) and pronounced them man and wife.

They further declared that said couple lived together as man and wife up to the time of his death, July 7th 1904; that they were never divorced or separated in any way; that S.A. Jacoby is dead; that neither John Robinson or Charlotte Robinson were married before they married each other as above; and that Charlotte Robinson has not married since the death of her husband John Robinson.[195]

Correspondence concerning burial benefits for the Widow
Date: 27 Mar 1911

Dear Sir:

Yours of Feb. 8th in re claim for pension of Rosa P. Robinson [minor child of John Robinson] has been referred to me for reply.

John Robinson, alias John Cashion, received a pension from the U.S. Government, the number of pension being 617092. After his death his widow, Charlotte Robinson, received the pension. She died on July 27, 1908, and her daughter, Rosa P. Robinson desires to collect the pension due her mother. If you will refer to your letter to me of March 21st, you will probably be able to locate the claim.

I am enclosing herewith certified copy of appointment of James S. Robinson as guardian for Rosa P. Robinson, with the seal of the court attached.

If you desire any further information, please let me know at once. Yours very truly, Jas. E. Peurifoy.[196]

---

[195] General Affidavit of Edward Tucker and Thomas Chisholm, in the matter of John Robinson alias John Cashion, Company D, 128th U.S.C.T (Round, Colleton, SC), dated 26 Jul 1904.

[196] Letter from, The First National Bank of Walterboro, S.C, legal representatives of Rosa P. Robinson), to Mr. J.L. Davenport, Commissioner, Bureau of Pensions, Washington, D.C, dated 27 Mar 1911.

Scott ROBINSON
alias
Scott Prince

Private, Company E: Born on 25 Dec 1840, at Charleston, Charleston, SC; a Slave of Mistress Rebecca Holmes (widow of Mr. John Holmes); Enlisted on 02 Mar 1865, at Georgetown, Georgetown, SC; Honorably Discharged on 10 Oct 1866, at Morris Island, Charleston, SC. Married to Isabelle Simmons (d. 08 Jan 1903, at Charleston, Charleston, SC), on 11 Jul 1873, Charleston, SC, by Rev. M. B. Salter. Children: William (b. 25 Dec 1883); and Frank (b. Nov 1884). **Scott Robinson** *died on 15 Nov 1911, at 33 Sumter St., Charleston, Charleston, SC.*[197]

Scott Robinson (Veteran Soldier)
Date: 02 Nov 1901
Residence: #4 Johnson Ct., Charleston, Charleston, SC
Occupation: Fisherman

My age is 56. I am the man who served in Company E, 128th U.S. Colored Troops as Scott Prince. I was born in Charleston, S.C., and was owned by Mrs. Rebecca Holmes – the widow of Mr. John Holmes. My mother was also owned by Mrs. Holmes and was her cook. My mother was name Julia. She was just called Julia, but she was married to my father Jacob Robinson – who was free. He was said to be a shoemaker. I never saw him; he died before the war. Mrs. Holmes died about the first part of the war and several slaves were sold. My mother was sold to Dr.

---

[197] Civil War Pension Record for Scott Robinson alias Scott Prince, SC No. 926.200, Pvt, Company E, 128th USCI, Records of the VA, RG 15, NARA, WDC; 1900 U.S. Federal Census, South Carolina, Charleston County, Charleston-WD 12, ED: 113, Page: 223A, Line: 27 (Roll: T623-1521).

Scott Robinson alias Scott Prince

Prince on King St., but I never knew her to live up there. She went to work at the Roper Hospital and worked there until I went into the army. I don't know whether I was sold to Dr. Prince for I staid with my aunt Hagar until I went in the army.

I suppose I got the name of Prince from Dr. Prince. I know that the boys never called me Prince until after my mother was sold, but I never lived with Dr. Prince and I did not think about where the boys got the name from. But that must be the way of it.

I was called Scott during slavery. My name was Scott Robinson but I was only called by my first name as was usual with slaves. Henry Martin (dead), and some of the others, who belonged to Mrs. Holmes would call me Prince when we were playing. So when I enlisted in the Army I just gave my name as Scott Prince. I don't know why I did it, but most of the slaves just gave any name that came into their heads. I had never been called anything but Scott up to that time. Henry Martin went in the army at the same time I did but he went in the 103rd Regiment and I in the 128th. After the war I took my father's name of Robinson and have been called Scott Robinson ever since by my neighbors, but the soldiers still call me Scott Prince.

In 1865 I went from here on a boat to Hilton Head, S.C. I think the boat was called the *Cosmopolitan*. From Hilton Head I went to Beaufort and, sometime in 1865, I enlisted at Beaufort in the U.S. Army. My regiment went to Hilton Head to be mustered in by Gen. [Milton S.] Littlefield* and then my Company E and Company K went to Parris Island and then my company went to Fort Sumter, S.C., and then we came over to Charleston and were mustered out.

Our colonel was [Charles H.] Howard, and [William M.] Beebe was our lieutenant colonel. My captain was [Eugene L.] Barnes and our lieutenant was [James K.] Van Vort. Our [first]/ordnance sergeant was William Gardner. Before Gardner, our [first]/ordnance sergeant was a white man by the name of George [Williams], but he deserted at Beaufort. There was also another man who acted as [first]/ordnance sergeant for a while. He was always trying to undermine Gardner but Captain Barnes stuck by Gardner. His name was Isaac Evans, but he was only the acting [first]/ordnance sergeant for a while.

I was never in the Confederate Service, but when the war was going on I would stay around the Confederate soldiers here and sometimes they would let me beat the drums but I never was paid anything and was living at home all that time. I would just hang around them like boys will do. Some of the officers got to know my name and would say – Scott beat that drum for them to fall in, and I would do it. I never went off with any of them.[198]

Alfred Simmons (Comrade of the Veteran Soldier)
 Date: 07 Nov 1901
 Residence: #254 Ashley Ave., Charleston, Charleston, SC
 Occupation: Laborer

My age is 56, and I served in Company K, 128th U.S. Colored Troops. Before the war I was owned by Mr. Jno. Tucker and lived near Georgetown, S.C. During the war I went to Georgetown and enlisted in the U.S. Service and was sent on a boat to Hilton Head, S.C. We stopped at Charleston and took on some more men. I was discharged before the company was mustered out on account of my eyes. Several of us were discharged from Hilton Head at the same time.

I know Scott Prince. He served in the 128th regiment, but I don't know what company. After I was mustered out I went back to Georgetown and lived up in that part of the state for 5 or 6 years and then came back here and lived here ever since. I met Scott Prince about a year or two after I came here. He was then known as Scott Robinson and has gone by that name ever since.[199]

Daniel Frazer (Comrade of the Veteran Soldier)
 Date: 07 Nov 1901
 Residence: #49 State St., Charleston, Charleston, SC
 Occupation: Laborer

---

[198] Deposition of Scott Robinson, case of Scott Prince (Charleston, Charleston, SC), dated 02 Nov 1901. * Note: Formerly the Commander of the 21st U.S.C.T. (Earlier the 3rd S.C. Volunteer Regiment).

[199] Ibid., Alfred Simmons.

Scott Robinson alias Scott Prince

My age is about 73, and I served in Company B, 128th U.S. Colored Troops. I was born and raised in this city but was sold to Mr. Frank Newton near Georgetown, S.C., about ten years before the war and lived there until I enlisted in the U.S. Service. I left Georgetown on the *Eliza Hancock* which came here for some men and then went to Hilton Head.

I was mustered out with my company on Morris Island and have lived in Charleston ever since.

I know Scott Prince who served in Company E, 128th regiment. He goes by the name of Scott Robinson. I knew him when he was a little boy just able to get about. I knew his uncle, Nero Johnson, in this city before I was sold and I saw Scott with him. Nero was sold just before I was and was sent South when we had our regiment made up at Beaufort.[200]

Hagar Rivers (Aunt of the Veteran Soldier)
Date: 08 Nov 1901
Residence: Charleston, Charleston, SC

I don't know my age but I was grown and married before the war and I mined [baby sat] Scott Robinson who is my nephew. We were all owned by Mrs. Rebecca Holmes. Scott's mother was Julia and she cooked for Mrs. Holmes. His father was Jacob Robinson who was free born. Scott's name before the war was Scott Robinson, but he was only called Scott. Since the war he has gone by the name of Scott Robinson.

Just before the war Mrs. Holmes died and we were divided up and some of us were sold. Scott's mother was sold to Dr. Prince but Scott was left with me and I kept him until I went to Columbia during the war and then I left him with my sister Matilda (now dead) but I came back in six months and took Scott home with me until he went off with the Union Soldiers. I did not see him again for over a year and then he came home with blue soldier clothes on and told me he had been in the army.

I don't know if what name he went by in service and can't remember that he ever told me. I have always called him Scott Robinson and never

---

[200] Ibid., Daniel Fraser.

knew him going by any other name. He was the oldest boy and was not grown during the war. He did not have any brothers in the army.[201]

Nero Johnson (Uncle and Comrade of the Veteran Soldier)
Date: 09 Nov 1901
Residence: #4 {Knacke} St., Charleston, Charleston, SC
Occupation: Laborer

My age is about 58. I served in Company G, 136th U.S. Colored Troops.* I was 4th Sergeant. I enlisted in Atlanta, Ga., and was mustered in Augusta, Ga. I was born and raised in this city and was owned by Mrs. Rebecca Holmes but I was sold in 1861 and sent to Columbus, Ga. I came back home as soon as I was mustered out of service and have lived here ever since.

Scott Robinson is my first cousin. I left him here when I was sold in 1861 and did not see him again until I came here after muster out. My regiment was mustered out early in 1866 and after I came home I met Scott here, He had on his uniform and said his regiment was one Morris Island and he just came to the city for a day and went back and was mustered out that week. I have never known him to go by any name except that of Robinson but he told me he went by the name of Scott Prince in service.

His mother was sold to Dr. Prince at the same time I was sold South, and I suppose Scott took the name of Prince from him when he went in the army.[202]

Ben Weston (Comrade of the Veteran Soldier)
Date: 16 Nov 1901
Residence: #102 Calhoun St., Charleston, Charleston, SC
Occupation: Driver

---

[201] Ibid., Hagar Rivers.
[202] Deposition of Nero Johnson, case of Scott Prince (Charleston, Charleston, SC), dated 09 Nov 1901. *Note: The 136th USCT was organized at Atlanta, Georgia on July 15, 1865; performed duty in the Department of Georgia; and Mustered out January 4, 1866.

Scott Robinson alias Scott Prince

My age is 55. I was born and raised in Georgetown, S.C., and was owned by Mr. Francis Weston. I enlisted at Georgetown and was mustered out on Morris Island. I lived over in Mt. Pleasant from muster out until 1876 and then I came over to the city and I have lived here ever since.

I know Scott Robinson. He served in Company E, 128th regiment, but in service he went by the name of Scott Prince. I first met him in Beaufort, S.C., when we were both members of the 128th. I knew Scott well in service. I helped Dr. [Henry K.] Durrant* for some time and would go with the doctor when he went to different companies and in that way I got to know a number of men in other companies and besides that Scott would beat the drum some and I knew him in that way.

I have seen him a number of times since the war. He used to work at the old police station which staid right where this post office building now stands. I don't know if he attended the horses or helped the police but he worked right here; that was about 1872 or 1873, and that is where I first knew him to go by the name of Robinson.[203]

John Nicholas (Comrade of the Veteran Soldier)
Date: 16 Nov 1901
Residence: Mt. Pleasant, Charleston, Charleston, SC
Occupation: Laborer

My age is about 60. I served in Company E, 128th U.S. Colored Troops. I was born and raised near Georgetown, S.C., and was owned by Mr. Francis Weston. I enlisted at Georgetown and was mustered out on Morris Island.

I know Scott Robinson. He served in the same regiment and company with me but in the service he went by the name of Scott Prince. I have lived in and near Charleston ever since the war and have seen Scott often and I know positively that he is the same man who served in Company E, 128th regiment as Scott Prince.[204]

---

[203] Ibid. Ben Weston, dated 16 Nov 1901. *Note: Dr. [Henry K.] Durrant was the Regimental Surgeon for the 128th USCT.
[204] Ibid. John Nicholas, dated 02 Nov 1901.

Robert RODGERS
alias
Robert McFarlan

Private, Company A: Born during 1835, at Cash's Depot, near Cheraw, Chesterfield, SC; a Slave of Col. Allan McFarlan; Enlisted on 08 Mar 1865, at Edisto Island, Charleston, SC; Honorably Discharged on 10 Oct 1866, at Morris Island, Charleston, SC. 1st Marriage to Elizabeth Ellerbe (d. Dec 1907), on 06 Oct 1869, at Cheraw, SC, by Rev. P. M. Hidler. Children: Binah (b. Aug 1868); Richard (b. Oct 1869); Isom (b. Apr 1887); Lottie (b. Nov 1889); and Ella (b. Oct 1892). 2nd Marriage to Mary Jane {Cautur}, on 04 Dec 1908, at Cheraw, SC, by Rev. J.W. Wright. Children: Edith (b. Feb 1910) and May (b. May 1913). ***Robert Rodgers*** *died during May 1923, at Cheraw, Chesterfield, SC.*[205]

Robert Rodgers (Veteran Soldier)
    Date: **12 Oct 1904**
    Residence: Cash Depot, near Cheraw, Chesterfield, SC
    Occupation: Farmer

I don't know my age but I think I am about 60. I was young and unmarried before I went in the Army. I am the Robert McFarlan who served in Company A, 128th U.S. Colored Infantry. I was born near where I now live and have lived here all my life except when I was in the Army. I was owned by Col. Allan McFarlan. I was working for him up to the time Sherman's Army came by here, when I was taken away and put to driv-

---

[205] Civil War Pension Record for Robert Rodgers alias Robert McFarlan, SC No. C-2.523.655, Pvt, Company A, 128th USCI, Records of the VA, RG 15, NARA, WDC; 1900 U.S. Federal Census, South Carolina, Chesterfield County, Steer Pen, ED: 28, Page: 190A, Line: 26 (Roll: T623-1523).

Robert Rodgers alias Robert McFarlan

ing a wagon. I drove for them until we got on the other side of Raleigh, N.C.,* when a man by the name of Capt. [Mirand W.] Saxton took me and a lot of others to Wilmington, N.C., and put us on a boat and sent us to Charleston and then to Edisto and then to Beaufort.

Captain [Mirand W.] Saxton was with us at Beaufort and we were all stripped and made to wash and examined and put on soldier clothes. Captain [Mirand W.] Saxton staid with us as our captain. Julius Simple was our lieutenant. James was our First Sergeant. General [Charles H.] Howard and Colonel [William M.] Beebe had charge of us. Our doctor's name was [Henry K.] Durrant.

We were camped at Beaufort most of the time, then we went to Grahamville and then to the Islands about Charleston, including time at Castle Pinckney, and then were mustered out on Morris Island.

I remember Broughton Hall, James Knight, Saxton and Ward, but have not seen any of them since the war.

My brother, Nero, who is getting a pension, was in the same company with me. He also went off with Sherman's Army but I did not see him until we met in Beaufort and were put in the same company. Roman and Lewis McFarlan were in the regiment with us but I don't think they were in the same company. Roman is dead. He left a child name Della but I don't know where she is but she lives near here. I think she is grown and married. Jet was with us in Beaufort. He was very young, but I think he was a soldier. I don't think he staid long. I don't think he ever had a wife. He died just after the war.

I know Lavania McFarlan who used to live about 20 miles from here in Marlboro. She was the wife of Frank McFarlan and never the wife of Jet. I never knew Jet to have a wife and don't know that he was a soldier.

I have only been married once and my wife is living. Her name was Elizabeth {Shoat}. She was never married and never had a child before she married me. We were married about a year or two after the war by a preacher.

We have eleven children living. Ella is the youngest and she is ten years old. She was born in August. Lottie is next. She is fifteen. Isom is next. He was born in October 1886. The others are all older.

I am known as McFarlan and also Rodgers. I go by both names. My father's name was Rodgers. And my name was McFarlan. I am called by both names.[206]

Geoffrey Broughton (Comrade of Veteran)
Date: 14 Oct 1904
Residence: Meeting St., Charleston, Charleston, SC
Occupation: Not Employed

My age is about 70 years old. I served in Company A, 128th U.S. Colored Infantry. I am a pensioner. I was born and raised on Cooper River and went back there after mustered out and was there for seven years, then came here and have been here ever since.

I remember Robert McFarlan, he was a corporal for a while and was then reduced again - I don't know why. He was in my company and he had a brother by the name of Nero also in there, and there were several other McFarlans in Company I. They all came from the same place – somewhere up in this state, but I don't know where. I have not seen Robert since we were mustered out.

Robert was a young man – dark skin, but not black. He had more sense than his brother Nero. I don't think he was as tall as Nero. I have not seen any of the McFarlans since we were mustered out.[207]

---

[206] Ibid., Robert McFarlan, dated 12 Oct 1904. *Note: Interesting that these men served as members of Sherman's Pioneer Corps before they enlisted in the Army.

[207] Ibid., Geoffrey Broughton, dated 14 Oct 1904.

40-Acres and a Mule

This term refers to the compensation that was to be awarded to freed slaves in America after the Civil War - 40 acres of land to farm, and a mule with which to drag a plow so the land could be cultivated.

The award - a land grant of 40 acres of land deeded to heads of households presumably formerly owned by land-holding whites - was the product of Special Field Orders, No. 15, issued January 16, 1865 by Major General William T. Sherman, which applied to black families who lived near the coasts of South Carolina, Georgia and Florida.

After the assassination of President Abraham Lincoln, his successor, Andrew Johnson, revoked Sherman's Orders. It is sometimes mistakenly claimed that Johnson also vetoed the enactment of the policy as a federal statute. In fact, the Freedmen's Bureau Bill which he vetoed made no mention of grants of land or mules. (Another version of the Freedmen's bill, also without the land grants, was later passed after Johnson's second veto was overridden.)

By June of 1865, around 10,000 freed slaves were settled on 400,000 acres in Georgia and South Carolina. Soon afterward, President Johnson reversed the order and returned the land to its white former owners. Because of this, the phrase has come to represent the failure of Reconstruction and the general public to assist African Americans.

Source: Special Field Order No. 15, dated 16 Jan 1865; Wikipedia: http://en.wikipedia.org/ wiki/40_acres_and_a_mule

Irvin ROWE
alias
Irwin Nero

Private, Company F: Born c1846, near Orangeburg, Orangeburg, SC; a Slave of Joshua Olener; Enlisted on 22 Mar 1865, at Charleston, Charleston, SC; Honorably Discharged on 10 Oct 1866, at Morris Island, Charleston, SC. Married to Rosanna Nabnett, on 15 Dec 1868, in Orangeburg County, SC, by Rev. Adam Williams. Children: James (b. 16 Dec 1869); William (b. 14 Aug 1871); Cornelia (b. 11 Apr 1873); Samuel (b. 20 Jun 1876); Milledge (b. 25 Jul 1878); Cephus (b. 15 Nov 1880); and Frances (b. 26 Mar 1882). **Irvin Rowe** *died on 26 Nov 1904, at Orangeburg County, SC.*[208]

Irwin Rowe (Veteran Soldier)
Date: 28 Aug 1901
Residence: near Advance, Orange, SC
Occupation: Farmer

I am 56 years of age. I served as a private in Company F, 128th U.S. Colored Infantry Regiment. I enlisted at Charleston, S.C., in March and served not quite two years. I was mustered out with my company at Morris Island, S.C., in November. I can't give the year. I served under the name of Irvin Nero. I had no other service, military or naval. I was never in any way connected with the Confederate Service. I am pensioned at $6.00 per month under the New Law. I have never filed a claim under the General Law.

---

[208] Civil War Pension Record for Irwin Rowe alias Irwin, SC No. 901.840, Pvt, Company F, 128th USCI, Records of the VA, RG 15, NARA, WDC; 1900 U.S. Federal Census, South Carolina, Orangeburg County, Caw Caw Township, ED: 51, Page: 100A, Line: 1 (Roll: T623-1538)

Irvin Rowe alias Irwin Nero

My first captain was James Scranton and he was replaced by James Justus. My lieutenants were James Sprague and Dick Swarts. My First Sergeant was William Emory; he took the place of a First Sergeant who died at Beaufort, S.C., in the service. Richard Humbert was my First Sergeant a while.

Daniel Green was a sergeant in my company. I don't recollect the names of my corporals. I think Quash Pinckney was a corporal in my company. My bunkmate was Russell Keller. He died in the service and I then bunked with Peter Green. Keller and Green were my messmates.

There was no other man in my company named Irwin Nero or Irwin Rowe. None of my comrades live in this county. Most of them came from down around Georgetown, S.C., and a few from Charleston, S.C. Amos Pipkins, Harry Miller, Every Stedman, Jackson McConnell, Brutus Nesbit and Fortune Walpool were some of the men in my company.

When I enlisted I was only about 17 or 18 years old as near as I can recollect. My old 'misses' told me my age soon after I was mustered out. I was not quite as tall then as I am now. I am now 5 ft & 7 inches high. My color is black and hair of same color. My eyes are sort of a bluish brown color. I weigh about 155 at present. I don't recollect what my weight was at enlistment.

After enlistment my company remained at Charleston a little over one week and then went to Beaufort, S.C., on boats, remaining there the remainder of our service except for a few days spent at Hilton Head doing garrison duty. We went back to Charleston a few weeks before muster out and were sent to Morris Island where they kept us until discharge. We generally did garrison and guard duty. We were in no battles or skirmishes.

I was in a hospital one month while stationed at Beaufort, S.C. I suffered with pains in my left side. I had dysentery and yellow jaundice in the service but nothing else. I contracted no permanent disabilities while in the U.S. Service. I lost no time from duty except that month spent in the Beaufort Hospital.

I was born and raised in Orangeburg County, S.C. My father was named Dennis Hagler. He afterwards called himself Dennis Young. My mother was named Katie Hagler. They belonged to John Hagler in slavery and lived eleven miles east of Orangeburg in Orangeburg County, S.C.

My owner at birth was John Hagler (dead) but by the marriage of his sister to Robert Rotenberg (dead) I became the property of the latter. After the death of Rotenberg his widow married Joshua Olener (dead) and I was in his possession until I got my freedom.

My parents are both dead. I have no brothers, but I have one sister, Jane Jenkins, of Cameron on the Coast Line Railroad.

Before enlistment I was known as Irvin Nero. I was christened with that name. My mother gave me that name at birth. I don't know where she got the name of Nero from. I was named after some powerful big man they said.

After discharge I took the name of my uncles who called themselves Rowe because I liked that name better than Nero. I had no better reason than this for changing my name. I have gone by the name of Irvin Rowe ever since. I have lived in the county since muster out. My discharge certificate got burned up about one month after I left the service.

I have been once married and then to Rosanna Nabnett who still lives with me. We were married on or about 15 December 1868. We had seven children; one is now under the age of sixteen years.[209]

Sheck Thomas (Comrade of Veteran)
    Date: 29 Aug 1901
    Residence: near Lone Star, Orangeburg, SC
    Occupation: Farmer

I served as a private in Company K, 128th U.S. Colored Infantry. I enlisted in March 1865 at Beaufort, S.C., and was discharged for disability in September 1865 at Parris Island, S.C. I served under the name of Jacob McAllister.

I have known Irvin Rowe since he was a small boy. His father was named Dennis Rowe and lived in this county during slavery the same as I. Irvin Rowe belonged to Joshua Olener when the war came up and I

---

[209] Deposition of Irwin Rowe, case of Irwin Nero alias Rowe (near Advance, Orangeburg, SC), dated 28 Aug 1901.

belonged to Russell Zimmerman. Their places were three miles and a half apart. I saw Irvin often during slavery and in the service. We were in the same regiment though in different companies.

    We were together at Beaufort, S.C., during our service, but at no other place. Since our discharge we have again lived in the same county and I have seen him on an average of once per year. He lives about 20 miles from me. During slavery I called him Irvin and nothing else. That was the way black folks talked to each other in those days.

    In the service he was known as Irvin Nero. I don't know why he took the name or where he got it. Since our discharge he has been called Irvin Rowe after his daddy, Dennis Rowe. He took that name soon after he got home. I think it was about 1868 that he did so. His reason for changing his name was to have himself called after his father.

    I know that Irvin Nero and Irvin Rowe are identical, and that he is the man who performed service with me in the 128th U.S. Colored Infantry.

    I do not recollect that there was any other man in that regiment with the name or a similar name. Irvin is a black man with black hair and eyes. He was about 20 or 21 at the time of enlistment, and weighed fully 140 or 145 pounds. I can't give the exact weight, but he was not as tall as I was at enlistment.[210]

Harry Dickson (Comrade of the Veteran Soldier)
    Date: 29 Aug 1901
    Residence: Raymond, Orangeburg, SC
    Occupation: Farmer

I am 68 years old. I served as a private in Company K, 128th U.S. Colored Infantry. I enlisted in 1864 and was mustered out in 1865. I served under the name of Harry Lewiston. I have known Irvin Rowe since we were together in the U.S. Service. I first saw him while we were drilling at Beaufort, S.C., soon after the organization of our regiment. He was not in my company. I can't state his company, but I sorter think it was Company F.

---

[210] Ibid., Sheck Thomas.

We were together right along in the service. We were not intimate associates for we were not thrown together as much as members of the same company were, but being from the same county we staid together as much as we could.

Only three men from Orangeburg County were in the 128th U.S. Colored Infantry and Irvin Rowe and I were two of them. The other one was Jacob McAllister. I was with Rowe at Beaufort and Hilton Head, S.C. and then this company was sent off and I never saw him again until after our muster out. Since the war we have lived in the same county- generally about four or five miles from each other, and are often together at just one place and another.

While in the service, Irvin Rowe was known as Irvin Nero. I never heard him called Irvin Rowe until since our discharge.

I don't know where he got the name of Nero from. All the fellows in the army called him just Irvin but I heard his name called as Irvin Nero by the officers.

Soon after we got home from the service he began to call himself Irvin Rowe and has since gone by that and I never hear Nero spoken of again except in his pension business.

I don't know where he got the name of Rowe from. I am positive that Irvin Nero and Irvin Rowe is one and the same person. I would say that if I was going to die. There was no other man in our regiment by either name so far as I know. The last time I saw Irwin Rowe was a couple of weeks ago.

He is a dark chunky full faced man about 60 years old, weigh 160 or 170 pounds and is about 5 ½ feet high.[211]

---

[211] Ibid., Harry Dickson, Dated 29 Aug 1901.

Explanation ~~Explanation~~ DEFINITONS

"Old Law"
Act of July 14, 1862

All references to the "Old Law" or "General Law" in this book pertain to the Civil War Pension Act of 1862. On July 14, 1862, Congress enacted a revolutionary pension system which provided benefits to soldiers and their dependents.

This Pension Law authorized benefits to veterans who suffer from service-connected disabilities, widow of veterans who died from injury or disease incurred during the War, and orphaned children in cases where both the veteran and his surviving widow is deceased.

"New Law"
Act of June 27, 1890

All references to the "New Law" in this book pertain to the Civil War Pension Act of 1890. On June 27, 1890, Congress passed the first "Social Security Act" which provided benefits to veterans with 90 or more days of service during the War; can no longer provide welfare for his family; and, his disabilities are not due to vicious habits (i.e., alcoholism, sexually transmitted diseases, etc).

Source: Megan J. McClintock, "Civil War Pensions and the Reconstruction of Union Families," *The Journal of American History*, 83 (September 1996).

Daniel SAMUELS
alias
Samuel Daniels

Private, Company H: Born on 02 Mar 1846, at Black Swamp, Beaufort (now Barnwell), SC; a Slave of Benjamin Lawton; Enlisted on 02 Mar 1865, at Savannah, GA; Disability Discharged on 01 Oct 1865, at Hilton Head, Beaufort, SC. Married to Rose Ella Best (b. c1850, Screven County, GA), during Aug 1870/1, at Mt. Zion Church, Allendale, Allendale, SC, by Rev. Frank Barnwell. Children: Mamie (b. 02 Jun 1874); John Wesley (b. 01 Jan 1876); Walter (b. 05 Jun 1878); Elliott (b. 10 Aug 1880; d. 03 Aug 1913); Nora (b. 12 Feb 1886); Willie (b. 02 Jun 1890); and Isabella (b. 01 May 1892). **Daniel Samuels** *died on 05 Oct 1922, at Luray, Hampton, SC.*[212]

Simon Meyers and Stephen Snider (Comrades of the Veteran)
Date: 15 Aug 1893
Residence: Hampton County, SC

Affiants, Simon Myers and Stephen Snider, testify on oath that they are well acquainted with Daniel Samuels and knew him during the war, and were with him when he was discharged for hernia and rheumatism which he contracted on Beaufort Island, S.C., in 1865. He was discharged at Hilton Head, S.C., on account of disability caused from above disease. Our knowledge of these facts is from being with the claimant. We testify further that these afflictions were not caused from vicious habits of the claimant, he being a man of good character and temperate habits. We

---

[212] Civil War Pension Record for Ella Samuel, widow of Samuel Daniel alias Daniel Samuel, WC No. 940.017, Pvt, Company H, 128th USCI; Records of the VA, RG 15; NARA, WDC; 1900 U.S. Federal Census, South Carolina, Hampton County, Goethe Township, ED: 55, Page: 65A, Line: 6 (Roll: T623-1531).

Daniel Samuels alias Samuel Daniels

know the claimant to be not able to support himself on account of hernia and rheumatism. Not being allowed to do any straining at all. We testify also that the above was written in our presence, and only from our oral stalemates, on the 15th day of August 1893 in Brunson, S.C. before R.E. Primus Notary Public and that in making the same, we did not use any printed matter nor aided or prompted by any written or printed statement or recital prepared by any person.[213]

Simon Meyers and Henry Brooks (Comrades of Veteran)
Date: 23 Mar 1901
Residence: Barnwell County, SC

Affiants, Simon Myers and Henry Brooks, testify that we have known Daniel Samuels from infancy and have always known him to be a peaceable and sober man in his habits and have no reason to say or think any disability claimant has is due to any vicious habits and we know that prior to March 10th 1892 claimant was a sufferer from rheumatism and complaining of hernia and distress in origins of his heart presumably had spells of difficulty in getting his breath on very little exercise and we know that during all this period to present date he has suffered from rheumatism and heart trouble and we also know that he has been growing worse and that on account of rheumatism, heart trouble and hernia this man has not from and before March 10th 1892 nor since been able to do any kind of manual labor to earn wages that will afford him support nor has he any vicious habits.[214]

---

[213] Genera Affidavit for Simon Meyers and Stephen Snider, in the matter of Pension Claim No. 1096522, of Daniel Samuel (Hampton County, SC), dated 15 Aug 1893.

[214] Ibid. Simon Meyers and Henry Brooks, dated 23 Mar 1901.

John SHINES
alias
John Tenant

Corporal, Company H: Born c1840, on James Island, Charleston, SC; a Slave of the Tenants; Enlisted on 13 Mar 1865, at Beaufort, SC; Honorably Discharged on 10 Oct 1866, at Morris Island, Charleston, SC. 1st Marriage to Diana [MNU] (d. 1873). 2nd Marriage to Susan Young (b. Sep 1859), on 18 Jan 1880, at Stono Lodge, James Island, Charleston, SC, by Rev. Nelson Richardson, AME Minister. Children: Julia (b. 17 Nov 1878); Malsey (b. 15 Aug 1883); John (b. 17 Feb 1887); and Susan (b. 01 Jun 1891). **John Shines** *died on 08 Jan 1891, on James Island, Charleston, SC.*[215]

Susan Shines (Widow of the Veteran Soldier)
Date: **22 Aug 1901**
Residence: **James Island, Charleston, SC**

I don't know how old I am. I was a small girl when the war broke out. I was born of slave parents right here on James Island, S.C. My father's name was Joshua Young and my mother's name was Judy. I was called Susan Young; named after my father. My father's master was named Croskey Royal; a planter who used to own the place where I now live.

I have never been married but once and never been known or called by any other name than Susan Shines since my marriage to John Shines. My husband's full name was John Shines. When my husband went into the war he enlisted as John Tenant, named after his master. I have heard

---

[215] Civil War Pension Record for Susan Shines, widow of William Shines alias Tenant, WC No. 410.739, Pvt, Company H, 128th USCI, Records of the VA, RG 15, NARA, WDC.

John Shines alias John Tenant

my husband called Tenant but that was not his name – only his army name. I don't know what company or regiment my husband served in. I never heard him say that he was wounded in any skirmish while in the army. My husband was a tall stout black man. He was a farmer. I don't know his age, but he was born on John's Island, S.C. I was married to John Shines at the African Methodist Church on James Island, S.C. I don't know what year it was, but my oldest child is now about 22 years old and she was born in about one year after my marriage.

My husband has been married before I married him and his wife died. Since the death of husband I have lived right here in this house with my children and have supported myself by working in the field and by washing and ironing and by my pension since I got it.

I have never remarried since the death of my husband. I am well acquainted with Peter Todd, a colored man who lives about a mile from my house. I used to keep company with Peter Todd and he wanted to marry me but I would not marry him. I have hired Peter to plow for me, but he did not board or live with me. I never had anything to do with him or any other man since my husband died.

I had three children living when my husband died and one, Susan, was born 4 months after his death.

My husband died here on James Island. I don't know what year. Dr. Lee and Dr. Ellis attended my husband in his last illness. Dr. Lee is dead, but Dr. Ellis lives here yet. I think my husband died of bronchitis. He had a bad cough. John Shines was a sound man when I married him but for about two years before his death he complained of his throat and breast. He had a bad cough and was not able to work. I have no other pension claim pending under any law.

I have lived in the house where I now live ever since my husband died. I have nothing by my 10 acres of land and my pension money to live on, and my work.[216]

---

[216] Deposition of Susan Shines, case of Susan Shines (Charleston, Charleston, SC), dated 22 Aug 1901.

* * * * * * * * * * * * *

Titus SIMMONS
alias
Titus DeHone

Corporal, Company I: Born during 1842, at Ashepoo, Colleton, SC; a Slave of Dr. Theodore DeHone; Enlisted on 07 Mar 1865, at Charleston, Charleston, SC; Honorably Discharged on 10 Oct 1866, at Morris Island, Charleston, SC. 1st Marriage to Maggie Magwood, on 24 Oct 1874, at Jacksonboro, Colleton, SC, by Rev. Lester Flood. Children: Frost (b. 05 Sep 1867); Richard (b. 1874); David (b. 30 Mar 1876); Elizabeth (b. 18 Apr 1879); Nancey (b. 18 May 1884); and Hester (b. 13 Mar 1885). 2nd Marriage to Miley [MNU], on 24 Nov 1923. **Titus Simmons** *died on 20 Aug 1925, at Jacksonboro, Colleton, SC.*[217]

Titus Simmons (Veteran Soldier)
Date: 27 Apr 1903
Residence: Jacksonboro, Colleton, SC
Occupation: Farmer

I think I am 64 years of age. My full and correct name is Titus DeHone. I was born at Ashepoo, Colleton, S.C. My father's name was Brass Poosa. My mother's name was Pender Poosa. My owner – Dr. DeHone. I have only one sister, Grace Simmons, and she resides in Edisto, S.C. Immediately after I came out of the army I took the name of Titus Simmons. Tambo Simmons, who also belonged to Dr. DeHone, raised me. My mother and father died when I was a child and I took the name of Simmons because Tambo Simmons raised me. Since the close of the war I

---

[217] Civil War Pension Record for Titus Simmons alias Titus DeHone , SC No. C-2.524.029, Pvt, Company I, 128th USCI, Records of the VA, RG 15, NARA, WDC. 1910 U.S. Federal Census, South Carolina, Colleton County, Fraser Township, ED: 117, Page: 265A, Line: 24 (Roll: T624-1456).

Titus Simmons alias Titus DeHone

have generally been known as Titus Simmons. I have been known also as Titus DeHone.

I resided here at Ashepoo until about Jan 1864 when the 25th Ohio, a white regiment, marched through here and I followed them to Charleston, S.C. I was with the regiment 6 or 7 months or more when I was drafted and put in the guard house at Charleston, S.C. and, with others, taken to Hilton Head Island, S.C., where I was forced (Page __) ~~(impressed   j.r.g.)~~ into service. At Hilton Head we were enlisted and taken to Beaufort, S.C., where we were examined and mustered into service in Company I, 128th U.S. Colored Infantry in February 1865.

I was discharged with my regiment at Morris Island, S.C. in October 1866. We were in camp within a half mile of Beaufort, for about one year and then went to Charleston, S.C., on the Steamer *Mayflower* and we were in the Charleston neighborhood about 6 months then mustered out. We were in camp on Sullivans Island across the river from Charleston, S.C. The various companies were distributed about doing guard duty at different places. Companies I and B did guard duty at the Charleston Jail two or three months.

We turned in our arms on Sullivans Island and then we were put out on Morris Island without a gun and shortly afterward mustered out there. I was given a discharge certificate and kept it about 4 years and my little child destroyed it.

I received $16 per month during the entire period of my service. Sometimes they paid us every three months and sometimes every several months. They did not have a regular time for paying us. When they enlisted me they asked the name of my owner and I answered DeHone and I was enrolled under that name and answered to that name at roll call. I did not give the name of Simmons or any name other than DeHone. I can't read or write and don't know how my discharge read, but I do know that I signed under the name of Titus DeHone and in Company I, 128th U.S. Colored Infantry.

My first tent mates were John Simmons and Louis ___. Louis died in the swamp at Beaufort, S.C. After Louis died, Adam Bennett tented with Simmons and myself until we went to Charleston. After that we were housed in Charleston and Sullivans Island.

Washington Granville, who died at Ashepoo, S.C., 3 years ago was the only member of my Company that I knew before the war and he and I were neighbors until his death. Sawney {Brown / Poosa}, a preacher residing at Lincolnville, S.C., served in my Company. I have seen him very frequently since the war. He began preaching in the neighborhood about 4 years ago.

Washington Gramville and Swaney {Brown / Poosa} were the only member of the Company I saw and communicate with from muster out until in December 1902 when I learned that some members of my Company resided in the neighborhood of Charleston and Ashley Junction and I went to that place and saw Samuel Ingram and Edward Allston and they readily identified me and I sent their testimony on to Washington.

I went to see Sawney {Brown / Poosa} at his house a Lincolnville, S.C. but he said "it been so long he couldn't tell whether I was the man." Israel {Anomn} was a member of my company and said he resided at Wadmalaw Island but I have not seen him since muster out.

About 10 years ago a colored man named {Pyhins} who then resided here, started a pension claim for me. He wanted to charge me so much that I became discouraged and didn't bother with it no more until last year when I had G.A. Bead write for me. I obtained the name of my Washington attorney, Nathan Bickerford, from {some} Ashley a {Sueds}. Mr. Bead wrote for me and obtained the necessary blanks and he filled out the papers, read them to me, I signed them and was sworn to truth of the content. Daniel W. Pubinon and J.S. Blount were present and witnessed my signature.[218]

Miley Simmons (2nd Wife of the Veteran Soldier)
Date: 08 Apr 1925
Residence: Jacksonboro, Colleton, SC

Miley Simmons takes oath that she is the wife of Titus Simmons, formerly known as Titus DeHone, having been married to the said Titus Simmons on or about the 24th of November 1923; that she lives with the said

---

[218] Deposition of Titus DeHone, case of Titus DeHone (Jacksonboro, Colleton, SC), dated 27 Apr 1903.

Titus Simmons alias Titus DeHone

Titus Simmons at Jacksonboro, and has been living with him since her marriage; that she has no children by the by the said Titus Simmons; that the said Titus Simmons has been, before and since their marriage, in very poor health, but commencing about six months ago his condition has rapidly declined;

That he suffers severely from rheumatism and with feebleness due to old age; that he is totally deaf in his left ear and almost totally deaf in his right ear, and his eyesight is rapidly failing; that he can do no work of any kind, and requires her constant attendance to wait upon him;

That he would be absolutely helpless without someone to wait upon him, and requires my constant regular attendance to minister to his personal wants and physical needs.[219]

---

[219] General Affidavit of Miley Simmons, case of Miley Simmons (Colleton County, SC), dated 08 Apr 1925.

Scott SMITH
alias
Scott Brooker

Sergeant, Company A: Born c1841, at the Brooker Plantation, Hancock County, GA; a Slave of Ted Brooker; Enlisted on 04 Mar 1865, at Beaufort, Beaufort, SC; Honorably Discharged on 10 Oct 1866, at Fort Pinckney, Charleston, SC. Married to Sylvia Williams (b. 26 Jul 1848, Screven County, GA), on 30 Jan 1871, at Savannah, Chatham, GA, by Rev. Houston. Children: Francis (b. c1879); Charlotte (b. c1881); Rainey (b. c1882); Elzey (b. c1883); Ethel (b. c1889); and Leola (b. 16 Jul 1892). ***Scott Smith*** *died on 18 July 1906, at Savannah, Chatham, GA.*[220]

Scott Smith (Veteran Soldier)
Date: 03 Sep 1902
Residence: #634 W. Bryan St., Savannah, Chatham, GA
Occupation: Watchman

I am 61 years of age. I am the identical person who was a soldier during the late war as a private, corporal and sergeant in Company A, 128th U.S. Colored Volunteer Infantry. I enlisted during the month of March 1865, at Savannah, Georgia, and was discharged during October 1866 near Charleston, S.C. We were discharged at Castle Pinckney, just opposite Charleston. We were carried to Morris Island to await payment, then mustered out and allowed to go. I served under the name of Scott Brook-

---

[220] Civil War Pension Record for Sylvia Smith (widow of Scott Smith alias Scott Brooker), WC No. 633.887, Private, Company A, 128th USCI, Records of the VA, RG 15, NARA, WDC; 1900 U.S. Federal Census, Georgia, Chatham County, Savannah – 1st District, ED: 31, Page: 203B, Line: 94 (Roll: T623-185).

er. I had no other army service than previously stated and never served in the U.S. Navy or Marine Corps.

I was born in Hancock County, Georgia, a slave of Ted Brooker. I was reared in the same county a few miles from Sparta, and was a slave of Mr. Brooker until emancipation. My mother was Rainey Brooker. My father was named Frank and was a slave of Jack Smith, of Hancock County, Georgia. I do not know if my parents were lawfully man and wife or not, as I now {saw} my father. I have two half brothers, a fellow named Elbert Brooker, of Sparta, Hancock County, Georgia; and Mashan Brooker, of the city. Elbert is about 70 years old of age and Mashan is about 25. I have no sisters. Mother is dead.

I left the plantation during the fall of 1864 and came here with Sherman's Army in his raid through Sparta. I left the plantation alone. A man named Henry - last name forgotten, and a man named Carter and I enlisted at the same time. Henry died before muster-in at Beaufort, S.C., with small pox. Carter served his time in my company – I think, but I don't know what became of him.

From enlistment we remained at Beaufort until just before the following Christmas, but we were then sent to Grahamville, S.C. to perform garrison duty. We were there two or three months. We then were sent to Paris Island, near Beaufort. We were there a month. We were then sent near Charleston, S.C. We were ordered then to {Roxall}, then to Edisto Island to perform garrison duty. We were there about two months when we were ordered to the fort near Charleston, and then to Castle Pinckney where we were discharged. I was never in no battle. The war was about won when I enlisted.

I was mustered into service as a private but was shortly made a corporal. Soon after this I was made Commissary Sergeant and sometimes during 1865 I was made a regular duty sergeant. I was paid $16 month as a private, $18 as a corporal and $20 as a sergeant.[221]

---

[221] Deposition of Scott Smith alias Brooke, case of Scott Smith alias Brooke (Savannah, Chatham, GA), dated 03 Sep 1902.

Sheck T. THOMAS
alias
Jacob McAllister

Private, Company K: Born c1837, at Orangeburg District, SC; a Slave of Mr. Zimmerman; Enlisted on 08 Mar 1865, at Beaufort, Beaufort, SC; Disability Discharge on 23 Sep 1865, at Hilton Head, Beaufort, SC. Married to Emily Shirer (b. c1839; d. 31 Jul 1920), on 25 Feb 1871, at Creston, Calhoun, SC, by Reverend Prioleau. Children: Mrs. Phillis Durant; Mrs. Adeline Johnson; Mrs. Josephine Sanders; Mrs. Simsie Riley; and Sheck D. **Sheck T. Thomas** *died on 24 Feb 1904, at Lone Star, Calhoun, SC.*[222]

Thomas Scheck (Veteran Soldier)
Date: 29 Aug 1901
Residence: Lone Star, Calhoun, SC
Occupation: Farmer

I am 64 years of age. I served as a private in Company K, 128th U.S. Colored Infantry regiment. I enlisted in March 1865 at Beaufort, S.C., and was discharged in September at Paris Island, S.C. I was discharged by my surgeon because of an affliction of my left foot caused by a horse throwing me about four years before my enlistment. I served under the name of Jacob McAllister. There was no other man in my company with that same name.[223]

---

[222] Civil War Pension Record for Emma Thomas (widow of Sheck Thomas alias Jacob McAllister), Private, WC# 675.831; Company K, 128th USCI, Records of the VA, RG 15, NARA, WDC; 1900 U.S. Federal Census, South Carolina, Orangeburg County, Pine Grove Township, ED: 70, Page: 183A, Line: 64 (Roll: T623-1538).

[223] Deposition of Sheck Thomas, case of Jacob McAllister (Lone Star, Calhoun, SC), dated 29 Aug 1901.

Sheck T. Thomas alias Jacob McAllister

My father was named Aleck Thomas and my mother was Sarah Thomas. My parents are both dead now. I have four living brothers – Abram, Shedrick, Aleck and Samson Thomas, all of this county, and three sisters who also live in this county.

At enlistment I took the name of Jacob McAllister - in this way. I fancied the name McAllister for I had somewhere heard of it and told the recruiting officer to put me down as Sheck McAllister on his paper. At first roll call I did not answer to my name because they called out Jacob McAllister. The sergeant came up to me and asked me about the matter and I told him I wanted the name of Sheck and McAllister. Pretty soon one of the big officers came around to me and requested me to answer to the name of Jacob McAllister for they had already gotten it down that way and did not want to change it. So I answered to name of Jacob McAllister ever afterward. I did so at the request of that officer and for no other reason. After I was discharged I took the name of my father and have since been known by that name and none other – that is, the name of Sheck Thomas.[224]

Emily Thomas (Widow of the Veteran Soldier)
Date: 09 Jul 1909
Residence: Lone Star, Calhoun, SC

I don't know my age, but I am nearly 70. I am the widow of Sheck Thomas alias Jacob McAllister who was a soldier and a pensioner. I claim pension as his widow. My correct name is Emily but most people call me Emma. I was born and raised in Orangeburg County and have lived in and near here all of my life. I was owned by Mr. John Sellers and Sheck was owned by Mr. Zimmerman. I was first owned by Mr. Adam Shirer and when he died I was sold to Mr. Sellers.

Before I ever had a husband I went by the name of Emily Shirer. The first man I ever lived with was Daniel Peston. I was not married to him but went to live with him during the war – before freedom come – and we had been together less than a year when the soldiers came by our

---

[224] Testament (hand written on plain paper) of Sheck Thomas to the Department of Interior, Bureau of Pension, dated 29 Aug 1901.

place and took him off. Cuffie Kei{t} and Bo{z} Holman went off with him, and when they came back home they told me he had died. I can't recall the place of death, but he died in this state – before they got to North Carolina. I don't think and never heard that he ever enlisted or joined the army. I have never put a claim for pension on his account.

I had one child by him – born after he left. He never came back after he left with the soldiers and I have never seen nor lived with him since freedom. I never married nor lived with a man after he died until I had Sheck Thomas. I knew Sheck before the war. I knew when he went off during the war and when he came back because they would not keep him. He never had a wife until he had me.

The year after he came home from the army he and I took up and went together as man and wife. That was at an old house 12 to 15 miles from here, and then about 2 years after, we came down here and were married by Rev. Prioleau. He married us in our house. We lived together from the time we first went together until he died in February – five years ago this month.[225]

May Durant (Son-in-Law of the Veteran Soldier)
Date: 06 Aug 1920
Residence: Lone Star, Calhoun, SC

Dear Sirs: I write to ask, what disposition you are going to make of the last check sent to Emily Thomas? The check came here this week but, I, not understanding the matter, did not take it. Emily Thomas died in my house July 31, 1920, 8:00 p.m.

I am Emily Thomas' son-in-law, having married her oldest daughter, Phillis Thomas-Durant, who also died two weeks ago leaving five children. Emily Thomas burial expenses is $120.00, and as I am already burdened with the burial expenses of my wife, I was thinking that you may be able to arrange for the last check to be used in helping to pay Emily Thomas' burial expenses, as I am old and already hard pressed. Should you wish to

---

[225] Deposition of Emily Thomas, case of Emily Thomas (Lone Star, Calhoun, SC), dated 09 Jul 1909.

Sheck T. Thomas alias Jacob McAllister

know more about the matter, write Probate Judge of Calhoun County: C. Zeagler, Magistrate at Lone Star, S.C. or the Post Master. Kindly let me hear from you at once. Very truly yours, [his signature] May Durant.[226]

Harry Dickson (Comrade and Friend of the Veteran Soldier)
Date: 29 Aug 1901
Residence: Raymond, Orangeburg, SC
Occupation: Farmer

I am 68 years old. I served as a private in Company K, 128th U.S. Colored Infantry regiment. I enlisted in about 1864 and was mustered out in 1865. I served under the name of Henry Livingston.

I have known Sheck Thomas since we served together in the same regiment. I did not know him prior to our enlistment. I got acquainted with him at Beaufort, S.C., while we were drilling. We slept in the same tent and belonged to the same mess from that time until Sheck was discharged. He was discharged before I was. Since our service together we have lived in the same county and have seen each other often.

Sheck went by the name of Jacob McAllister while serving in Company K, 128th U.S. Colored Infantry. I knew him then by that name only and so did our comrades. I don't know where he got the name of Jacob McAllister from. I don't know why he changed his name after he was discharged.

He once told me that the white people were no longer his masters and he was not going to bear their name. Soon after the war ended he began to call himself Sheck Thomas and the name stuck to him.[227]

(Last Will and Testament of Sheck T. Thomas)
Date: 30 Dec 1902
Residence: Orangeburg, Orangeburg, SC

---

[226] Letter from May Durant, Lone Star, Calhoun, SC to Department of the Interior, Bureau of Pensions, Washington, DC, dated 06 Aug 1920.

[227] Deposition of Harry Dickson, case of Jacob McAllister (Orangeburg, Orangeburg, SC), dated 29 Aug 1901.

Know all men by these presents that this is my last Will and Testament. In the name of God, Amen.

I Sheck T. Thomas, farmer, in the County of Orangeburg, and State of South Carolina, being of sound and disposing mind and memory, and calling to mind the precautions of life, do make, ordain and publish this my last Will and Testament in the following manner:

My Will is that all just debts shall by my Executors be paid out of my estate as soon after my death as practicable.

I give and bequeath to my beloved wife, Emily Thomas, my house and tract of land, containing forty-nine (49) acres, more or less, for her life time, and after her death to my daughter, Phillis Thomas Durant, or to her children, in the event of her death.

I give and bequeath to my daughter, Adeline Thomas Johnson, the "Spigener" Tract of land, containing fifty (50) acres, more or less.

I give and bequeath to my daughter, Josephine Thomas Sanders, the "Zeagler" Tract of land, containing fifty-one (51) acres, more or less.

I give and bequeath to my daughter, Simsie Thomas Riley, about one hundred and thirteen (113) acres, of my "Caw Caw" Tract of land, on the side adjoining the "Swinney" Tract of land.

I give and bequeath to my step-son, Preston Thomas, one hundred (100) acres of my "Caw Caw" Tract of land, that contains most of my woodland.

I give and bequeath unto my aforesaid daughters, Phillis, Adeline and Josephine each, fifty (50) acres of my "Caw Caw" Tract of land.

And the remaining portion of my "Caw Caw" Tract of land to be sold by my son, Sheck D. Thomas, and the proceeds from said tract to be applied to my debt. In the event that the proceeds shall be more than enough to satisfy my debts, the balance shall be given by him to my beloved wife, Emily Thomas.

I give and bequeath to my son, Sheck D. Thomas, one lot and building thereon in the town of Crestor, S.C., known as my

Sheck T. Thomas alias Jacob McAllister

Hotel Lot, also one-half (½) of the lot adjoining said lot, to be cut off next to the "Hotel" lot. And I also give and bequeath to my son, Sheck D. Thomas, all my "Tindle" Tract of land, containing about three hundred and seven (307) acres, more or less.

I give and bequeath unto my aforesaid daughter, Simsie, my other one and one-half lot of buildings thereon in the town of Creston, S.C.

I give and bequeath unto my daughter, Phillis, my lot in the town of Lone Star, S.C., being the nearest lot I own to 3rd St.

I give and bequeath to my daughter, Josephine, my lot in the town of Lone Star, S.C., being the lot nearest to second St. That I own.

I give and bequeath to my daughter, Adeline, my lot in the town of Lone Star, S.C., being the nearest lot I own to 1st St.

It is my desire that my children shall maintain and keep my beloved wife, Emily, comfortably provided as long as she may live.

Balance of my estate, all the rest of my estate, both real and personal or mixed, of which I shall die seized and possed(sp), or to which I shall be entitled at the time of my decease, shall be sold and applied first to any debt that I may justly owe, and after my debts are satisfied, then to be equally divided between my heirs.

And, lastly I do nominate and appoint Sheck T. Thomas and May Durant as Executors of this my last Will and Testament. In testimony whereof I set my hand & seal this 30th day of December Anno Domini, 1902, and in the One Hundred and Twenty-seventh year of the Soverity and Independence of the United States of America.

Signed, Sealed and Delivered, In the presence of us: Thomas E. Whaley, Frank Simpson, Isah Wright.[228]

---

[228] Last Will and Testament of Sheck Thomas (Orangeburg, Orangeburg, SC), dated 30 Dec 1902.

Alex TRAPIER
alias
Elick Trapier

Private, Company F: Born during Jun 1846, at Sampit, Georgetown, SC; a Slave of William Dorsey; Enlisted on 27 Mar 1865, at Georgetown, Georgetown, SC; Medically Discharged on 26 Jul 1865, at Beaufort, Beaufort, SC. Marriage to Louisa Skelly (d. 15 Mar 1893, Sampit, Georgetown, SC), by Parris Harrison. Children: Mrs. Elizabeth Duncan (b. 02 Apr 1872); Alex Trapier (b. 12 May 1874); Mrs. Isabella {Doby} (b. 06 Nov 1884); Mrs. Mary (Gaskey} (b. 10 Aug 1886); and {Jakey} (b. 01 Apr 1893). **Alex Trapier** *died on 31 Jul 1913, at Sampit, Georgetown, SC.*[229]

Alex Trapier (Veteran Soldier)
Date: 025 Oct 1909
Residence: Georgetown County, SC

State of South Carolina, Georgetown County
Personally appeared before me, Alex Trapier, and made oath, that the bible in which my age was recorded was destroyed by fire about ten years ago and that is why I do not know the exact day in Jun in the year 1846 I was born. Alex Trapier
Sworn before me, October 20, 1909
A.J. Tilton, Magistrate[230]

---

[229] Civil War Pension Record for Alex Trapier alias Elick Trapier, SC No. C-2.487.630, Pvt, Company F, 128th USCI, Records of the VA, RG 15, NARA, WDC; 1900 U.S. Federal Census, South Carolina, Georgetown County, Gourdin Township, ED: 46, Page: 36B, Line: 65 (Roll: T623-1528).

[230] Affidavit of Alex Trapier (Georgetown County, SC), dated 25 Oct 1909.

Alex Trapier alias Elick Trapier

Alex Trapier, Jr. (Son of the Veteran Soldier)
Date: 07 Oct 1913
Residence: Sampit, Georgetown, SC

Sir: Your claim for reimbursement in the case of Alex Trapier, Certificate No. 1.133.026, is rejected on the ground that the pensioner left assets consisting of real estate valued at $50; sufficient to meet the approvable expenses of his last sickness and burial.

Your charges in this case are $56.60, but of this amount the charge of $32 for merchants' supplies is not approval, for the reason that such items are held not to have been due to nor the result of the pensioner's last sickness and burial. Deducting this amount leaves the approvable charges of $24.60, but as this amount is covered by the assets left by the pensioner, the accrued pension cannot be paid to any one for any purpose.

The above action is, however, subject to your right of appeal to the Secretary of the Interior, if the same be taken within a year from date hereof. Very Respectfully, G.M. Saltzgaber, Commissioner.[231]

---

[231] Letter from the Commissioner of the Board of Review, Office of the Secretary of the Interior, to Mr. Alex Trapier, Jr., 7 RFD No. 1, Sampit, Georgetown County, SC, dated 07 Oct 1913.

Stephen VIRENE
alias
Stephen Ward

Private, Company A: Born during Mar 1844, at Brook Green, Georgetown, SC; a Slave of Joshua Ward; Enlisted on 27 Mar 1865, at Beaufort, Beaufort, SC; Honorably Discharged on 10 Oct 1866, at Morris Island, Charleston, SC. Married to Catherine Conyers (b. c1851, Brook Green, Georgetown, SC; d. 08 Jun 1916, Charleston, SC), on 22 Oct 1872, at Charleston, SC, by Reverend W.D. Middleton. Children: Paris (b. 03 Nov 1874); and Lucille (b. 12 Aug 1876). **Stephen Virene** *died on 06 Mar 1913, at Charleston, Charleston, SC.*[232]

Stephen Virene (Veteran Soldier)
Date: 11 Dec 1906
Residence: #17 Queen St., Charleston, Charleston, SC

I think I am about 63 of age. I am the Stephen Virene who is claiming pension under the name of Stephen Ward, for I served in Company A, 128th U.S. Colored Infantry. I was born and raised in Georgetown County on the Waccamaw River and was owned by Josh Ward and lived with him until I went into the army. I was mustered out on Morris Island and come into Charleston and have lived here ever since.

Before I went in the army I was called Virene by the colored people and Ward by the white people, and when I joined the army the officer asked me the name of my owner and put me down as in his name

---

[232] Civil War Pension Record for Catherine Virene (widow of Stephen Virene alias Stephen Ward), WC No. 761.998, Pvt, Company A, 128th USCI, Records of the VA, RG 15, NARA, WDC; 1910 U.S. Federal Census, South Carolina, Charleston County, Charleston – Ward 3, ED: 22, Page: 76A, Line: 27 (Roll: T624-1452).

Stephen Virene alias Stephen Ward

(Ward), but when I mustered out I took back my father's name of Virene and have gone by that name ever since.

I claim pension on account of lung disease, shortness of breath and stomach trouble and general debility. For several years before I put in for a pension I worked on the docks loading ships (at Charleston) as they came in, but about the time I put in for my first claim I began to weaken and before I put in my last claim I had to give up that work a short time before Mr. Minges filed my last claim in August 1904. Just before I put in that claim I had a spell of diarrhea that lasted me for over two months. Dr. Jackson attended me all the time but could not stop it. I had never had it before but have it several times since.

I married my present wife, Catherine, with whom I now live, in 1872. Her maiden name was Conyers, and neither of us had been married before and neither had ever lived with anyone else and she had not had a child before she married me. She was born in the same place where I was born and was brought here (at Charleston) by her aunt at the close of the war. I found her here when I was mustered out of the army.[233]

Catherine Virene (Wife of the Veteran Soldier)
    Date: **11 Dec 1906**
    Residence: **Charleston, Charleston, SC**

My age is about 55 and I am the wife of Stephen Virene. I married Stephen in 1872 and have lived with him ever since. He and I were both owned by Colonel Josh Ward, on the Waccamaw River in Georgetown, S.C., before the war.

I can remember when Stephen and the others went off during the war to join the army. Before he went we called him Stephen Virene but while he was in the army he wrote to his mother and told her where he was and that she must write to him as Stephen Ward, as that was the name he was going by in the army.

At the close of the war my aunt brought me here and I met Stephen here about that time. I think he had just been mustered out because he had on soldier clothes, and from what I saw and from what I heard at home and after I came here I know that he was a soldier.[234]

---

[233] Deposition of Stephen Virene, case of Stephen Virene (Charleston, Charleston, SC), dated 11 Dec 1906.
[234] Ibid. Catherine Virene.

Cyrus WHALEY
alias
Cyrus Vaily

Private, Company I: Born c1834, at South Edisto Island, Charleston, SC; a Slave of Benjamin Whaley; Enlisted on 08 Mar 1865, at Beaufort, Beaufort, SC; Honorably Discharged on 10 Oct 1866, at Morris Island, Charleston, SC. 1st Marriage to Charlotte Griffin (d. c1887), c1859, at Edisto, Charleston, SC, by Rev. Caesar Small. Children: Mrs. Charlotte Griffin. 2nd Marriage to Elsie Ellington, c1903/05, local Magistrate. **Cyrus Whaley** *died on 17 Nov 1908, at Goose Creek, Charleston, SC.*[235]

Cyrus Whaley (Veteran Soldier)
Date: 14 Oct 1902
Residence: #145 Calhoun St., Charleston, Charleston, SC
Occupation: Unemployed (Incapacitated)

I am 68 years of age as near as I can tell. My full and correct name is Cyrus Whaley (It is difficult to determine, from the way he pronounces his name whether it is Whaley or Vaily – Special Examiner). My father's name was John Brown. My mother's name was Emma Brown. Cyrus Frasier was my old time name. Just how I got that name I can hardly tell. The boys in my neighborhood called me Frasier when I was a boy, and that name still stick to me out in the Ashley Phosphate-Goose Creek community, but my owner's name was Ben Whaley and that is the name I have been known by and gone by since I have grown up.

---

[235] Civil War Pension Record for Cyrus Whaley alias Cyrus Vaily, SC No. C-527.097, Pvt, Company I, 128th USCI, Records of the VA, RG 15, NARA, WDC.

Cyrus Whaley alias Cyrus Vaily

I was born on Edisto Island, Charleston County, S.C., and I have resided in this county all my life. I was with my owner at Goose Creek when the recruiting officers picked me up and brought me here to Charleston and put me in the guard house and then they took me to Hilton Head Island, S.C., where they had a great way many colored men they wanted to make soldiers. They brought us in from Hilton Head Island to Beaufort, S.C. where they searched us and separated the good from the bad. They examined me at Beaufort and found that I was "good" and I was sworn in and assigned to the regiment they were forming Company I, 128th U.S. Colored Infantry.

As soon as the regiment was organized we marched to Gillionsville, Hampton County, S.C., where we remained about one month, and then back to Beaufort and from Beaufort to Morris Island until muster out. We were not in any battles.

My captain's name was [James C.] Rundlett. My 1st lieutenant was O.P. Boyd. My 2nd lieutenant was [George] Keef. Samuel Ferguson, Dennis Floyd, Clarence Palmer and Thomas Lasty, all of Charleston, S.C., served with me in Company I of the 128th U.S. Colored Infantry. My tent mates were Billy Singleton, Ward Bennett, Sammy Brown and James Brown. They came from Cooper River. I don't know where they live now.

After discharge I went back to Goose Creek and resided there until February 1901 when I came to Charleston and then resided there from then to the present time. I was not in the hospital but I was sick once with some kind of bump in my head. I don't know what the doctors called it but I had sort of aches in my head for about two days. Then I had cramp in my arms and hands for 3 or 4 days. I was on detached duty here in Charleston for about one week, guarding the jail. A half dozen of my comrades came over from Sullivans Island to guard the jail and I was one of them.[236]

---

[236] Deposition of Cyrus Whaley, case of Cyrus Whaley (Charleston, Charleston, SC), dated 14 Oct 1902.

Isaac WHITE
alias
Isaac Lester

Private, Company F: Born c1841, at Georgetown, Georgetown, SC; a Slave of William Lester; Enlisted on 27 Mar 1865, at Georgetown, SC; Disability Discharge on 25 Sep 1865, at Hilton Head, Beaufort, SC. Married Betsy {Booby} (b. Johns Island, Charleston, SC), during 1867, at Mt. Pleasant, Charleston, SC, by Rev. Scott. Children: Abraham (b. 1878); and, Julia (b. 1880). ***Isaac White*** *died 24 Nov 1901, Stono, Charleston,, SC.*[237]

Isaac White (Veteran Soldier)
Date: 17 Oct 1901
Residence: Johns Island, Charleston, SC
Occupation: Farmer

I was born in Georgetown, S.C., a slave to a man by the name of William Lester, and that is why I am sometimes called Lester. He lived 10 miles from Georgetown. My father's name was Prince White and his master's name was Hugh S. Thompson. The name of White was selected by my father with the permission of his master.

I enlisted in Georgetown, S.C., in Company F, 128th U.S. Colored Infantry Regiment. I can't tell how old I was at enlistment but I call myself about 63 years old. I was recruited by a man named Woods from Ohio. He said my pay would be $16 per month and if I stayed three years

---

[237] Civil War Pension Record for Betsy White (widow of Isaac White alias Isaac Lester), WC No. 553.472, Private, Company F, 128th USCI, Records of the Veteran's Administration, RG 15, NARA, WDC; 1900 U.S. Federal Census, Charleston County, Johns Island, ED: 123, Page: 105A, Line: 45 (Roll: T623-1521).

I would get a bounty of $300.00. He sent me to Hilton Head and General [Milton S.] Littlefield swore me in.

I was examined. I was stripped naked and made to run about the room. I was in service from March till the following December – I think it was. I was discharged at Hilton Head, S.C. This was the only service I had in the U.S. Army. I was with my master, Mr. Lester, in the Confederate Army as a waiter. I was a servant to him during most of the war. I was not a soldier in the Confederate Army and never carried any arms – only worked for my master.

During my service in the U.S. Army I was frequently detailed to unload coal at Lands End, S.C. I was often detailed to the saw mill after lumber to be used about the camp. I would only be gone from the camp a day or so at a time. Sometimes Sergeant Cage Clark would go with us on the details and sometimes Sergeant William Emory would go.

When I was discharged I went back to Georgetown and lived there about 6 months and then came back to Charleston and have lived near Charleston ever since. I lived at Mt. Pleasant, in this county, for about years, but I have not lived at Mt. Pleasant for 15 years.

My tent mates were Monday Bryan and Snow Flagg. I was in hospital No. 4 at Beaufort. I went to the hospital on account of a cold I had contacted. I stayed in the hospital about a month then went back to the camp but answered sick call every morning until was discharged for disability. I had pneumonia in the hospital and it left me with a pain in left side and I was discharged by General Littlefield.

I was a waiter with my boss when I enlisted. I get a pension of $6.00 per month under the Act of June 27, 1890. My witnesses in my claim were Scipio Johnson, Moses Gallant, and Archie Geddes. Archie Geddes is sometimes called Jenkins. I was not a witness for any of them.

Moses Gallant and Scipio Johnson swore they were in the same company with me and that I was discharged for disability. Moses was called Wilson by his home folks. Archie Geddes swore that he had known me ever since I came out of the army.[238]

---

[238] Deposition of Isaac White alias Lester, case of Isaac White alias Lester (Charleston, Charleston, SC), dated 17 Oct 1901.

Jupiter WHITE
alias
Jupiter Gardner

Private, Company G: Born during Feb 1839, at St. Simons Island, Glynn, GA; a Slave of the Postells; Enlisted on 08 Mar 1865, at St. Simon Island, Glynn, GA; Honorably Discharged on 12 Jan 1867, at Charleston, Charleston, SC. Married to Queen Victoria Merchant, during 1868, at St. Simons Island, GA, by Rev. Jack Dent. Children: Floyd (b. 06 Jun 1873); Willard (b. 17 Dec 1875); Lurina (b. 28 Oct 1876); Arthur (b. 13 Feb 1885); and Estella (b. 15 Jun 1892). **Jupiter White** *died on 24 Apr 1910, at St. Simons Island, Glynn, GA.*[239]

Jupiter White (Veteran Soldier)
Date: 07 Jan 1903
Residence: St. Simons Mills, Glynn, GA
Occupation: Farmer

I am 65 years of age. I was born right here on this island of St. Simons and was owned by the Postells. My father was {Ruben} White. I hardly know how I got the name of Jupiter Gardner in service, but I think my grandfather's father was a Gardner. I served during the War of the Rebellion in Company G, 128th U.S. Colored Volunteer Infantry.

I enlisted in Beaufort, S.C., but I cannot give the year or month and was in the army for about 2 years. This was my only service in the Army or Navy of the United States. After enlistment at Beaufort they took us to

---

[239] Civil War Pension Record for Victoria White (widow of Jupiter White afterward known as Jupiter Gardner), WC No. 709.787, Pvt, Company G, 128th USCI, Records of the VA, RG 15, NARA, WDC; 1900 U.S. Federal Census, Georgia, Glynn County, St. Simon's Island, ED: 37, Page: 139A, Line: 18 (Roll: T623-200).

Jupiter White alias Jupiter Gardner

Pocotaligo and then to Morris Island and to Sullivan's Island and then to Charleston. I was discharged at Charleston. We were never in any battle but was in a skirmish at Pocotaligo and Morris Island. No men were ever killed out of my Company. I was never wounded or sick in service. I was always on duty.

Peter King, Isaac Owens and Joe Hilliard ate and slept with me in service. After the war they wanted me to join the regular army but I said I could not do it and I returned here and have been here ever since.

I have only been married once. I married Queen Victoria Merchant. We were married the 3rd year after the war. We were married by Justice of the Peace Gould. We were married right here and my wife was never married before I married her.

Only one of my children is under 16 years of age – Estella. She was born in April 1892.[240]

Jupiter White (Veteran Soldier)
Date: 07 Jan 1903 (Supplement)
Location: St. Simon's Mills, Glynn, GA

I was in jail once while I was in Charleston during my service in the army. I was taken off of guard one morning and carried straight to jail with a number of others. I do not know now why I was arrested and put in jail. I was with the other men. I can't tell you why they were arrested. I think I was in jail about 2 months. When I was taken out of jail I was taken to Castle Pinckney and a month or six weeks. I was sent over to Charleston and got my discharge and pay. My regiment had been mustered out near a month or more when I was discharged.[241]

---

[240] Deposition of Jupiter Gardner alias Jupiter White, case of Jupiter Gardner alias Jupiter White (St. Simons, Glynn, GA), dated 07 Jul 1903. Note: The 128th U.S.C. Infantry Regiment mustered out of service on October 10th 1866, but Private Jupiter White was discharged on January 2nd 1867.
[241] Ibid., Supplement.

Charles WILLIAMS
alias
Charles Owens

Corporal, Company H: Born c1842, in Colleton County, SC; a Slave of William or Clarence Owens; Enlisted on 07 Mar 1865, at Beaufort, SC; Honorably Discharged on 10 Oct 1866, at Morris Island, Charleston, SC. Married to Eliza Owens (b. c1843; d. 05 May 1911, Elko, Barnwell, SC), on 15 Oct 1860, in St. Peters Church, Elko, Barnwell, SC, by Rev. James W. Talbert. Children: John (b. c1863); Carrie (b. c1864); and James Samuel (b. Nov 1880). Charles Williams died on 10 Aug 1889, at Elko, Barnwell, SC.[242]

Eliza Williams (Widow of the Veteran Soldier)
Date: 05 Feb 1900
Residence: Elko, Barnwell, SC

My age is about 57. I am the legal widow of Charles Williams who served in Company H, 128th U.S. Colored Troops as Charles Owens.

Before the war we were both owned by Mr. William Owens of Colleton County, S.C. We took each other for husband and wife before the war when we were nothing but children. I had three children by him before he went in the army. Neither one of us had ever been married before. He ran away and joined the army just before freedom and was gone about one year and ten months. He never was away before nor since, therefore, I know that he was only in the service that one time.

---

[242] Civil War Pension Record for Eliza Williams, widow of Charles Williams alias Charles Owens, WC No. 492.133, Pvt, Company H, 128th USCI, Records of the VA, RG 15, NARA, WDC; 1880 U.S. Federal Census, South Carolina, Barnwell County, Wiliston Township (Elko Town), ED: 27, Page: 341, Line: 21 (Roll: T623-1518).

Charles Williams alias Charles Owens

When he came home he told me he had served as a Corporal in Company H, 128th and he had his soldier's clothes and discharge papers. He has since lost his discharge papers. We lived near our old house for about a year and then moved up here. I have been here since and soldier was here with me until he died.

After we came here we were married over again by Reverend James Talbert. We were married in the local church right here one Saturday night. Soldier and I lived as man and wife from the day he came home from the army until the day he died and I nursed him up to the last and he died in my house. He died twelve years ago last August. I have not remarried nor lived with a man since and I have not had a child. I have lived right here with my children ever since my husband died.

He was a preacher and had charge of the church here for years. We were married over again and then he married a number of people around here over again. We had thirteen children in all. The youngest one living when soldier died was James Samuel Williams. He was born in November 1880. I have no record of that but I remember the date. He was the only one under sixteen when I applied for pension.

Soldier went by the name of Charles Williams after he came out of the army, but during slavery and during the war he went by the name of Owens. Owens was his master's name and Williams was his father's name. My two oldest living children were born during the war before Charles ran away and they are about 37 and 36 years old.

I do not own any property nor income except this little place of 1/4 of an acre, worth about $100.[243]

Duncan Williams (Son of the Veteran Soldier)
Date: 05 Feb 1900
Residence: Elko, Barnwell, SC

I am 36 Years of age. Eliza Williams is my mother and her late husband, Charles Williams, was my father. I know that I am 36 for I have kept my age ever since I was a child. My father and mother lived as man and wife

---

[243] Deposition of Eliza Williams, case of Eliza Williams (Elko, Barnwell, SC), dated 05 Feb 1900.

from the time I can remember until my father died in August 1887. They were never divorced nor separated. I was present when my father died.

My mother has lived with us ever since 1887 and I know that she has not remarried nor lived with a man. When my father died he left this place of 1/4 of an acre and this little house, worth about $100 to my mother and two acres of land to us children. He did not own anything else and my mother has nothing except what he left her.[244]

Jerry Wallace (Friend of the Veteran Soldier)
Date: 09 Mar 1896
Residence: Hendersonville, Colleton, SC

I am aged 52 years. I have known Eliza and Charles Owens all of my life. We belonged to the same owner, Clarence Owens, and lived on the same place before the war. Clarence Owens married Charles Owens to Eliza before the war commenced and they lived together until Charles went to war. When Charles came out of the army he went back to her and took her from the place where we were all living to Walterboro to be remarried and when he came back he told me he was married to Eliza by one Reverend J.W. Talbert. They lived together up to his death and Eliza has never been remarried since. She has nothing with which to support herself other than her labor and she is not in good health.

The statement above was made by me to J.F. Brown (Notary Public) at White Hall, S.C., March 9th 1896, who reduced to writing in my presence. In making these statements I was not aided or prompted by any written or printed statement or recital prepared or directed by any other person and attached as an exhibit to this testimony.[245]

Nellie Wilson (Mother of the Veteran Soldier)
Date: 18 Apr 1896
Residence: Elko, Barnwell, SC

---

[244] Ibid. Duncan Williams.
[245] General Affidavit of Jerry Wallace, in the matter of Eliza Owens, widow of Charles Owens (Colleton County, SC), dated 09 Mar 1896.

Charles Williams alias Charles Owens

Nellie Wilson declares that she is aged 75 years; that she knows Eliza Owens and did, to the time of his death, know Charles Owens; that they were man and wife and lived together as such up to the time of the death of Charles Owens; that there is no public record of the marriage of Eliza Owens and that the law of this state does not require any record to be kept; that Charles Owens was a slave up to the time of his running away and joining the Union Army; and that he died in August A.D. 1887, and that deponent knows the above to be true of her own knowledge; that the deponent and Eliza Owens having been slaves are unable to read or write. I have not been aided by any person in making this statement and it is made solely from my own knowledge.[246]

James Williams (Son of the Veteran Soldier)
Date: 18 Apr 1912
Residence: Elko, Barnwell, SC
Occupation: Farmer

I am 31 years of age. I am the son of Eliza Williams, who was a pensioner of the United States, and who lived with me. My mother died May 5, 1911 at her home, near Elko. She did not leave any children under 16 years of age at date of her death.[247]

---

[246] Ibid., Nellie Wilson, dated 18 Apr 1896.
[247] Deposition of James Williams, case of Eliza Williams (Elko, Barnwell, SC), dated 18 Apr 1912.

William C. WILLIAMS
alias
Cuyler McCall

Private, Company A: Born on 22 Jun 1846, Savannah, Chatham, GA; a Slave of Phillip McCall; Enlisted on 08 Mar 1865, at Beaufort, Beaufort, SC; Honorable Discharge on 10 Oct 1866, Morris Island, SC. 1st Marriage to Eliza Vormick (d. 15 Aug 1882, Woodsville, Chatham, GA). Children: James Adolphus (b. 31 Oct 1875). 2nd Marriage to Mary J. Kyles (b. c1850; d. 24 May 1926). **William C.** *Williams died on 20 Sep 1902, at Savannah, Chatham, GA.*[248]

Mary J. Williams (Widow of the Veteran Soldier)
Date: 02 Jan 1905
Residence: #47 St. Gaul St., Savannah, Chatham, GA
Occupation: Laundress

I am 52 years of age. My maiden name was Mary J. Kyles. My father was Abram Kyles. My mother was Clarinda Kyles. I was born in Jefferson County, Ga., and resided there with my owner, Mr. Henry McAlpin, until freedom when I came to Savannah and have resided there ever since. When I was 17 years of age and employed as a servant in the home of Dr. Schley, I had a child by Alvin Miller. I was never married to Miller and never lived with him.

Two years after I had the child by Miller I had a child by Robert Irvine, who was a married man who roomed with me covering a period of three years. During those three years I was employed as a servant and

---

[248] Civil War Pension Record for Mary J. Williams (widow of William C. Williams alias Cuyler Mackall), Pvt, WC No. 604.470; Company A, 128th USCI, Records of the VA, RG 15, NARA, WDC; 1900 U.S. Federal Census, Chatham County, Savannah, ED: 34, Page: 243A, Line: 33 (Roll: T623-185).

William C. Williams alias Cuyler McCall

Irvine spent the nights with me. I was not married to him and did not take his name. I had two children by Irvine. The last one was born in 1879. As a fact, I never lived with Irvine as his wife. I was a servant in the house of Henry McAlpin at his farm out of the city, for three years. Robert Irvine was a field hand on the McAlpin place and he came to my room and shared my bed at night but the McAlpins did not know that and no one knew it until my children were born and then I told them who the father was.

I was never married and never lived with any man, as wife, until my marriage to William C. Williams on November 19, 1884. We were married by Rev. Nesbit, Pastor of Bethlehem Church. Nesbit died many years ago. We were married at the home of my aunt, Julia Nichols, dead, on Prendergrast Street. Benjamin Houston and Sarah Wilson are the only living witnesses to my marriage. William and myself were never separated but lived together from the time of our marriage until his death which occurred here in Savannah, GA., on September 20, 1902. I have not remarried nor have I lived with any man since the death of my said husband. I have lived at 47 St. Gaul Street for 18 years. Phoebe Miller who has a stand at the market, and her child, and myself occupy the house. We have lived together two years. Before Phoebe Miller moved into the house with me, Frank Williams and his wife and three children lived in a part of the house.

I first knew William C. Williams in 1878. He told me that he belonged to Philip McCall in slavery time. He told me also, that he served in Company A, 128th U.S. Colored Infantry under the name Cuyler McCall. His full name was William Cuyler Williams and he served, so he told me, under the name of Cuyler McCall.

Scott Smith and Franklin Jones served in the army with my husband. Scott Smith used to visit my house when my husband was in life and from what Smith and my husband told me I know that Franklin Jones was in the same Company with them.

When he and I lived together he would go off and live with some other woman for two or three months at a time and then come back to me but I have heard of only two wives prior to his marriage to me. He resided in Savannah from the close of the war until his death. It is my understanding that he brought the first wife, Agnes, out of the army; that she was his army wife and that they lived together three or four years after the war. I never saw Agnes. I heard that she was living with another man when she died and that she died on Bryan Street, this city, and that is all I know about Agnes.

When I first et the soldier he was living with "Eliza" whom, I am informed, was his second wife. Eliza. She and I belonged to the same beneficial society and when she died the society, through Sarah Butler, Secretary, paid $100.00. Eliza died at 4 mile Hill, Woodsville, at the home of her sister, Jane Stephney. Isaac Vormick is Eliza's brother and can tell you all about Eliza. John White, Scott Smith and Louisa Anderson knew Agnes, the first wife, so they have informed me.[249]

Scott Smith (Comrade and Widow of the Veteran Soldier)
Date:　　　02 Jan 1905
Residence:　#634 Bryan St., Savannah, Chatham, GA
Occupation:　Laborer

I am 66 years of age. I served in Company A, 128th U.S. Colored Infantry under the name of Scott Brooker. I enlisted in March '65 and was discharged in October 1866. I first knew Cuyler McCall at enlistment. He served in my Company and I well knew him from enlistment until his death. He and I were neighbors and friends from discharge until his death 3 years ago. I attended his funeral. I knew him in the service as Cuyler McCall. After the war he was known as Cuyler Williams. He told me his father's name was Williams and that is the reason he took the name Williams after the war.

I first knew Mary J. Williams as the wife of Cuyler Williams, alias McCall. I visited claimant and her husband when they were living together and know that this claimant is the widow of Cuyler McCall who served in my Company. I have knowledge of her history prior to the time she began living with the soldier, but she has not remarried nor has she lived with any other man since his death, to my knowledge. I live with

---

[249] Deposition of Mary J. Williams, case of Mary J. Williams (Savannah, Chatham, Georgia), dated 02 Jan 1905.

William C. Williams alias Cuyler McCall

one block of her and frequently see her and I am certain that she has not taken up with any man since soldier died.

While were stationed at Grahamville, Beaufort, S.C., soldier was married to a woman named "Agnes." The ceremony was performed by [Mirand W.] Saxton, the Captain of our company. That was in 1865. Agnes was with the soldier and his regiment until Muster Out and they came here to Savannah, and lived together for a time. I do not know how long. I was in New York for a time right after the war and when I came back here in the Fall o 1869 I met Williams and he told me that Agnes was dead or that they had parted and I cannot now remember which statement he made, but or the other.

I never saw Agnes after 1868. Later Williams had a wife named "Eliza" but I saw her only a few times. I heard that Eliza died but I have no personal knowledge of her death. I was invited to Cuyler's wedding when he married this claimant but was working in the Swamp at the time and did not attend. I know from hear say that they were married by ceremony. Williams was a bad man and I don't know how many women he had.[250]

John White (Friend of the Veteran Soldier)
    Date: 04 Jan 1905
    Residence: #650 Cohen St., Savannah, Chatham, GA
    Occupation: Drayman

I am 62 years of age. I knew Cuyler McCall from the time we were small boys. He belonged to Phillip McCall. His father's name was Williams and Cuyler took the name of Williams after the war. He did not have a slave wife but he brought home from the Army a wife called "Agnes" and he and Agnes lived together as husband and wife in Waccamaw and my deceased wife and myself visited them and they visited us and they were known and recognized as husband and wife for five or six years, when they separated and she took up with another man and died a year or two later.

---

[250] Ibid., Scott Smith.

After Agnes died Cuyler was married to Eliza, by ceremony. Eliza died out at Woodsville prior to the time Cuyler began living with claimant. I do not know when and how the soldier and claimant were married. I only know that they lived together a number of years and that she has not remarried nor has she lived with any man since the death of the soldier.[251]

Isaac Vormick (Brother-in-Law of the Veteran Soldier)
    Date: 06 Jan 1905
    Residence: Bay St. & Styles Ave., Savannah, Chatham, GA
    Occupation: Laborer

I am 70 years of age. I first knew Cuyler Williams soon after the war. Some three or four years after the war he was married to my sister, Eliza Vormick. They were married here in Savannah in about 1870 and lived together some time then separated. They lived together several years and Eliza had two children by him and then he left her, and she took up with Isom Lawson and lived with him a year or two when she died.

Eliza died under the name of Williams. She died at Woodsville, within the city limits, and was buried at the New Hope Grave Yard. I bought the coffin from Dorsey, a colored undertaker, and carried her body to the New Hope Grave Yard, 10 miles from Savannah. No tombstone marks her grave and there is no record of burials in that country Grave Yard. The grave yard is on the old Holliday Plantation and all the colored people who lived in the community are buried there.

One of the children of Eliza and Cuyler is living, [James] Adolphus Williams, and he is between 20 and 30 years of age.[252]

Adolphus Williams (Son of the Veteran Soldier)
    Date: 08 Jan 1905
    Residence: #617 West Bryan St., Savannah, Chatham, GA
    Occupation: Laborer (at Merchants and Miners Docks)

---

[251] Ibid., John White, dated 04 Jan 1905.
[252] Ibid., Isaac Vormick, dated 06 Jan 1905.

William C. Williams alias Cuyler McCall

I am 30 years of age. William Cuyler Williams who died on September 20, 1902, was my father. Eliza Williams was my mother. My mother died on August 15, and was buried at the New Hope Grave Yard on August 16, 1882. I now exhibit to you a book in which was transferred by me from an old book my father had, which book was destroyed as it was falling to pieces. I was born on October 31, 1875. My father was born June 22, 1846. My mother, Eliza, died August 15, 1882. I well remember my mother and when she died.

I never heard that my father had a wife, Agnes, before he had my mother. He had only two wives, to my knowledge, my mother and this claimant, Mary J. Williams. My father was married to the claimant after the death of my mother. I did not witness the ceremony but know from hear say that they were married and I know that they lived together as husband and wife and that she has not remarried. My father and claimant were separated at time for two or three months at a time but they were never legally separated.[253]

---

[253] Ibid., Adolphus Williams, dated 08 Jan 1905.

Gabe WILSON
alias
David Spaulding

Private, Company E: Born on c1844, at Sapelo Island, McIntosh, GA; a Slave of Randolph Spaulding; Enlisted on 27 Feb 1865, at Beaufort, Beaufort, SC; Honorably Discharged on 10 Oct 1866, at Morris Island, Charleston, SC. Married to Mary Grant, on 20 Dec 1868, in McIntosh County, GA, by Rev. O'Neal (colored). Children: Glasco (b. c1870); Harriet (b. c1872); Charles (d. c1874); March (d. c1876); Hattie (d. c1880); Amelia (d. c1882); Duncan (d. c1885); Richard (d. c1888); and Ellen (d. c1891). **Gabe Wilson** *died on 19 Oct 1913, at St. Simons Island, Glynn, GA.*[254]

Gabe Wilson (Veteran Soldier)
Date: 05 Aug 1903
Residence: St. Simons Mill, Glynn, GA
Occupation: Farmer

I am 58 years of age and I am the David Spaulding who served as a private in Company E, 128 U.S. Colored Volunteer Infantry during the war of the rebellion and was pensioned at $8.00 a month under the Act of June 27, 1890.

I was born on Sapelo Island, Ga., the slave of Randolph Spaulding and I remained his slave until freedom. My young Missus, Mrs. McKinly, now lives where I was born. My father was named Cuffy Wilson. I titled after my owner until I came out of the army when I took the name

---

[254] Civil War Pension Record for Gabe Wilson alias David Spaulding, SC No. 981.902, Pvt, Company E, 128th USCI, Records of the VA, RG 15, NARA, WDC; 1900 U.S. Federal Census, Georgia, Glynn County, St. Simons Islands, ED: 37, Page: 128A, Line: 35 (Roll: T623-200).

of my father and have kept that name ever since. I am Gabe Wilson in all things except pension matters. The name David was given me by my mistake when I enlisted. I was never called David before I went in the army. In slavery I was Gabe from a baby until freedom. I am known now by no other name except Gabe Wilson. I was married under that name and vote under that name.

I enlisted in Beaufort, S.C. I can't give the date. It was in the spring or late winter. I had a naked medical examination. I had to run and squat and kick and open my mouth.

We first went to Charleston, thence to Fort Sumter. We remained there until we were sent over tow Morris Island to be discharged. I was with my company all the time and was never on detached duty. Since my discharge I lived on Sapelo Island until two years ago when I came here. I lost my original discharge.

[William M.] Beebe was my colonel and Dallas was major. I can't give the lieutenant colonel. I can't recall the surgeon. [Eugene L.] Barnes was my captain. I can't recall the lieutenant. Isaac Havens was [first]/ordnance sergeant. Abram Beaton and Minus McNeal were my tent mates.

I keep my own pension papers and I execute my quarterly vouchers before the Postmaster at my post office. I carry both papers. I never go before the 4th of month and he swears me each time and I pay him twenty-five cents.

I have been married but once. My wife died this 16th day of July [1903]. I have two children under age 16; Ellen – aged 12 and Richard – aged 13.[255]

---

[255] Deposition of David Spaulding, case David Spaulding (St. Simons Mill, GA), dated 05 Aug 1903.

William WINE
alias
William Lawton

Private, Company F: Born c1846, in Savannah, Chatham, GA; a Slave of the Lawtons; Enlisted on 28 Feb 1865, at Savannah, Chatham, GA; Disability Discharged on 15 Jun 1865, at Beaufort, Beaufort, SC. Married to Eugenia {Houzer} (d. 26 Sep 1897, Brighton, Hampton, SC), during Feb 1872, by Rev. George {Shuiasam}. Children: Laura (b. 01 Mar 1877); John (b. 01 Apr 1879; d. 06 Mar 1898); Henry Paul (b. 07 Aug 1881; d. 26 Nov 1901); Jane (b. 18 Sep 1886); and Molsey (b. 11 Dec 1888; d. 09 Sep 1898). **William Wine** *died on 03 Nov 1891, at Brighton, Hampton, SC.*[256]

Eugenia Wine (Widow of the Veteran Soldier)
Date: 03 Sep 1892
Residence: Brigton, Hampton, SC

Eugenia Wine declares that she is the widow of William Lawton alias William Wine; that her said husband enlisted in Company E, 128th U.S. Colored Troops under the name of William Lawton, the name Lawton being that of his master during his period of slavery; that he served under that name to June 1865 when he was honorably discharged and then assumed the name of William Wine, by which latter name he was generally known in the community in which he resided; that her said husband William Lawton alias William Wine, died at Brighton, County of Hampton, State of South Carolina on or about the 2nd day of September 1891, and that this affidavit is made for the purpose of perfecting and completing

---

[256] Civil War Pension Record for Jane Wine (minor of William Wine alias William Lawton), MC No. 457.682, Pvt, Company F, 128th USCI, Records of the VA, RG 15, NARA, WDC.

William Wine alias William Lawton

his pending claim for pension under the Act of June 27th 1890. That she was married to the said William Lawton alias William Wine during February 1872 at Brighton in the State of South Carolina;

That she had not been married; that her husband been previously married to a woman who died seven months after marriage; that she hereby makes application to complete her said husband's pending claim for pension. She hereby appoints, with full power of substitution and revocation, R.B. Donaldson and Company of Washington, D.C., her true and lawful attorney's to prosecute her claim, the fee to be ten dollars payable as prescribed by law; that her post-office address is Brighton, County of Hampton, State of South Carolina.[257]

Lawrence McKnight (Notary Public)
Date: 03 Oct 1892
Residence: Hampton County, SC

I, Lawrence McKnight, Notary Public, for the State of South Carolina, resident in the County of Hampton, do hereby certify to all whom it may concern, that in this the third day of October A.D. 1892, the book in which are recorded the father of children of William Lawton alias William Wine and his wife Eugenia was brought to me for examination and find the same to be the "Life of Christ" "printed and published by Case, Lockwood & {Brainard} – Hartford, Conn. 1869.

The corners of the book have been torn off ({as} {on} also a few of the {last} {leaves} but in other respects the book has been {considerably} well preserved. Opposite page 334 it should be page 335 is a blank page on which it is written as follows –

Belle	was born	Dec 10, 1872
Anna	"	Feb 19, 1875
Laura	"	March 1, 1877
John	"	April 1, 1879*
Henry Paul	"	Aug 7, 1879*

---

[257] General Affidavit of Eugenia Wine, in the matter of Eugenia Wine (Brighton, Hampton, SC), dated 03 Sep 1892.

~~Jane~~	"	~~Oct 9, 1886~~**
Jane	"	Sept 18, 1886
Mille	"	Dec 11, 1888

The erased line was evidently an attempt to record the birth of Jane by someone who could not give satisfaction and was erased and afterward recorded in a different handwriting. A part of the record is in ink and a part in pencil and has every appearance and, I believe, same {an} {gen} {wine} and {made} if not at the time of birth soon thereafter. When Dr. Walter W. Smith made a copy of birth he omitted "Bella" – she being dead to his knowledge. On reverse of page 335 is a picture "Destruction of the Temple foretold." I further certify by that I have no interest in said claim for pension nor concern in its prosecution.[258]

Walter W. Smith (Guardian of Minor)
Date: 09 Nov 1901
Residence: Brighton, Hampton, SC

I am 52 years of age. I am the guardian of Jane Wine, the minor of William Wine (deceased), and have charge of her person and estate. Her sole and only estate is her quarterly pension paid by the government to her, or to me as her guardian, on account of the services of her father, William Wine, as a private in Company E, 128th U.S. Colored Infantry during the War of the Rebellion and death.

I was appointed guardian of the persons and estate of the minors of William Wine, May 28, 1896 – by the Probate Court of Hampton County, S.C. There were three minors when I was appointed – Henry P., Jane and Molsey. Henry has past his 16th year, Molsey is dead and Jane, the only remaining one now living with her aunt, Mary Nix. She is well cared for and has a better home and comforts of life than other girls in her class.

---

[258] Certification made by Lawrence McKnight, Notary Public (Hampton County, SC), dated 03 Oct 1892. *Note: Undoubtedly an error between the dates of birth of John and Henry exist – being only four months apart. **Note: An entry for Jane was 'struck-through' in the original document.

William Wine alias William Lawton

I make an annual report to the Probate Court and to the Pension Bureau of my receipts and expenditures and I am not now behind with my reports. My reports have all been approved to date. I was very well acquainted with the father of these minors and helped in the preparation of the papers to procure the pension and I am satisfied that these minors are his legitimate heirs, born in wedlock, and that William Wine was the soldier as alleged in the declaration for pension.

William Wine formerly belonged to the Lawtons and I know that is where he got his name. The name Wine, he has held, I think, ever since the war. I do not know how he came about it. Many of the old slaves adopted new names of their own notion and abandoned their former name without apparent reason.

These are my pension papers. I have sent the voucher to Knoxville for the May [1901] payment. I keep these papers in my own possession and have never pledged them for money or thing

Tobias WRIGHT
alias
Cuffy Wright

Private, Company A: Born on c1840, at Kenningston Plantation, Ashley River, Charleston, SC; a Slave of Mr. Ingram then Mr. Ball; Enlisted on 07 Mar 1865, at Beaufort, Beaufort, SC; Honorably Discharged on 10 Oct 1866, at Morris Island, Charleston, SC. 1st Marriage to Sallie Bowen (d. 1867), during c1860. Children: George (b. c1862); and Judy (b. c1866). 2nd Marriage to Lucy Roberson, during Sep 1870, at Rice Hope, Nazareth Church, by Rev. Paul {Combs}. Children: {6} (b. c1882); {Peter} (b. c1887); {Lorraine} (b. c1889); Stephen (b. c1892); Annie (b. c1894); Mary (b. c1896); Isaiah (b. c1900) and Toby (b. c1902). **Tobias Wright** *died after Feb 1906, at Unknown.*[259]

Hannah Wright (*Alleged* Widow of the Veteran Soldier)
Date: 20 Feb 1895
Residence: Charleston, Charleston, SC
Occupation: Cook

I do not know my age but I am somewhere between 65 and 70 years old. I go by the name of Hannah Wright. I make my living by washing and odd jobs, and when I was able, I was a cook. I am entirely dependent without property or income of any kind and no one to take care of me. I am helped some by charity.

---

[259] Civil War Pension Record for Tobias Wright alias Cuffy Wright, SC No. C-2.481.042, Pvt, Company A, 128th USCI, Records of the VA, RG 15, NARA, WDC; 1880 U.S. Federal Census, South Carolina, Charleston (Berkeley) County, St. Johns Berkeley, ED: 88, Page: 267A, Line: 28 (Roll: T9-1223). Note: The application for Widow's Pension filed by Hannah Wright was rejected "on the ground that special examination shows that soldier is not dead, and for further reason that applicant is not the legal wife of soldier."

Tobias Wright alias Cuffy Wright

I was married to Cuffie Wright on the 17th of October 1865 at Beaufort, S.C., by Parson DeForrest; a Methodist preacher. My husband was then a member of Company A, 128th U.S. Colored Troops. I went with him some four or five months before we were married and we lived together in Beaufort. We were there about nine months when the regiment came here to Charleston to be mustered out. He sent me up here ahead of him coming up with the regiment.

He was stationed on Sullivans Island until muster out and during the time he was stationed there he would come over on furlough and see me. He was not here a great while before he was mustered out. He left me as soon as he was mustered out of the army saying that he was going up in Cooper River where he had formerly lived to get some land then he would come for me and that was the last I ever saw of him.

I never had any children by him, but I am the mother of eight children; four are living and four are dead and they were born before the war and by a white man who was the overseer of my owner. He was an Englishman and died in 1863. I have not had any children by any one since his death and I have not lived or cohabitated with any one since Cuffie left me. I supported myself after my husband left me by cooking and washing. I have not gone by any other name than Hannah Wright since my marriage in 1865.

Brown was my maiden name which was my father's name. My owner's name was Charles Waller of St. Johnsberg, Berkeley, S.C., and in Ashepoo Parish. My living children as follows:
Anna Holmes, somewhere in New York City; Grace Harding, somewhere in New York City; George Waller, 22 Spring St., Charleston, S,C.; and Charles {Snowden}, Six Mile House, Berkeley County, S.C. George is my owner's son and he is blind.

I do not know the date of the death of my husband of my own knowledge.[260]

---

[260] Deposition of Hannah Wright, case of Hannah Wright (St. James Settlement, Berkeley, SC), dated 20 Feb 1895. Note: The deposition attested to by Hannah Wright is in stark contrasts with the deposition prepared by Judy Segar (daughter of the veteran soldier).

Charles Hutson (Comrade of the Veteran Soldier)
Date: 23 Feb 1895
Residence: #137 Spring St., Charleston, Charleston, SC

I am 65 years old. I served in Company I, 128th U.S. Colored Troops. I enlisted March 7, 1865 at Hilton Head, S.C., and was discharged in the fall of 1866 at Morris Island, S.C. I knew Cuffy Wright prior to his enlistment either in Company A or B, 128th U.S. Colored Troops. I was present at his marriage to Hannah at Beaufort, S.C. It was in 1865 and we had been in the service about half a year prior to the marriage. They were married by a white minister and I do not remember his name.

I knew Hannah a long time before she was married. The last I saw them together was in 1867 at her home on Warren Street and I have not seen him since 1868. I do not know if he is dead or alive.[261]

Judy Segar (Daughter of the Veteran Soldier)
Date: 04 Apr 1895
Residence: St James Settlement, Berkeley, SC

I am 25 years old and I am the wife of Alex Segar. I am the daughter of Cuffie and Sallie Wright. My father and mother were owned by the Irving Family and they were married before the war by their owner, Dr. Irving. My father was in the army. I have no knowledge of his service. I am the third child born to him and my mother after he came out of the army. I was told that he came immediately here after his discharge from the army. He lived with my mother continuously up to her death about 12 years ago, after he came from the army. He left here soon after my mother's death and I heard two months ago he was alive at Georgetown, S.C., and living under the name of Toby Wright. I do not want you to mention this as he does not want anyone around here to know of his whereabouts. My brother George and myself are the only children of our parents alive. When father went away he left Benjamin, Annie, and {Jenny}. {Jenny} has since died. George was born before the war and is the oldest child.

---

[261] Ibid., Charles Hutson, dated 23 Feb 1895.

Tobias Wright alias Cuffy Wright

I do not know that I have heard my father speak of a woman as Hannah who did his washing while he was in the army and to whom he gave a house and lot at Beaufort, S.C., when he came out of the army. He never spoke of her as his wife. I have never seen her.[262]

Mr. R. J. Phillips (Acquaintance of the Veteran Soldier)
  Date: 04 Apr 1895
  Residence: Medway Plantation/Cordesville, Berkeley, SC
  Occupation: Housekeeper

I am 52 years old. I have lived in this vicinity all of my life. I know Cuffie Wright, who was a slave owned by the Irving Estate and since the war lived about a half mile from me. He had a wife while a slave, named Sallie, by whom he had some five or six children; some born before freedom and some since. Sallie Wright died about 12 years ago and while Cuffie resided in this neighborhood I do not know where he lives or whether he is alive. He stole some hogs from Mr. Naber Windom and to keep from being punished for the theft he ran away from the county and I do not think any of the white people knew anything of him or if he is alive. I do not know whether he was in the army or not.[263]

---

[262] Ibid., Judy Segar, (St. James Settlement, Berkeley, SC), dated 04 Apr 1895.
[263] Ibid., Mr. R.J. Phillips, (Medway Plantation, Berkeley, SC).

* * * * * * * * * * * * *

July YOUNG
alias
July Tenant

Private, Company H: Born on 11 Mar 1847, at St. James, Goose Creek Parish, Charleston, SC; a Slave of Dr. Charles Tenant; Enlisted on 11 Mar 1865, at Beaufort, Beaufort, SC; Disability Discharged on 01 Oct 1865, at Hilton Head, Beaufort, SC. Married to Sarah Lucinda Richardson (b. 05 Nov 1858, Brick Hope Plantation, near Goose Creek, Charleston, SC; d. 14 Oct 1937, Oakley, Berkeley, SC), on 31 May 1875, at Howe Hall Church, Goose Creek, SC, by Rev. S.W. Hazel, A.M.E. Children: Thomas (b. Feb 1876); Edward (b. 13 Apr 1880); Maggie Lucinda (b. 15 Feb 1882; d. bef 10 Apr 1915); Sarah Elizabeth (b. 20 Apr 1884; d bef 10 Apr 1915); Mrs. Fannie Watson (b. 20 Feb 1887); Joshua Augustus (b. 12 Jun 1889); Elijah Peter (b. 28 Jul 1891); Rebecca Eliza (b. 14 Nov 1893); Harriet Victoria (b. 29 Mar 1896); Harry James (b. 01 Jun 1898); and Mrs. Josephine Washington (b. 17 Oct 1902). **July Young** *died on 09 Oct 1922, at Oakley Depot, Berkeley, SC.*[264]

Marie Haynes Heyward (Friend of the Veteran Soldier)
Date: 22 Jan 1923
Residence: Oakley Depot, Berkeley, SC

Deponent, Marie Haynes Heyward, made oath that she has lived near Oakley Depot, Berkeley County, South Carolina, since her early childhood; that she knew July Tenant, generally known as July Young, and

---

[264] Civil War Pension Record for Sarah Lucinda Young (widow of July Tenant known as July Young), WC No. 928.928, Pvt, Company H, 128th USCI, Records of the VA, RG 15, NARA, WDC; 1900 U.S. Federal Census, South Carolina, Berkeley County, St. Johns Township, ED: 30, Page: 237B, Line: 98 (Roll: T623-1519).

July Young alias July Tenant

Sarah Lucinda Young for several years prior to October 17th 1902, up to the time of the death of the said July Young. That during all these years, the said July Young (or July Tenant) and the said Sarah Lucinda Young (whom deponent knew as "Lucinda Young") lived together as husband and wife, and were generally recognized as husband and wife; that deponent has never heard any suggestion that either of them had ever divorced; and since they both lived continuously in South Carolina during the twenty-five or thirty years previous to the death of July Young, and, to the best of deponent's information, during all of their lives, they could not legally obtain a divorce.[265]

Thomas Young (Son of the Veteran Soldier)
Date: 29 Apr 1938
Residence: Berkeley County, SC

The petition of Thomas Young shows: that Sarah Lucinda Young, who last dwelt in Oakley, S.C., in the County of Berkeley and State of South Carolina, died intestate on the 14th day of October A.D. 1937, leaving as her heirs at law the following persons, to wit:[266]

Name	Age	Residence	Relationship
Thomas Young	64	Oakley, SC	Son
Fannie Watson	56	Charleston, SC	Daughter
Rebecca Young	47	Charleston, SC	Daughter
Victoria Young	38	Charleston, SC	Daughter
Harry J. Young	36	Charleston, SC	Son
Josephine Washington	34	Charleston, SC	Daughter

---

[265] Deposition of Marie Haynes Heyward, case of Lucinda Young, widow of July Tenant known as July Young (Berkeley County, SC), dated 22 Jan 1923.
[266] Probate Court, in re: Estate of Sarah Lucinda Young (deceased), Ex Parte: Thomas Young (Petitioner), (Berkeley County, SC), dated 29 Apr 1938.

Appendix A

Cross-Reference: County to District

There are currently forty-six (46) counties in the State of South Carolina. In 1868, when district localities were redesignated as counties, in accordance with the post-war state Constitution of the same year, there were only thirty-one (31) counties in the state. Some of the present-day counties are split-off from earlier counties. The table below depicts the relationship between earlier counties and present-day counties. The table is not entirely accurate because some counties (*)[i] were derived from two or more counties. The number in parentheses indicates the year the original localities were incorporated.

Before 1868 the geographical area represented as counties were called districts. The table below also shows the relationship between counties and districts. As of the year 1800 there were a total of twenty-six (26) districts.[ii]

County (Yr 2000)	County (Yr 1868)	District (Yr 1800)
Abbeville (1785)	Abbeville	Abbeville
Aiken (1871)	Barnwell	Barnwell
Allendale (1919)	Barnwell	Barnwell
Anderson (1826)	Anderson	Pendleton
Bamberg (1897)	Barnwell	Barnwell
Barnwell (1785)	Barnwell	Barnwell
Beaufort (1785)	Beaufort	Beaufort
Berkeley (1882)	Charleston	Charleston
Calhoun (1908)	Orangeburg	Orangeburg
Charleston (1670)	Charleston	Charleston
Cherokee (1897)*	Spartanburg	Spartanburg
Chester (1785)	Chester	Chester

---

[i] In 1888, Florence County was formed from parts of Marion, Darlington, Williamsburg, and Clarendon Counties, and in 1897, Cherokee County was formed from parts of Spartanburg, Union, and York Counties; Dorchester from Berkeley and Colleton; and Greenwood from parts of Abbeville and Edgefield. In 1902, Lee emerged from parts of Darlington, Kershaw, and Sumter.

[ii] Compiled by Historical Records Survey, Works Project Administration, 1938.

Appendix A – Cross-Reference: County to District

County (Yr 2000)	County (Yr 1868)	District (Yr 1800)
Chesterfield (1785)	Chesterfield	Chesterfield
Clarendon (1855)	Clarendon	Clarendon
Colleton (1798)	Colleton	Colleton
Darlington (1785)	Darlington	Darlington
Dillon (1910)	Marion	Marion
Dorchester (1897)*	Colleton	Colleton
Edgefield (1785)	Edgefield	Edgefield
Fairfield (1785)	Fairfield	Fairfield
Florence (1888)*	Marion	Marion
Georgetown (1769)	Georgetown	Georgetown
Greenville (1786)	Greenville	Greenville
Greenwood (1897)*	Barnwell	Barnwell
Hampton (1878)	Beaufort	Beaufort
Horry (1801)	Horry	Georgetown
Jasper (1912)	Beaufort	Beaufort
Kershaw (1791)	Kershaw	Kershaw
Lancaster (1785)	Lancaster	Lancaster
Laurens (1785)	Laurens	Laurens
Lee (1902)*	Sumter	Sumter
Lexington (1785)	Lexington	Orangeburg
Marion (1790)	Marion	Marion
Marlboro (1804)	Marlboro	Marlboro
McCormick (1916)	Abbeville	Abbeville
Newberry (1785)	Newberry	Newberry
Oconee (1860)	Oconee	Pendleton
Orangeburg (1769)	Orangeburg	Orangeburg
Pickens (1826)	Pickens	Richland
Richland (1785)	Richland	Richland
Saluda (1895)	Edgefield	Edgefield
Spartanburg (1785)	Spartanburg	Spartanburg
Sumter (1798)	Sumter	Sumter
Union (1785)	Union	Union
Williamsburg (1785)	Williamsburg	Williamsburg
York (1785)	York	York

Appendix B

Cross-Reference: District to County

Prior to the Civil War local municipalities were divided into Circuit Court Districts. After the Civil War, in accordance with the requirements of the 1868 Constitution, they were redesignated as counties. The table below depicts a relationship between districts and counties. Since each soldier was born before 1868, this table will serve as a guide to determine the geographical area where he was born.

The date in parenthesis is the date a particular municipal locality was originally incorporated. In most cases municipalities were first incorporated as districts, and in 1868 were redesignated as counties. An asterisk next to the date of incorporation indicates that the district/county was formed from more than one district.

District (as of 1860)	County (as of 2000)
Abbeville	Abbeville (1785)
" "	Greenwood (1897)
" "	McCormik (1916)
Barnwell	Aiken (1871)*
" "	Allendale (1919)*
" "	Bamberg (1897)
" "	Barnwell (1785)
Beaufort	Beaufort (1785)
" "	Hampton (1878)
" "	Jasper (1912)
Charleston	Charleston (1882)
" "	Berkeley (1882)
Chester	Chester (1785)
Chesterfield	Chesterfield (1785)
Colleton	Colleton (1798)
" "	Dorchester (1897)
Darlington	Darlington (1785)
Edgefield	Edgefield (1785)
" "	Saluda (1895)

Appendix B – Cross-Reference: District to County

County (Yr 2000)	County (Yr 1868)	District (Yr 1800)

Georgetown .... Georgetown (1769)
"   " .... Horry (1801)
Greenville .... Greenville (1786)
Kershaw .... Kershaw (1791)
Lancaster .... Lancaster (1785)
Laurens .... Laurens (1785)
Marion .... Florence (1888)*
"   " .... Marion (1790)
Marlboro .... Dillon (1910)
"   " .... Marlboro (1785)
Newberry .... Newberry (1785)
Orangeburg .... Calhoun (1908)
"   " .... Lexington (1785)
"   " .... Orangeburg (1769)
Pendleton .... Anderson (1826)
"   " .... Oconee (1860)
"   " .... Pickins (1826)
Richland .... Richland (1785)
Spartanburg .... Cherokee (1897)
"   " .... Spartanburg (1785)
Sumter .... Clarendon (1855)
"   " .... Lee (1902)
"   " .... Sumter (1798)
Union .... Union (1785)
Williamsburg .... Williamsburg (1785)
York .... York (1785)

Appendix C

Cross-Reference: Community to County

This table lists the associated local community to a particular county as it exist at the most recent census (2000).

Community (Yr 1860)	County (Yr 2000)
Aiken	Aiken
Alcolu	Clarendon
Andrews	Georgetown
Andrews	Williamsburg
Awendaw	Charleston
Beaufort	Beaufort
Black Swamp	Hampton
Bonneau	Berkeley
Branchville	Orangeburg
Brookgreen Garden	Horry
Camden	Kershaw
Charleston	Charleston
Cordesville	Berkeley
Cross	Berkeley
Dalzell	Sumter
Dillon	Dillon
Eadytown	Berkeley
Edisto (Island)	Charleston
Elliott	Lee
Ellore	Orangeburg
Eutaw/Eutawville	Orangeburg
Frogmore	Beaufort
Georgetown	Georgetown
Goose Creek	Berkeley
Gourdin	Williamsburg
Green Pond	Colleton
Hanahan	Berkeley
Hilton Head (Island)	Beaufort
Holley Hill	Orangeburg

Appendix C – Cross-Reference: Community to County

County (Yr 1860)	County (Yr 2000)
Honey Hill	Jasper
Huger	Berkeley
James Island	Charleston
Jamestown	Berkeley
Johns Island	Charleston
Kingstree	Williamsburg
Ladson	Dorchester
Lane	Williamsburg
Lugoff	Kershaw
MacBeth	Berkeley
Mayesville	Sumter
Moncks Corner	Berkeley
Montmorenici	Aiken
Mt. Pleasant	Charleston
Nesmith	Williamsburg
Oceda	Georgetown
Oceda	Williamsburg
Orangeburg	Orangeburg
Paxville	Clarendon
Pineville	Berkeley
Pinewood	Sumter
Pocotaligio	Beaufort
Ravenel	Charleston
Rembert	Sumter
Rimini	Clarendon
Ritter	Colleton
Robertville	Jasper
Round	Colleton
Statesburg	Sumter
St. Stephens	Berkeley
Summerton	Clarendon
Sumter	Sumter
Wando	Berkeley
Wedgefield	Sumter
Yauhannah	Georgetown

Appendix D

South Carolina Volunteers Colored Infantry Regiments

During January to July 1863, five volunteer Colored Infantry Regiments were organized in South Carolina, and served with the Department of the South. Enlisted soldiers consisted of ex-slaves and freedmen drawn, predominately, from the states of South Carolina, Georgia, and Florida. Officers were drawn from northern (Union) regiments assigned in the Department of the South.

1st South Carolina Volunteer Infantry Regiment
Jan 31, 1863 -   Organized at Beaufort, SC
Feb 8, 1864 -   Redesignated as the 33rd USCT

2nd South Carolina Volunteer Infantry Regiment
May 22, 1863 -   Organized at Beaufort/Hilton Head, SC.
Feb 8, 1864 -   Redesignated as the 34th USCT

3rd South Carolina Volunteer Infantry Regiment
Jun 19, 1863   Organized at Hilton Head, SC.
Mar 14, 1864   Consolidated with the 4th SCV and Redesignated as the 21st USCT

4th South Carolina Volunteer Infantry Regiment
July 1863   Organized at Fernandina, FL.
Mar 14, 1864   Consolidated with the 3rd SCV and Redesignated as the 21st USCT

5th South Carolina Volunteer Infantry Regiment
Organization not completed.
Transferred to 3rd and 4th SCV

Appendix E

South Carolina United States Colored Troops (USCT)

On May 22, 1863, the U.S. War Department issued General Order No. 143, which established the Bureau of Colored Troops. As a result, future regiments and all state designated regiments, of African Descent, were redesignated as United States Colored Troops.[i]

21st U.S. Colored Infantry Regiment
Mar 14, 1864 -   Organized from 3rd and 4th Regiments, SCV Infantry (African Descent)
Oct 7, 1866 -   Mustered Out at Mount Pleasant, SC

33rd U.S. Colored Infantry Regiment
Feb 8, 1864 -   Organized from 1st Regiment, SCV Infantry (African Descent)
Jan 31, 1866 -   Mustered Out at Morris Island, SC

34th U.S. Colored Infantry Regiment
Feb 8, 1864 -   Organized from 2nd Regiment, SCV Infantry (African Descent)
Feb 28, 1866 -   Mustered Out at Jacksonville, FL

103rd U.S. Colored Infantry Regiment
Mar 10, 1865 -   Organized at Hilton Head, SC
Apr 5-20, 1866 -   Mustered Out at Fort Pulaski, GA

104th U.S. Colored Infantry Regiment
Jun 25, 1865 -   Organized at Beaufort, SC
Feb 5, 1866 -   Mustered Out at Mount Pleasant, SC

---

[i] Ibid. Dyer Compendium. Approximately 160 Infantry Regiments and 10 Artillery Batteries were organized or redesignated by the Bureau of Colored Troops. They provided service to the Federal Government, consisting of nearly 200,000 volunteers.

Appendix E – South Carolina USCT

128th U.S. Colored Infantry Regiment
Apr 1865 -   Organized at Hilton Head, SC
Oct 20, 1866 -   Mustered-out at Morris Island, SC[ii]

Battery G, 2nd U.S. Colored Light Artillery Regiment
May 24, 1864-   Organized at Hilton Head, SC
Aug 12, 1865-   Mustered-out at Hilton Head, SC[iii]

[ii] During the last weeks before muster-out, companies of the 128th regiment were detached to various locations about the Charleston area.

[iii] During muster-out companies of Battery G were serving on Post and Garrison duty at Beaufort and Hilton Head, SC.

Appendix F

The Structure of a Civil War Regiment

The basic fighting unit in the Union Army during the Civil War was a regiment. On April 29, 1863, General Orders No. 110 specified the official organization of regiments and companies of the Volunteer Army of the United States. Although many changes occurred in the organization tables during the war, those governing the Volunteer Army after April 1863 generally clung to the prescriptions of General Orders No. 110. Thus, the size and composition of regiments remained fairly constant, at least as spelled out in organization tables. The regiments raised for the United States Colored Troops were organized in accordance with General Orders No. 110, described as follows:[272]

Infantry Regiment

1 Colonel	1 Surgeon	1 Commissary Sergt
1 Lieutenant Colonel	2 Assistant Surgeons	1 Hospital Stewart
1 Major	1 Chaplin	1 Principal Musician
1 Adjutant (Lt)	1 Sergeant Major	
1 Quartermaster (Lt)	1 Quartermaster Sergt	

Infantry Company
(10 Companies)

1 Captain	1 First Sergeant	2 Musicians
1 First Lieutenant	4 Sergeants	1 Wagoner
1 Second Lieutenant	8 Corporals	

and

(64 Privates - minimum); (83 Privates - maximum)

---

[272] Hondon B. Hargrove. *Black Union Soldiers in the Civil War.* Jefferson, NC: McFarland & Company, Inc. 1988. p.125.

250

Appendix G
Officer of the 128th USCT

Field & Staff Officers	
Commanding Officer	Col. Charles H. Howard
Executive Officer	LtCol. William M. Beebe
Major	Maj. William H. Danielson
Adjutant	2ndLt. Clarence J. Lemen
Quartermaster	
Surgeon	Surg. Henry K. Durrant
Assistant Surgeon	AsstSurg. Edward C. Fox[i]
Chaplain	Chap. Thomas K. Noble

Company or Line Officers	
Company A	**Company B**
Capt. Mirand W. Saxton	Capt. Benjamin H. Manning
1stLt. Oliver P. Boyd[ii]	1stLt. Edwin W. Sanborn
1stLt. Julius Simple	2ndLt. George W. Quimby
2ndLt. Joseph A. Bedoll	2ndLt. Wm. G. Bradford[iii]
Company C	**Company D**
Capt. Rufus Johnson[iv]	Capt. Frederick K. Fields
1stLt. Julius Simple	1stLt. Levi Waters[vi]
1stLt. James Sprague[v]	2ndLt. William R. Flagler
1stLt. Richard L. Swartz	
2ndLt. Henry Pichot	

---

[i] AsstSurg. Fox was dismissed fm service by G.C.M.
[ii] 1stLt. Boyd was dismissed fm service, 06 Jul 1865.
[iii] 2ndLt. Bradford was prom to 1stLt and xfrd to Co. H.
[iv] Capt. Johnson was dismissed fm service, by S.O. 353, War Department, WDC.
[v] James Sprague mustered as a 2ndLt, 27 Mar 1865, with Co. E, then prom to 1stLt, 04 Nov 1865, and xfrd to Co. C.
[vi] 1stLt. Waters was dismissed fm service.

Appendix G - Officers of the 128th USCT

Company E	Company F
Capt. Eugene L. Barnes 1stLt. James Justice[vii] 1stLt. James Sprague[viii] 2ndLt. Alexander Whyte	Capt. Edwin J. Scranton[ix] Capt. James Justice[x] 1stLt. Richard L. Swartz 2ndLt. James Sprague[xi] 2ndLt. Edward M. Stoeber
Company G	**Company H**
Capt. Dexter W. Howard[xii] 1stLt. Lester Hall 2ndLt. James B. Berry[xiii]	Capt. Alexander Ketchum 1stLt. William. G. Bradford[xiv] 2ndLt. James M. Pearson[xv] 2ndLt. Frank J. Manning[xvi]
Company I	**Company K**
Capt. James C. Rundlett 1stLt. Oliver P. Boyd[xvii] 2ndLt. Thomas Callan 2ndLt. George Keef	Capt. Robert Aiton 1stLt. James K. Van Vort 2ndLt. James B. Berry[xviii]

[vii] James Justice, mustered as a 1stLt, 27 Mar 1865, then prom to Capt and xfrd to Co. E.
[viii] James Sprague, prom to 1stLt, and transferred from Co. C to Co. E.
[ix] Dismissed fm service, 16 Sep 1865, by sentence of G.C.M
[x] James Justice, prom to Capt, 05 Nov 1865, and xfrd fm Co. F as a replacement for Capt. Scranton.
[xi] James Sprague, prom to 1stLt, 04 Nov 1865, and xfrd to Co. C.
[xii] Capt. Howard died at home, 21 Jun 1866, at Leeds Centre, ME
[xiii] 2ndLt. James Berry, discharged fm service, 06 Jul 1865.
[xiv] William Bradford, prom from 2ndLt of Co. B and xfrd to Co. H.
[xv] 2ndLt. James Pearson, dismissed fm service, 06 Jul 1865.
[xvi] Frank Manning, prom to 2ndLt from Sergeant.
[xvii] 1stLt. Boyd, dismissed fm service, 06 Jul 1865.
[xviii] 2ndLt. James Berry, discharged fm, service, 06 Jul 1865.

List of Sources

Begley, Paul R. and Steven D. Tuttle. *African-American Genealogical Research (Pamphlet).* Columbia, SC: South Carolina Department of Archives & History, March 1991.

Côté, Richard N. *City of Heroes: The Great Charleston Earthquake of 1886.* Mount Pleasant, SC: Corinthian Books, 2006.

Devlin, George A. *South Carolina and Black Migation, 1865-1940: In Search of the Promise Land.* New York: Garland Publishing, Inc., 1989.

Dyer, Frederick H. *A Compendium of the War of the Rebellion.* Dayton, OH: Press of Morningside Book Shop, 1978.

Gladstone, William A. *United States Colored Troops, 1863-1867.* Gettysburg: Thomas Publications, 1990

Glasson, William H. *Federal Military Pensions in the United States,* ed. David Kinley. New York: Oxford University Press.

Gourdin, J. Raymond, ed. *Voices from the Past: 104th Infantry Regiment – USCT, Colored Civil War Soldiers from South Carolina.* Bowie, MD: Heritage Books, Inc., 1997.

Hargrove, Hondon B. *Black Union Soldiers in the Civil War.* Jefferson, NC: McFarland & Company, Inc. 1988.

Linares, Claudia. "The Civil War Pension Law." University of Chicago (2001).

Marion, John Francis. *The Charleston Story: Scenes from a City's History.* Harrisburg, PA: Stackpole Books, 1978.

McClintock, Megan J. "Civil War Pensions and the Reconstruction of Union Families," *The Journal of American History,* 83 (September 1996).

Microfilm Publication No. M589: *Index to Compiled Service Records of Volunteer Union Soldiers who Served with the United States Colored Troops*, National Archives and Records Administration, Washington, DC.

List of Sources

Microfilm Publication No. T288: *General Index to Pension Files, 1861-1934*, National Archives and Records Administration, Washington, DC.

Microfilm Publication No. T289: *Organization Index to Pension Files of Veterans Who Served Between 1861 and 1900*, National Archives and Records Administration, Washington, DC.

Shaffer, Donald R. "An Ambiguous Victory: Black Civil War Veterans from a National Perspective."

Special Veterans Census (1890): *Surviving Soldiers, Sailors, and Marines, and Widows, etc*, National Archives and Records Administration, Washington, DC.

Taylor, Alrutheus Ambush. *The Negro in South Carolina during the Reconstruction.* 1924; New York: AMS Press, Inc., 1971 (1924).

United States Population Census, 1870-1930 (except 1890). Washington, DC: NARA.

United States. War Department. *The War of the Rebellion: A Compilation of the Official Records of the Union and Confederate Armies.* Series I—Volume XLVII [47], Part I—Reports. Washington, DC: GPO, Harrisburg, PA, 1971 and 1985 (1895).

Name Index

____, Agnes 224-226
____, Caroline 43
____, Carter 200
____, Charlotte 159
____, David 227-28
____, Diana 193
____, David 227-28
____, Della 126
____, Essie 35
____. Henry 200
____, Jane 61
____, Jane Anna 129
____, Louis 196
____, Margaret 21
____, Maria 93
____, Mary 147, 148
____, Miley 195
____, Phillis 69, 70
____, Phyllis 99, 159
____, Zacharias 161
ADAMS, Annie 57
  Benjamin 57
  John 57
AIKEN, Carrie 1
  Edmund 50
  Joseph 1
  Snow 1, 2
  William 1
ALBANY, ____ (Rev) 65
ALBRIGHT, Joseph 50
ALLSTON, ____ (Rev) 90
  (Gov) 115
  A.P. 69, 70
  Anthony, ____ (Rev) 89
  Benjamin 69
  Frederick 115
  Nat 78, 79, 115
  Nathaniel 167

  Tony 78, 115, 167
ALSTON, Edward 26
  Nat 166
ANDERSON, Louisa 223
ANDREW, Driver 104
{ANOMN}, Israel 197
ANSON, Cipio 95
ARMSTRONG, {Sue} 4
  Harry 3, 4
  Henry 4
  Martha 11
  Peter 3, 4
  Rena 3, 4
  William 4
  William M. 85
AUSTIN, Adeline 125, 126
BAILEY, Constantine 29
  Edward 90
  John 10
  Nancy 89
  Sam 76
BAKER, Benjamin (1stSgt) 76
  Benjamin 150
  John, 122
BALL, ____ 72, 233
  Coming 74
  Elias 73
  W.J. 139
  William 71-74
BAPTIST, John 87
BARNES, Eugene L. (Capt) 176, 228
BARNETT, Harriett 161
BARNWELL, Frank (Rev) 191
BEAD, G.A. 197
BEATON, Abram 228
BEATY, Charlotte 5
  William 5

Name Index

BECKETT, ____ (Dr) 158
   Edith 5
   Randol 5-7
BEEBE, William M. (Col) 166, 182. 228
   William M. (LtCol) 12, 76, 160, 176
BEECHER, William M. (Col) 106, 107
BELLINGER, Charlotte 171-174
   John, 173
BENJAMIN, Chubby 78
BENNETT, Adam 26, 196
   David 13
   Harriet 11-14
   Laurence 76
   March 26
   Mary Ann 81
   Ward 212
BERRY, James B. (2ndLt) 78
BEST, Ella Rose 191
BETTERSON, Anna 9
   Chloe 9
   Duncan 9
   Harry Rabbit 9
   Henry 10
   January 9
   Maggie 9
   Martin 9
   {Murvin} 10
   Samuel 9, 10
   Stephen, 9, 10
BICKERFORD, Nathan 197
{BLACK}, Charles 78
BLAKE, Seabron 146
BLOUNT, J.S. 197
BLUMENBERG, W.D. 15
BLOUNT, Paul 94
{BOGERS}, ____ (Maj) 36
BONNET, Viney 121, 123
{BOOBY}, Betsy 213
BOONE, G.C. (Rev) 33

{BORDECH}, {Hilton} 144
BOSTICK, Aron Elijah 11
   Charity 11
   Hilton 11
   Hilton R. 11, 13-14
   Hilton Reddy 11
   Lula, 11
BOWEN, Sallie 233
BOYD, Benjamin 149
   Moses 150
   O.P. 212
   Richard 148, 150
   William 150
BOYKIN, Ellen 1
BRAGG, ____ (General) 155
   Ephraim 144, 155
BRANT, Adam 32
BROOKER, Elbert 200
   Masham 200
   Rainey 200
   Scott 199, 223
   Ted 199, 200
BROOKS, ____ (Dr) 124
   Henry 192
BROTTON, Charley 200
BROUGHTON, Geoffery 127, 183
BROWN, Amelia 22
   Boston 17, 19
   Dafney 82
   Daphney 81
   Della 158
   Emma 211
   Francis 17, 19
   Frank 18
   Hammond 155
   Isaac 133
   J.F. (Notary) 219
   James 212
   John 21-23, 211
   John Samuel 21
   Jonas 21
   Juliana 91

Name Index

Linda 77, 80
Louisa 17
Mandy 57, 59
Mike 21
Morris 21
Nelson 91
Phoebe 67-68
Sammy 212
Sawney 197
Swaney 197
BRUNSON, Elizabeth 103
BRYAN, Monday 214
{BURST}, Robert (Dr) 76
BUSH, Mike 162
BUTLER, Brutus 26, 144, 155
   Joe 10
   Laura 155
   Susanna 121
   Susannah 123
BYRD, Maria 56
BYTHEWOOD, R.F. (Rev) 67
CANADY, Gracie 25
   Richard 25
CARLEY, Dora 118
   Henry 119
   Augustus 114
   Augustus T. 113
   Israel 6-7, 166, 170
CARROLL, ___ (Judge) 133
CARTER, Leonora 129
CARY, John 56
CASH, Patience 27
CASHION, ___ 173
   John 171-173
   Mark, 68
{CAUTHER}, Mary Jane 181
CHAMBERLAIN, ___ 41
CHARLES, Samuel 143-144
CHISHOLM, Amelia 67-68
   Eliza 75
   Thomas 163, 173
CHRISTENSEN 68

CLARK, Cage (Sgt) 214
CLARKSON, Boston 18
CLAYTON, Jane 65
COBB, ___ 133
   Matilda 131-133
COHEN, Caesar 78
COLE, Murray (Min) 47
COLEMAN, Ephraim 29
   G.W. 30
   Gibson W. 29
   Gibson Westpoint 30
   Huckey 29
   Moses 29
   Samuel 29
   William 29
COLLINS, (Rev) 139
{COMBS}, Paul (Rev) 233
CONYERS, Catherine 209-210
COONER, Darkis 54
   Henrietta 55
   Isham 54
   James 53, 55
   Jim 55
   Mary 54
   Lewis S. 53
   Sarah 55
   Squire 54
   William 54, 55
COOPER, Rose 35
COPE, David 31-32
   George 31
CROSBY, ___ (Rev) 93-94
DAISE, Yanekey 169
DALLAS (Maj) 228
   Lydia 71-72, 74
DANIELS, Samuel 191
DANIELSON, William H. (Maj) 12, 160
DAVID, Allen 31-32
   Francis 31
   Stewart 31
   Wesley 31

Name Index

DAVIS, Eliza 61
  Sylvia 43
  William 68, 160
DAYS, Fortune 200
DEAS, Annie V. 33
  Emily 33
  Frank 33
  George 33
  George Washington 33-34
  {Gretus} 33
  Rosa E. 34
  {Silbina} 130
  Washington 34
DEFORREST, ____ (Parson) 234
DEHONE, ____ 196
  Theodore (Dr) 195
  Titus 195-196, 198
DENNIS, Julia 159
DENT, Jack (Rev) 215
DICKERSON, Samuel (Rev) 25
DICKSON, Harry 35-37, 188, 204
  Harry J. 35
DISS, Washington 33
DOBSON, Isabella 30
  Isabella Rebecca 29
  {DOBY}, Isabella 207
DOE, D.K. (Special Examiner) 106
{DOIL}, ____ (Dr) 58
DORSEY, William 207
DOSIER, Bill 32
DUNCAN, Elizabeth 207
  Frank, 110
DURANT, May 203-204, 206
  Phillis 201
DURRANT, Henry K. (Dr) 50, 122, 180-182
  Henry K. (Surgeon) 156
DWIGHT, Isaac 90
EDNA, Ben 90, 92
EDNEY, Benjamin 122
EDWARDS, Millie 21
EDWIN, Daniel 59

ELLERBE, Elizabeth 181
ELLINGTON, ____ (Dr) 92
  Elsie 211
ELLIOTT, Stephen 161
ELLIS, ____ (Dr) 194
  David 18
  {Lavay} 18
  Louisa 17-18
ELLIS-WASHINGTON, Annie 69
EMORY, Bill (1stSgt) 110
  William (1stSgt) 186
  William (Sgt) 214
EVANS, Isaac (OrdSgt) 176
  Thomas (Rev) 111
EVERETTE, John (Rev) 41
{FARM}, Toby 4
FARMER, {I}.K. (Dr) 134
FAVORS, Daniel 39-40
  Lucinda 39
  Quintus 39
  Susan 39
FELDER, W.R.A. (Rev) 75
FERGUSON, Samuel 212
FEWELL, E.F. 14
FIELD, F.K. (Capt) 12
  Frederick (Capt) 156
  Frederick K. (Capt) 36, 108
FINICK, Canning 157
FINLEY, Eliza 130
FINNICK, Canning 157
FLAG, Snow 110
FLAGG, A.B. 5
  Arthur (Dr) 1
  J. Ward (Dr) 5- 6
  Snow 1, 214
FLOOD, Lester (Rev) 195
FLOYD, Dennis 41-42, 212
  Jacob 41
  Rebecca 41
FOLK, Jesse 32, 108
FORD, ____ (Cpl) 82
  George 157-158

Name Index

Jackson (Cpl) 160
Rosanna 158
Rosanna F. 157
FRANKLIN, Ben 56
  Josephine 53
FRASIER, Cyrus 211
FRAZIER, Caroline 45
  Daniel 148, 177
  Frank (Cpl) 48
  Henry 44
  Jacob 43
  Joe 10
  Robert 43
  Susie R. 43
FREEMAN, Richard 54
  Robert 143
  Theodore 143
FROST, Daniel (Rev) 145
GADISON, Eliza 165
  Frank 47
  Louisiana 48
GAINEY, Eliza 166-167
GALLANT, Moses 214
  William 94
GALLEN, Michael 76
GARDNER, ____ 45, 215
  Jupiter 215
  William (OrdSgt) 176
GARRETT, Andrew 63-64
  Corina 64
  Edward 26
  {Rivan} A. 64
  {Rivana} 61
GARY, Benjamin 129
{GASKEY}, Mary 207
GEDDES, Archie 214
GEDDIS, Lewis 50
  Primous 51
  Rebecca 51
  Richard 49-51
GELZER, Frank 50
GEORGE, Daniel 32

GIBBS, J.T. 86
GILES, Sarah 99
GILLARD, Aaron 111
GILYARD, Henry 59
GIN, E.R. 32
GLOVER, Julius 53
  Lewis 53
  Mary 65
  Tom, 55
GOODIN, Mike 32
GOODWIN, Alfred 57, 60
  Berry 59
  Eugene 57
  Jim 59
  John 60
  Molly 60
  Simon 57
  Willie 57
GOODWINE, Frederick 50
GORDON, Leila 53
GOULD, Peace 216
GOURDINE, Elvira 170
  Jack 169
  Joseph 169
  Joshua 169
GRAHAM, John (Rev) 157-158
GRANDERSON, John 13
GRANT, Mary 227
  Prince 92
  Ulysses S. (Gen) 79
GRANVILLE, Washington 197
GRAY, Frank 129-130
GREEN, Anthony 152
  C.S. (Rev) 70
  Catherine 135
  Charles S. (Rev) 69
  Daniel 186
  Hector 78
  John 152
  John A. 152
  Peter 186
  Renty 110

Name Index

GREENE, A. (Postmaster) 162
  C.R. (Postmaster) 162
GRIFFIN, Alonzo 68
  Charlotte 211
  Green 26
GRIMES, Jim 56
GYLES, Herbert E. 66
HAGLER, Dennis 186
  John 187
  Kattie 186
HALL, Broughton 182
  Lester (1stLt) 78
  Lester (Lt) 160
HAMILTON, Edward (Sgt) 200
  Prince 50
  Thomas 32
HANKERSON, Butter 62
  John 61
  Milledge 61, 63-64
  Robert 62
HANNIBAL, Richard (OrdSgt) 69
HARDING, Grace 234
HARE, Emile L. 2
HARLESTON, William 1
HARRIET, John (Dr) 134
HARRIS, Henry (Rev) 53
  W.L. (Special Examiner) 107
HARRISON, J. Turner (Rev) 169
  July 69
  Parris 207
  Thomas 65-66, 122
  Thomas J.D., 151
HARVEY, Adaline 31
  Henry 32
HASEL, Francis 165
  Jack 68
HATCHER, Judie 65
HAVENS, Isaac (1st/OrdSgt) 228
HAWKINS, Peter 77
HAYES, Coleman 78
HAYNES, Coleman 78
  Margaret 143

{HAYNES}, {Friday} {Charles} 80
HAYWARD, Julia 71
HAZEL, Francis 166
  S.W. (Rev) 237
HEDDELSTON, Charles 68
  Daniel 67-68
  Mary 68
HEDDELSTON-SIMMONS, Rose 68
HENDERSON, Daniel 67, 68
{HEREFORD}, Peter 155
HERIOT, {Allison} 69
  Abraham 69
  Annie 70
  Eddie 69
  Gabriel 69
  Gilbert 69
  Isaac 69
  July 69-70
  Sarah 69
  Wallace 69
HEYWARD, Charles 71
  Hannibal 71, 73-74
  Marie Haynes 237
  Phillis 71
HICKMAN, J.C. 98
HICKSON, ___ 118
  Ella, 117-118
HIDLER, P.M. (Rev) 181
HILL, Sam (Rev) 61
HILLARD, Joe 216
HINCKLEY, Thomas (Magistrate) 1
{HOLE}, {Phelps} 59
HOLMAN, Bo{z} 203
  Ella 118-119
HOLMAN-STALEY, Ella 118
HOLMES, Anna 234
  John 175
  Rebecca 175, 178-179
  Samuel 26

Name Index

HOPKINS, ____ (Dr) 117-118
HOUSTON, ____ (Rev) 199
   Benjamin 222
   Louisa 153
{HOUZER}, Eugenia 229
HOWARD, Charles H. (Col) 12, 76, 78, 176
   Charles H. (Gen) 182
   Dexter (Capt) 160
   J. 100
   {Ned} 71
   {S.K.} 71
   {Ted} 71
HOWELL, Arnold (Rev) 99
HUGER, {Beaver} 75
   Ben 148
   Benjamin 75, 94, 95
HUGGINS, Betty 79-80
   Hagar 77
   James H. 77
   Peter 77, 79, 166
HUMBERT, Richard (1stSgt) 186
HUNT, Quintus 39
   William 39-40
HUTSON, Charles 235
INGRAM, ____ 233
   Rebecca 139
INSON, Cipio 95
IRVINE, Robert 221
IRVING, ____ (Dr) 235
IZZARD, ____ 68, 80, 135-137
   Mary Jane 33-34
   R.S. 77, 79
   Robert 135-137
   Tony (Rev) 135
JACKSON, Boston 26
   Carrie 65
   Samuel 72
JACOBY, S.A. (Magistrate) 172-174
JAMES, (1stSgt) 182
JAUNT, Lydia 147-148

JENKINS, Alfred 81, 83
   Annie 103
   Archie 214
   Betsy 81
   Hector 81-83
   Jane 187
   Joseph 50
   Josephine 81
   Maggie 81
   Martha 81
   Mary 81
   Renty 150
   Sara Ann, 81
JOHNSON, ____ 132
   Adeline 201
   Alex 85
   Alfred 85-87
   Becky 123
   Cipio 95
   Clarinda 89
   Elias 92
   Ella 86, 88, 153
   Emma 153-154
   Frank 89, 91
   Henry 146, 153
   Henry (2ndSgt) 78
   Isabella 89, J., 101
   J.H. 163
   James R. 85, 88
   John 93
   John Henry 154
   Joseph 148
   Kate 94
   Lacey 89
   Lancey 91
   Mary Jane 89, 91
   Nancy 85, 91
   Nero 179
   Pleasant 162
   Rebecca 85
   Sam 92
   Samson 89-91

Name Index

Samuel 89
Scipio 93, 214
Sippy 93
Timothy 90-91
Tom 55
JONES, Arrington 97, 98
  Frank 32
  Franklin 222
  Hagar 139
  {Hippy} 18
  James 97
  Jim 97, 98
  John 102
  Sarah 97
  Seaborn 48
  Thomas 18, 99-102
  Tisby 153, 155
  Tishby 154
  Tom 18
JUSTUS, James (Capt) 69
  James (Lt) 166, 186
KANNEDY, Richard 28
KEADDER, Cyrus (JP) 117-119
KEARSE, Stephen 31
{KEE}, John 171
KEEF, George (2ndLt) 212
KEI{T}, Cuffie 203
KELLER, Russell 186
KENNEDY, Elsey 26-27
  Richard, 25-26, 28
KILPATRICK, Andrew 99
  Calvin 99-102
  Elizabeth 99
  George 98
  J.F. 100
  J.H. 99, 101
  James 97, 99
  W.L. 97
KIMBLE, Mahalia 47
KING, Ellis, 151-152
  Mallory P. (Capt) 3, 4
  Peter 3, 216

Stephen Clay 151
KINLOCH, Andrew 103
  Caty 104
  Ester 103
  Napoleon 104
  Napoleon B. 103-104
  Rachel 139
KINSEY, C.E. (Dr) 21-23
KITT, Daniel 43
  Jacob 43
KNIGHT, James 182
KOOGER, Amarita 105
  Arthur 105
  Hector 105-107
  Joseph 105
  Sarah 105
KYLES, Abram 221
  Clarinda 221
  Mary J. 221
LADSON, Alex 22
LANCE, W.S. 149
LASTRY, Alfred 81
  Edward 81
  Richard 83
  Thomas 19, 82
LASTY, Thomas 25, 212
LATSON, Sarah 141
LAURENCE, Hercules 91
  Robert 91
  Sam 91
  Susana 91
LAWRENCE, Adam 109
  John 109
  Sue 109
LAWTON, Benjamin 191
  Francis 17
  Hager 145
  Joe 9
  Stephen 9
  William 229-230
  William J. 145-146
LEE, ____ (Dr) 194

Name Index

Robert E. (Gen) 79
LESTER, ___ 214
  Isaac 213
  William 213
LEWIS, ___ (OrdSgt) 166
  Charley 200
  Cyrus 50
  Ellen 41
  Frank 102
LEWISTON, Harry 35-37
LITTLEFIELD, Milton S. (Gen) 176, 214
LIVINGSTON, Harry 35, 37
LIVINGISTONE, John 35-36
{LLOYD}, Henry 26
LUCAS, Benjamin 111
  Catherine 111
  Henry 111
  John 111
  Mary Jane 111-112
  Sallie 111
LYKER, Jesse D. 33
MAGGETT, July (Rev) 131-133
MAGWOOD, Maggie 195
MALLORY, John 200
MANDORA, Robert 167
  Sarah 167
MANDY, Emma 53
MANNING, Benjamin H. (Capt) 26, 166
MARCH, Benjamin 159
MARGOOD, Major 159
MARTIN, Georgiana 105
  Henry 176
  Rosa E. 33
MASHAW, June 135-136
MAYHAMS, Alice 113-116
  Cain 113, 115-116
  Delia 116
  Delilah 114-115
  Eugenia 113-114, 115-116
  Frederick G. 113

  Norridge 113-116 Sarah 114-116
{MCABOUT}, Robert 4
MCALLISTER, Jacob 37, 189, 201-202, 204
  Sheck 202
MCALPIN, Henry 221-222
MCBRIDE, Sylvia 126
MCCALL, Cuyer 200
  Cuyler 221-224
  Philip 221-222, 224
  W.A. ___ (Judge) 43
MCCLAY, George P. 94-95
{MCCLELLAN}, ___ (Dr) 76
{MCCLENAN}, ___ (Dr), 17
MCCLOUD, Elmira 75
MCCONNELL, Jackson 186
MCCOY, Julia Ann 98
MCCREA, Henry 117
  Isaac 121
MCCREARY, Bob 121
  Chester 122
  Cora 117
  Edward 122
  Effie 121, 123
  Ella 118-119
  Emma 121
  Henry 117-119, 121-124
  Isaac 121-124
  J., 117
  J.H. 117
  John 122
  Lillie 117, 119
  Neal 117
  Paul 121
  Robert 117, 121-124
  Robert W. 123
  Rosetta 123
  Rosie 121
  Sam 122
  Samuel 121, 123
  Stella 117

Name Index

Viney 122
MCDONNELL, Betsie 11
  Elizabeth 11
MCFARLAN, Adeline, 127
  Allan 125
  Allan (Col) 181, 125
  Della 126, 182
  Frank 182
  Jet 126, 182
  Lavinia 182
  Lewis 126, 182
  Nero 125-127, 182-183
  Robert 126, 181, 183
  Roman 126, 182
MCINTYRE, Tyra 4
MCKINLY, ___ 227
MCKNIGHT, Lawrence (Notary) 230
MCNEAL, Minus 228
MCNEILL, Beatrice 129-130
  Edward 129
  Emma 130
  Frank 129-130
  Fred 129
  Magdaline 129
  Mahala 130
  Samuel, 50
MCPHERSON, Rosanna 157
{MEAT}, Adam 78
MEDLOCK, Mary 65
MERCHANT, Queen Victoria 215-216
METTS, Oliver 54
MEYERS, Simon 191, 192
{MICHBORO}, John 76
MIDDLETON, Jolly (Rev) 159, 160
  Lucinda 39
  March 50
  W.D. (Rev) 209
  William 89-91
MILE, Burn 56

MILES, Samuel 145
  Simon 145-146
MILLER, Adam 131-133
  Alvin 221
  Cicero 131, 134
  Esau 131
  Goull 131
  Gurantee 131, 133-134
  Harry 186
  Isaac 131
  Laney 131
  Matilda 132-133
  Misher 131
  Octavia 131
  Phoebe 222
  Priestly 131
  Rosy 131
  Stephen 131-133
  Zilla 131
MILLIGAN, J. 144
  John 144
MINGES, ___ 210
MITCHELL, Annie 137
  Bob 78
  Eloise 135
  George 136
  January 68
  Jonas 15, 135-137, 148
  June 136
  Mary 91
MOLE, Phoebe 31
MOLSEY, {James} 59
MONDAY, John 68, 160
MORSE, Henry 44
MOSLEY, W.H. (Rev) 65
MOULTRIE, Anna Retta 139
  Christina 139
  Humphrey 139-140
  Levi 139
  Mamie 139
  Peter 139
  Rebecca 113, 139

Name Index

Sukey 139
Susan 139
MUNGEN, Henry 141
  Stephen 141
MURCHINSON, ___ (Rev) 161
MURPHY, Flora 143
  Mary 144
  Rachel 143
  Rebecca 143
  Robert 144
  Samuel 143-144
  Samuel C. 143
  Samuel Charles 143
  Steven 143
  Helfus 139
  Holfus 139-140
MYERS, Alice 145
  Ben 145
  Caroline 145
  Edie 145
  Margaret 145
  Rebecca 145
  Rena 145
  Simon 145
  Tamah 145
NABNETT, Rosanna 185, 187
{NELSON}, ___ (Dr) 59
NELSON, Elsey 27
  Elsie 25
  Laura 149-150
NERO, Edwin 200
  Irvin 187-189
  Irwin 37, 185-186
NESBIT, ___ (Rev) 222
  Brutus 186
  Cain 147-148
  Harriet 148
  John 71-72, 74
  Julia 71
  Lydia 73, Maria 147-148
  Rose 147-148
  Susan 75

NICHOLAS, John 180
NICHOLS, Julia 222
NOBLE, ___ (Chaplain) 156
NORTH, ___ (Rev) 39, 40
NORTON, Elizabeth 149
NOVILLE, Alexander 149-150
  Charlotte 149
  Dillard 149
  Grace 149-150
  James 149
  Paul 150
  Richard 148, 150
OLENER, Joshua 185, 187
OLIVER, Clarinda 89
  Frank 90
ONEAL, ___ (Rev) 227
  Andrew (Rev) 3
OWENS, Amos 151
  Charles 22, 217, 219-220
  Clarence 217, 219
  Eliza 217, 219-220
  Ellis 151, 152
  Henry 151
  Isaac 216
  James 151
  John 21-22, 108
  Minnie 151
  Ned 151
  Rosa 151
  William 21, 151, 217
PAGE, Nancy 65
PALMER, Clarence, 26, 33, 34, 148, 212
  John S. (Dr) 103, 104
PARKER, Francis (Dr) 67, 93
PEAGLER, James 155
  Laura 155
PEAGLER-BUTLER, Laura 155
PEASE, Lymas 159, 160
PEGLER, Carolina 153
  Martha 153
  Mary 153

Name Index

Samuel 153
Simon 153
PESTON, Daniel 202
PEURIFOY, Jas. E. 174
PHILLIPS, R.J. 236
PHOENIX, Dick 164
  Elias 33, 34
PIATT, Cain 147
  John 147
  William J. 148
PINCKNEY, Canning 157
  E.M. (Rev) 129
  Edward 157
  Henry 158
  Isaiah 158
  Johnson 157
  {Leon} 166
  Mary 157
  Quash (Cpl) 186
  Richard 157-158
  Sara Ann 157-158
  Teana 157
PINO, Joe (OrdSgt) 160
  Joseph (1stSgt) 48
PIPKINS, Amos 186
POLITE, James 136-137
POOS, Pender 195
POOSA, ____ 132
  Brass 195
  John 131
  Sawney 197
  Simon 131, 133, 134
  Swaney 197
POPE, Josiah 32
PORCHER, William 50
POSTEL, Daniel 49
POSTELL, 215
  Jim 4
POTTER, Edward E. (Gen) 73, 154-156
POWELL, Charlotte 160
  Eliza 159

Elizabeth 159
Flora 159
Isaiah 159
James 159
Julia 160
Lymas 159
Phyllis 160
Wellington 159
PREAGLER, Carolina 154
  Daniel 153
  David 154
  Emma 154
  Frank 153
  Harriet 153, 154
  James 155
  Jane 153
  Phoebe 153
  Rosalie 153, 154
  Samuel 153-154
  Scipio 153
  Simon 153
  Tisby 154
PREGLER, Carolina 156
  Emma 156
  Louisa 156
  Samuel 155, 156, Simon 155, 156
  Tisby 156
PRESLEY, Sylvia 43
PRICE, Loby 146
PRIMUS, R.E. (Notary) 192
PRINCE, ____ (Dr) 175-176, 178-179
  Scott, 175-177, 180
PRIOLEAU, ____ (Rev) 201
PUBINON, Daniel W. 197
PURCELL, Janie 127
  William J. 127
PYATT, Frank 6
  John S. 113, 115
RAMSEY, Sarah 103
RANKIN, Richard 32

Name Index

RECTOR, ___ (Dr) 122
REED, Bradboy 78
  Clara 161
  Harriet 162, 163
  Henry 161-162, 164 Jestine 161
  Thomas 60
REEVES, Henry 161, 163
  Renty 162
RICHARDS, Dick 49, 50
RICHARDSON, Brass 165, 167
  Henry 165
  John 165
  Johnnie 165
  Mary 165
  Nelson (Min) 193
  Rosa 165
  Sarah Lucinda 237
RIGHT, Ameritta 169
RILEY, Simsie 201
RIVERS, Hagar 176, 178
  Matilda 178
  Sarah 111
ROBERSON, Lucy 233
ROBERTSON, ___ (Rev) 75
ROBINSON, Andrew 169
  Anna Lois 171
  Annie 172, 173
  Archie 169, 170
  Charles 161, 162
  Charlotte 171-174
  David 50
  Emmaline 171-173
  Frank 175
  Hector 171
  Hester 69
  Irene 171
  Isabella 171
  Jack 172
  Jacob 175
  James 171-174
  John 171-172, 174
  Julia 3, 175
  Leonard 170
  Lizzie 171
  Rosa 172-173
  Rosa P. 174
  Rosa Pearl 171
  Samuel 171
  Scott, 175-177, 179-180
  {Simon} 4
  Susan 75
  Susie 169
  {Tona} 4
  William 175
RODGERS, Binah 181
  Edith 181
  Ella 181-182
  Isom 181-182
  Lottie 181-182
  May 181
  Richard 181
  Robert 181, 183
ROGERS, Elina 91
  Israel 91
  Mark 91
  Nero 125-126
  Susana 91
  Samuel (Rev) 85-86
ROTENBERG, Robert 187
ROWE, Cephus 185
  Cornelia 185
  Dennis 187-188
  Frances 185
  Irvin 185, 187-189
  Irving 36-37
  Irwin 186
  James 185
  Milledge 185
  Samuel 185
  William 185
ROYAL, Croskey 193
RUNDLETT, James C. (Capt) 212
RUSSELL, S.D. (Magistrate) 143
RUTLEDGE, Caroline 109-110

Name Index

RYAN, Marshall 122
   Sam 122
SALTER, M.B. (Rev) 175
SALTERS, Paris 91
SALTZGABER, G.M. (Commissioner) 208
SAMUELS, Elliott 191
   Isabella 191
   John Wesley 191
   Mamie 191
   Nora 191
   Walter 191
   Willie 191
   Daniel 50, 146, 191-192
SANDERS, Josephine 201
SAPP, Bill 61
SAUNDERS, William 41-42
SAUNDERSON, Josh 59
SAXTON, Mirand W. (Capt) 182, 224
   Rufus (Gen) 79
SCHELY, ___ (Dr) 221
SCOTT, ___ (Rev) 213
   Winfield (Commissioner) 48
SCRANTON, James (Capt) 186
SEABROOK, ___ 83
SEGAR, Alex 235
   Judy 235
SELLERS, John 202
{SETON}, Rosanna 61
SEYMOUR, Luella 151
SHERMAN, William T. (Gen) 141, 142
SHINES, John 193, 194
   Julia 19
   Malsey 193
   Susan 193, 194
SHIPMAN, F.N. 11, 144
   Harman 155
   Hilton 11, 14
SHIRER, Emily 201, 202
{SHIVER}, Irena 59
   Peter 59
{SHOAT}, Elizabeth 182
SHOEMAKER, Seaborn 61
SHUBRED, ___ 74
   Jane 72
SHUBRICK, Lucretia 113-114
{SHUIASAM}, George (Rev) 229
SILAS, Cherry 57
   Houghton 57n
SIMMONS, Alfred 177
   Cuffie 22
   David 195
   Elizabeth 195
   Frost 195
   Grace 195
   Hester 195
   Isabelle 175
   John 76, 196-197
   Miley 197-198
   Nancey 195
   Richard 195
   Tambo 195-196
   Titus 195, 198
   Witty 134
SIMPLE, Julius (Lt) 182
SIMPSON, Frank 206
SINGLETON, ___ (Rev) 91
   {Aushie} 59
   {Cashil} 59
   {Cushile} 59
   Billy 212
   Scipio 78
SKELLY, Louisa 207
SKENLORE, Napoleon 103
SMALL, ___ (Rev) 18
   Caesar (Rev) 211
   Charles (Rev) 17-18
   Ella 153
   Emma 154
   Rebecca 49-51
SMITH, Charlotte 199
   Darcus 53

Name Index

Elzey 199
Florence J. 43, 45
Francis 199
Jack 200
John 111
Josie 21
Julius 154
Leola 199
Press 154
R. Press 39
Rainey 199
Rosa 25
Rose 25
Scott 199, 222-223
Tony 80
Walter W. (Dr) 231
SNIDER, Stephen 191
SNIPE, John 144
{SNOWDEN}, Charles 234
SNYDER, Stephen 146
SOLOMON, Jerre 10
{SOUTH}, Robert 78
SPANN, Jack 27
SPARKMAN, ___ (Dr) 80
SPAULDING, David 227
   Randolph 227
SPRAGUE, James 76
   James (Lt) 186
{ST. OLIVER}, Sam 42
STALEY, ___ 118
   Ella, 118
STEDMAN, Boston 122
   Emery 122
   Every 186
STEPHNEY, Jane 223
STEWARD, Diana 18
STOKES, Ben (Notary) 105
   Henry 48
STONE, ___ (Capt) 93
STONEY, Isaac D. 27
SUMTER, Carolina 153-154, 156
SWARTZ, Richard L. (Capt) 76

Dick (Lt) 186
TALBERT, J.W. (Rev) 219
   James (Rev) 218
   James W. (Rev) 217
TAYLOR, Gilbert 9
   Harry (Rev) 103
TENANT, Charles (Dr) 237
   John 193
   July 50, 237-238
TERRELL, Stephen 26
{TERRIEL}, Dennis 4
THOMAS, Aleck 202
   Emily 202-203, 205-206
   John 44
   John T. 44
   Major 44
   Major G. 44
   Preston 205
   Sarah 202
   Sheck 36-37, 187, 201, 203-204
   Sheck D. 201, 205, 206
   Sheck T. 201, 204-206
THOMAS-DURANT, Phillis 203, 205-206
THOMAS-JOHNSON, Adeline 205-206
THOMAS-RILEY, Simsie 205-205
THOMAS-SANDERS, Josephine 205-206
THOMPSON, Ella 21
   Hugh S. 213
TILTON, A.J. (Magistrate) 207
TINGMAN, Julius 144
TIZER, Charles (Cpl) 78
TODD, Peter 194
TRACY, Hector 22, 32, 105
TRAPIER, {Jakey} 207
   Alex 207
   Alex, Jr 208
   Elick 207
TRAPPIER, John 109, 110
   Sue 110

Name Index

William 109
TRAPPIN, William 109
TROWELL, James 47
   Thomas 47
TRUE, James 159
TUCKER, Edward 173
   Jno. 177
VAILY, Cyrus 211
VALION, Ella 85, 88
VAN VORT, James K. (Lt) 176
VARENE-GOURDINE, Elvira 169
VERGEN, Peter 155-156
VERMIN, Stephen 148
VIRENE, Catherine 210
   Lucille 209
   Paris 209
   Stephen 166, 209-210
VORMICK, Eliza 221, 225
   Isaac 223
WADE, Drayton 65
   John 66
   Richard D. (Magistrate) 66
   Thomas 65, 122
WALKER, ____ (Rev) 11
   Delilah 113
WALLACE, Jerry 219
WALLER, Charles 234
WAPOOL, Fortune 186
WARD, ____ 182
   Alfred 85-87
   Archie 6, 169
   Brant 167
   Brass 148, 165, 167
   J.J. 6
   Josh (Dr) 5
   Josh 209
   Josh (Col) 210
   Joshua 85, 87, 165, 169-170
   Joshua (Col) 209
   Joshua J. 165
   Randall 170
   Randol 5, 7

   Stephen 148, 209
WARING, Cato 50
WARREN, ____ (Dr) 111
   Amelia 21
   Caroline 18
   John 23, 111
WASHINGTON, Diana, 41
   Frazier 79
   Jeff 70
   Josephine 237-238
   Josh 59
   March 112
   Mollie 59
   Molly 57
   Rebecca 135
WATSON, Benjamin 75
   Fannie 237
   Kate 93
   Martha 93
   Susana 93
WAY, Henry H. 141-142
   Samuel (Dr) 141-142
   Willie 142
   Willie J. 142
WEBB, ____ 12
WELTON, Anita 135
{WENGER}, {Jeremiah} 159
WEST, Aaron 135-136
WESTBROOK, Emma 56
   Ki 56
WESTON, Ben 179
   Benjamin 75, 94
   Francis 33, 75, 179-180
   Isora 75
   Israel 59
   James 59
   Rosana 75
WESTPOINT, Gibson 29-30, 50
   Hardtime 29
   Peter 30
WETZEL, ____ 132
   Adam 131

Name Index

John 131
WHALEY, Ben 211
  Benjamin 211
  Cyrus 211
  Thomas E. 206
WHEATON, Edward E. 43n
  Selina B. 43
WHEELING, Thomas (3rdSgt) 69
  York (Cpl) 69
WHITE, Abraham 213
  Arthur 215
  Betty 4
  Estella 215-216
  Floyd 215
  Isaac 213
  J. (Notary) 63
  James (1stSgt) 12
  John 223
  Julia 213
  Jupiter 4, 215-216
  Lazarus 74, 140, 148
  Lurina 215
  Robert 4
  Willard 215
WHITE, Jr. Robert 4
WILKINSON, Martha 47, 48
WILLIAMS, Adam (Rev) 185
  Adolphus 225
  Bruce H. (Rev) 165
  Bunch (Rev) 30
  Carrie 217
  Charles 217-218
  Corinne 61
  Cuyler 223, 225
  Duncan 218
  Eliza 217- 218, 226
  Fibbie 61
  Frank 222
  George 130
  George (OrdSgt) 176
  Henry 32
  J. Bunch (Rev) 29
  James 220
  James Adolphus 221, 225
  James Samuel 217- 218
  Joe 98
  John 217
  Lydia 61
  Mahala 129
  Mary J. 221, 223, 226
  Princilla 151
  Sarah 97-98
  Sylvia 199
  William C. 221
  William C. (Rev) 222
  William Cuyler 222, 226
WILLIS, Paul (Rev) 77
WILLSON, Della 125
WILSON, A.J. (Rev) 125
  Amelia 227
  Charles 227
  Della 127
  Duncan 227
  Ellen 227-228
  Gabe 227-228
  Glasco 227
  Harriet 227
  Hattie 227
  March 227
  Nellie 219-220
  Richard 227-228
  Sarah 222
  Tamar 9
WIMBERLY, Ed 62
  Edward 61
  Milledge 61-63
WIMLEY, Millege 122
WINDOM, Naber 236
WINE, Anna 230
  Bella 231
  Belle 230
  Billy 10
  Eugenia 229
  Henry P. 231

Name Index

    Henry Paul 229-230
    Jane 229-231
    John 229-230
    Laura 229-230
    Mille 231
    Mosley 229, 231
    William 229-232
WINRY, Lois 5
WINS, Hercules 148
WOOD, Wesley 55
WOODWARD, Laura 66
WRAGG, Nancy 81-82
WRIGHT, Annie 233, 235
    Benjamin 235
    Cuffie 234, 235
    Cuffy 233, 235-236
    George 233, 235- 236
    Hannah 233
    Isah 206
    Isaiah 233
    J.W. (Rev) 181
    {Jenny} 235
    Judy 233
    Lavinia 29-30
    {Leonia} 233
    {Lorraine} 233
    Margaret 103
    Mary 233
    {Peter} 233
    Sallie 235- 236
    Stephen 233
    Tobias 233
    Toby 233
YANEY, Allen 32
    David 31
    John 31
    Wyman 31
YOUNG, Dennis 186
    Edward 237
    Elijah Peter 237
    Harriet Victoria 237
    Harry J. 238
    Harry James 237
    Joshua 193
    Joshua Augustus 237
    Judy 193, 237-238
    Lucinda 237-238
    Maggie 237
    Rebecca 238
    Rebecca Eliza 237
    Sarah Elizabeth 237
    Sarah Lucinda 238
    Susan 193
    Thomas 237-238
    Victoria 238
    W.M.D. 85
    Watson Fannie 238
ZEAGLER, C. (Probate Judge) 204
ZIMMERMAN 201-202
    Russell 188

ABOUT THE EDITOR

John Raymond Gourdin, a native South Carolinian, was born, raised and attended the public school system in Williamsburg County. Shortly after graduating from high school he enlisted in the U.S. Marine Corps and continued his education attending evening school and the military degree completion program. During 1978, John earned a B.A. in Economics and Business Administration from Chapman University, Orange, California, and during 1980, he earned an M.S. degree in Economics from the University of Southern California.

Over the years John developed his hobby as a genealogist and family historian, and in 1995, published his family genealogy and history—*GOURDIN: A French-African-American Family from South Carolina, 1830-1995*. Having discovered an ancestral connection with Civil War soldiers during his research, John initiated a more detailed research of service and pension records of veteran soldiers from the low-country of South Carolina, and in 1997, published a resource book—*Voices from the Past: 104th USCT, 1865-1866*. During the spring of 2003, he compiled, edited and published a fact-book citing the participation and contributions of black soldiers during the Civil War—*First, Last, Etcetera: Black Soldiers during the Civil War Era, 1861-1867*.

John is a long time member of the South Carolina Historical Society; the Hilton Head Heritage Library Foundation; past president of the Central Maryland chapter of the Afro-American Historical and Genealogical Society; instructor of a *Practical Genealogy* course for Anne Arundel Community College (Md.); a board member of the United States Colored Troops Living History Association (Md.); and, a Senior Fellow and board member of the United States Colored Troops Institute (N.Y.).

www.ingramcontent.com/pod-product-compliance
Lightning Source LLC
Chambersburg PA
CBHW062004220426
43662CB00010B/1230